FOREIGN POLICY AND ETHNIC INTEREST GROUPS

Recent Titles in
Contributions in Political Science

FOREIGN POLICY AND ETHNIC INTEREST GROUPS

American and Canadian Jews Lobby for Israel

DAVID HOWARD GOLDBERG

Contributions in Political Science, Number 256

Bernard K. Johnpoll, Series Editor

GREENWOOD PRESS

New York • Westport, Connecticut • London

E
183.8
I75
G65
1990

Library of Congress Cataloging-in-Publication Data

Goldberg, David Howard.
   Foreign policy and ethnic interest groups : American and Canadian
Jews lobby for Israel / David Howard Goldberg.
      p.   cm. — (Contributions in political science, ISSN 0147–1066
; no. 256)
   Includes bibliographical references.
   ISBN 0–313–26850–9 (lib. bdg. : alk. paper)
   1. United States—Foreign relations—Israel.   2. Israel—Foreign
relations—United States.   3. American Israel Public Affairs
Committee.   4. Jews—United States—Attitudes toward Israel.
5. Zionism—United States.   6. Canada—Foreign relations—Israel.
7. Israel—Foreign relations—Canada.   8. Canada-Israel Committee.
9. Jews—Canada—Attitudes toward Israel.   10. Zionism—Canada.
11. United States—Ethnic relations.   12. Canada—Ethnic relations.
I. Title.   II. Series.
E183.8.I75G65   1990
327.7305694—dc20   89–26019

British Library Cataloguing in Publication Data is available.

Library of Congress Catalog Card Number: 89–26019
ISBN: 0–313–26850–9
ISSN: 0147–1066

First published in 1990

Greenwood Press, Inc.
88 Post Road West, Westport, Connecticut 06881

Printed in the United States of America

The paper used in this book complies with the
Permanent Paper Standard issued by the National
Information Standards Organization (Z39.48–1984).

10 9 8 7 6 5 4 3 2 1

Parts of Chapter 5 of the present work appeared in a slightly different version in *The Domestic
Battleground: Canada and the Arab-Israeli Conflict*, edited by David Taras and David H. Goldberg,
102–24. (Montreal: McGill-Queen's University Press, 1989)

For my wife Sheri
and our daughters
Adara, Shayna, and Rebecca

Contents

Acknowledgments

I wish to express my gratitude to the many people whose contributions were so important to the completion of this study. In particular, I would like to acknowledge the assistance of Professor Harold M. Waller at McGill University, as well as the support of the McConnel Memorial Fellowship, the Max Binz Fellowship, and the Faculty of Graduate Studies and Research, McGill University.

Many colleagues have offered their comments and criticisms at various stages in the preparation of this manuscript. I note in particular the advice and support of my colleague and collaborator, David Taras at the University of Calgary, and David Dewitt, Director of the Centre for International and Strategic Studies, York University.

I also wish to take this opportunity to acknowledge the vital contributions made by a number of politicians, governmental officials, and nongovernmental political activists, in both the United States and Canada, who gave so freely of their time and expertise in support of my research.

Special gratitude is due to Joseph Solovitch, who did a masterful job of helping to research and edit the manuscript, and Corinne Altman, who helped prepare it for publication. At Greenwood Press, Mildred Vasan has been extremely helpful and patient. Finally, I owe much to my family, for their continued love and encouragement.

Theory and Background

Israel has always been considered something of an enigma amongst members of the international community of states. A geographically small and distant country, comprising but a tiny segment of the world's total population, Israel nonetheless receives a disproportionate amount of scrutiny and attention. Its domestic politics evoke considerable debate and controversy; so too does its foreign relations. One of the most controversial of Israel's foreign relations is its relationship with Jewish communities throughout the world.

From its inception, modern Zionism anticipated a special relationship between *Eretz Yisrael* and Jews of the diaspora. For although envisioned by its principal exponent, Theodore Herzl, as a liberal, secular nation-state on the nineteenth century European model, Israel was conceived of as much more than that. Israel was to be not only "a state of Jews" but also "the Jewish state" (Herzl's *Der Judenstaat*). Israel was to be the physical manifestation of Jewish nationhood, offering true political emancipation to the Jewish people as well as safe refuge to those fleeing antisemitism. It was also to be the spiritual center uniting together all of world Jewry. The dual function conceived for Israel made it unique amongst the nation-states achieving independence in the second half of the twentieth century. It also imposed on Israel a special relationship with Jews of the diaspora.

Most immediately, the relationship was to be manifested through immigration. One of the principal disappointments of Israel's forty years of modern political history has been its failure to attract massive waves of Jewish immigration from the West. The redefining of its relationship with the Jews of the Western democracies, in the light of their failure to respond en masse to the siren call of *aliyah*, has long represented one of the major challenges confronting Israel and Zionism.

As it has evolved, the redefined relationship has come to rest on two pillars: philanthropy and political action.[1] Each has elicited its share of controversy.

However, much of the most critical fire has been reserved for Jewish political action in support of Israel, especially as it has manifested itself in the North American context. Over the years political action has come to take varied and diverse forms, including the aggressive promotion of *hasbara*, the staging of mass public rallies in solidarity with Israel in times of crisis, "educating" media and government about the "strategic realities" of Israel and its adversaries, and the formation of organized lobby groups and political action committees (PACs). The organized Jewish communities of the Western democracies have proved particularly well-disposed toward and adept at political action, performing what has become a crucial function in the defense of Israel and Zionism.

This book addresses the pro-Israel political activities of the organized Jewish communities in the United States and Canada. The goal is not simply to describe each community in isolation. Rather, I compare the two communities and especially their respective designated pro-Israel lobby groups—the American Israel Public Affairs Committee (AIPAC) and the Canada-Israel Committee (CIC)—on the basis of a series of criteria. Each group is analyzed according to organizational characteristics, patterns of behavior, and level of political influence during the period between October 1973 and December 1988. Finally, my concern is with the impact of two similarly motivated ethnic foreign policy interest groups functioning in different decisional environments: the American presidential-congressional system of government and the Canadian parliamentary process.

THE IMPACT OF ETHNIC INTEREST GROUPS ON FOREIGN POLICY

The 1980s have witnessed tremendous intellectual and popular concern with the political activities of ethnic interest groups, especially those concerned with foreign policy. This increased attention to ethnicity and ethnic foreign policy interest groups reflects the combination of several heretofore unrelated tendencies in the analysis of group behavior.

The first of these tendencies focuses on the group as an important participant in the domestic governing process. Arthur F. Bentley's *The Process of Government* (1908) represented the seminal work in the field of group behavior. He organized, in a systematic fashion, many of the diverse theories evolving out of late nineteenth century liberal pluralism concerning the important functions performed by organized groups and other less formal "particles" of politics. David Truman's *The Governmental Process* (1951) significantly enhanced the existing research domain by focusing attention on, among other things, the organizational and political dynamic of the group. Truman also examined the impact upon the group's organization and political efficacy of such factors as countervailing forces and the way in which government makes decisions. Interest groups are now recognized as an ubiquitous and accepted part of political life in virtually all cultures and systems of government.

A second tendency in political analysis contributing to the current attention on ethnic foreign policy interest groups relates to the impact of organized interests upon the state's foreign policy-making process. Elmer Eric Schattschneider's *Politics, Pressure and the Tariff* (1937) is typical of its generation's concern with the alleged influence of business groups and trade associations in determining a government's international commercial policies. Schattschneider's image of an all-powerful business foreign policy lobby was to some extent undermined by the research of Bauer, Pool, and Dexter who, upon examination of the policy process associated with the formation of the U.S. Trade Excise Act of 1962, discerned that there is often a wide gulf between the perceived potency of an interest group and the group's actual influence over governmental foreign policy decisions (1964, 397). Subsequent research has broadened significantly the definition of *group* to include not only business associations but various other types of nongovernmental organizations concerned with foreign policy. Much of this literature reinforces Schattschneider's original premise of the significant impact (real or anticipated) of organized groups upon the making of foreign policy.

Yet a third tendency in group behavior literature concerns the increased appreciation of ethnicity as a natural base for group formation and organized political action. Scholars and practioners alike have, for several decades, recognized ethnicity as a factor of some relevance in the domestic political affairs of North America (Glazer and Moynihan 1970). Numerous studies have analyzed the ethnic group from a historical-sociological perspective, focusing on the group's pattern of arrival in and acculturation to North America as well as its internal political and organizational dynamics (Elliott 1971; Gerson 1964; Glazer and Moynihan 1970; Glazer and Young 1983).

The unprecedented concern with ethnic consciousness throughout the 1970s and 1980s increased significantly the attention scholars have given to the distinctly political behavior undertaken by groups formed on the basis of common place of origin or ethnic orientation. Ethnicity has become an essential ingredient in the domestic politics of North America; it was only natural that scholars should begin to focus on the ways in which ethnic groups interact with their governments in the making of foreign policy decisions of interest to the group and the constituency that it represents.

The combination of these various tendencies within group research has resulted in a large body of literature focusing on the attempts of ethnic interest groups to intervene in, and have influence over, the making of foreign policy (Said 1981; Trice 1974, 1976a, 1976b, 1977a, 1977b; Watanabe 1984). Many of these studies are case-specific, focusing on the activities of particular organized ethnic constituencies with regard to specific foreign policy decisions or issue areas.

With rare exceptions, these studies tend to suggest the existence of a strong causal relationship, either direct or indirect, between ethnic group political activism and the product of the government's foreign policy decision-making.

Especially since the mid-to-late 1970s, many of the studies postulating such ethnic interest group impact on foreign policy have focused on the pro-Israel lobbying activities of the Jewish communities in the United States and Canada.

THE NORTH AMERICAN PRO-ISRAEL ETHNIC LOBBIES

The North American domestic context of the Arab-Israeli conflict, and in particular the political activities of the various ethnically Jewish groups in the United States and Canada acting politically in support of Israel, is rich territory for the enterprising researcher. This is so not only because of the Jewish community's receptivity to fairly intense scrutiny relative to many other ethnic foreign policy interest groups (including much of the North American Arab community), but also because of the highly institutionalized nature of both the American and Canadian Jewish communities. Prompting further intellectual curiosity is the significant amount of controversy associated with each community's pro-Israel activism over the past fifteen or twenty years.

Given the size and status of the American Jewish community in international Jewry, it is not surprising that a great many analysts have focused critical attention on this community and its Israel-related political agencies and activities. Some studies are basically descriptive, concentrating on the intellectual and historical roots of American Zionism (Cohen 1975; Halperin 1961; Neusner 1985; Urofsky 1975). Others focus on the organizational makeup of the American Jewish community and attempts to develop a coordinated and unified voice on Israel-related matters in an ethnic community that is characterized by its diversity (Elazar 1980; Kenen 1981). Still others provide either an overview of the role of the Jewish community in the history of U.S.-Israel relations (Safran 1981; Spiegel 1985; Trice 1976b) or a detailed case study of a particular historical incident (Pollock 1982; Stern 1979; Teslik 1982).

A series of controversial developments in U.S.-Israeli and Israeli-American Jewry relations, especially since the late 1970s, has given rise to a large and diverse body of critical literature on American Zionism. The only common aspect of much of this literature is its conclusion that the organized American Jewish community wields extraordinary, and probably excessive, influence on the making of American foreign policy toward the Middle East and the Arab-Israeli conflict (Findlay 1985; Green 1984; Grose 1983; O'Brien 1986; Tivnan 1987).

There is, then, certainly no lack of material upon which to examine the pro-Israeli political activities of the American Jewish community; in many cases the challenge is to separate the pertinent from the mundane, the scholarly from the overtly political.

In contrast to its American "cousin," the literature on Canadian Jewry and its Zionist activity is comparatively small. This is in part a function of the small size and relative youthfulness of the Canadian Jewish community. It is also a reflection of Canada's traditionally low level, relative to that of the United States, of concern with and involvement in the core Middle East issues.

The literature on Canadian Zionism, though still limited, is nevertheless sufficiently diverse and intellectually rich to support enhanced research. Since at least the mid-1970s several factors have combined to influence the production of a small but empirically rich body of literature. These factors include an increased intellectual concern among Canadian scholars with ethnicity (Abu-Laban 1980; Elliott 1971; Weinfeld, Shaffir, and Cotler 1981), pressure-group politics (Pross 1975), and the domestication of foreign policy-making (Munton 1985; Nossal 1983–1984, 1985, 1989; Stairs 1977–78). The Canadian government's effort to significantly upgrade Canada's bilateral and multilateral commercial and diplomatic relations with the Middle East has also contributed to this increased interest (Dewitt and Kirton 1983; Stein 1976–77).

Some of this literature focuses on the historical evolution of the Canadian Jewish community and the role of Zionism as a unifying (and sometimes as a divisive) force within it (Hart 1926; Kallen 1977; Paris 1980; Rosenberg 1970–71); some, on the organizational dynamic and institutional idiosyncracies of Canadian Zionism (Hayes 1966, 1979; Waller 1974, 1980, 1981a, 1981b). An insightful overview of the first thirty years of Canada-Israel relations is offered by Bessin and Kaufman (1979).

A particularly important dimension of the relevant literature is an increasingly large number of case studies describing in detail the political behavior of Canadian Jewry in response to specific challenges to Israel and/or Canadian policy toward the Middle East (Bercuson 1985, 1989; Kay 1962–63, 1978; Stanislawski 1981a, 1981b, 1983, 1984, 1989; Stein 1976–77; Takach 1980, 1989; Taras 1983, 1984, 1989). As in the United States, though at an obviously reduced scale, a large body of literature critical of Canadian Zionism and its alleged impact on Canada's Middle East policy has emerged (Ismael 1976, 1984; Lyon 1982b, 1984; Noble 1983). One recent publication (Taras and Goldberg 1989) seeks to bring together literature on Canada-Israel and Canadian Jewry-Israeli relations.

The increasing size and the descriptive and analytic richness of the literature on American and Canadian Jewry notwithstanding, one serious deficiency remains: there has yet to be a serious attempt to systematically compare the two communities on the basis of their lobbying efforts in support of Zionism and Israel. To be fair, a few exceptions to this assertion must be cited (Hayes 1966; Stanislawski 1984; Taras 1984). These studies, however, tend to be so narrow in scope and focus as to make definitive comparative generalizations virtually impossible or at least intellectually dubious.

Detailed comparative analysis of the two Zionist communities should yield more enduring findings than those based on either the obvious size differential between the communities or the disproportionate amount of formal American involvement in the Middle East and the Arab-Israeli conflict relative to Canadian involvement. Rather, to have significance, such comparative analysis must reveal more fundamental similarities and diversities between the two ethnic communities. This type of study should stem from the unique histories and organizational characteristics, the particularities of the political cultures, and the foreign policy decision-making systems within which each organized community must function.

This book undertakes a comparison of the organized American and Canadian Jewish foreign policy lobbies. In the process of addressing this specific research objective, the book will also produce a series of generalizations concerning the study of ethnic politics and the impact of ethnic interest groups on the making of foreign policy in different political systems.

METHOD

The comparative analysis employed in this book is achieved in various ways. First, the activities of the American and Canadian Jewish communities are compared during the fifteen-year period between the Yom Kippur War of October 1973 and December 1988. This period was selected for two reasons: the tremendous amount of development on the Middle East landscape and in United States and Canadian policy toward the region beginning with the Yom Kippur War and culminating with the Palestinian disturbances and associated political developments (ongoing at the time of this writing); and the unprecedented level of internal debate and political activism on the part of the organized American and Canadian Jewish communities in response to those developments.

The chronology provides a convenient base of analysis. The purpose, however, is not to examine each historical incident in isolation, but rather to discern from the cases patterns of significant consistency and variance with regard to the political activities, organizational characteristics, and relative influence of the two subject ethnic interest groups.

Given the diverse and varying interests of the American and Canadian governments toward Israel and the Middle East, a full and complete comparison of the 1973–88 period is impossible. In order to provide a more credible base of comparison, the concentration is on developing a cross section of change or consistency in the respective lobby group's organizational and political response to developments in the Middle East and/or its government's policy initiatives or responses to regional developments.

In order to facilitate comparison, the historical period is divided into a series of policy issues of concern to each of the ethnic interest groups. The American Jewish community is examined on the basis of eight issues: the Yom Kippur War, the Kissinger diplomatic offensive, antiboycott legislation, Jimmy Carter's diplomatic strategy, the F-15 controversy, the AWACS (Airborne Warning and Command System) sale, Lebanon and the Reagan Plan, and the Palestinian disturbances. The Canadian pro-Israel lobby is analyzed on the basis of seven issues: the Yom Kippur War, the PLO in Canada, antiboycott legislation, the initiation of the Jerusalem embassy pledge, the reversal of the embassy initiative, the Lebanon War, and the Palestinian disturbances.

In selecting the policy issues for examination, I was guided by a number of considerations. Obviously, an issue had to be of concern to the interest group and the ethnic constituency that it represented. The issue had to have sufficient effect on U.S. and Canadian relations with Israel and the Middle East to necessitate some type of policy response or initiative from Washington and Ottawa. (There is, however, no suggestion that the ethnic interest group and the government necessarily perceived the policy issue in the same way. Similarly, the government's policy response need not have come in the form of substantive action; the decision not to act often says as much about a government's position concerning a particular issue as does dramatic behavior). Finally, in selecting the issues for consideration, I have been sensitive to the often fine distinction between chronic (that is, long-term noncrisis issues of concern) and crisis (that is, perceived crisis) aspects of each ethnic community's Israel-related agenda.[2]

Comparison of the American and Canadian Jewish ethnic lobbies is also facilitated through reference to a series of six factors that help to explain an ethnic interest group's potential impact upon governmental foreign policy.[3] These factors include the following:

1. *The behavioral attributes of the group, including its level of activity, policy objectives, timing, targets, and targeting strategies.* Much of the literature suggests that the different levels of influence experienced by interest groups is in part a function of their differing policy objectives. For example, distinctions are frequently drawn between permanent groups and temporary or ad hoc associations. A. Paul Pross differentiates between "institutionalized" and "issue-oriented" groups. He assumes that the group aspiring to establish permanent, long-term relations in the policy process over a wide range of issues of concern to its constituency will be more circumspect in its political behavior than will the group organized for the exclusive purpose of addressing one policy issue (Pross 1975). In a similar fashion, Trice distinguishes between "advocate" and "antagonist" groups; while dedicated to its causes, the advocate will tend to be perceived by other political players as behaving in a more constructive way than will the antagonist (Trice 1976b, 9). The literature also suggests that the timing of a group's behavior has an important bearing on its level of influence. The basic distinction is between group intervention in the formulative stage of policy development and reactive behavior; only intervention during policy formulation can directly affect the making of a policy decision, although the response of a group to a particular policy decision may help to establish the context for subsequent decisions pertaining to the group's concerns (Trice 1976b, 9). The timing of a group's behavior, as well as its selection of strategies and techniques, tends to be system-specific. For example, with reference to the Canadian public policy process, William Stanbury divides timing into four phases: preparliamentary, parliamentary-cabinet, parliamentary-legislative, and postparliamentary. The

statist quality of the Canadian system tends to favor techniques that ensure a group's access to the preparliamentary and parliamentary-cabinet phases of the policy process (Stanbury 1978). The more open American system tends to favor other stages of the policy process (Milbrath 1967; Trice 1976b).

2. *The organizational characteristics of the group, including its level and scope of development, wealth, structure, size, and participation and its level and extent of cohesion.* The literature suggests that there is significant variance between interest groups on the basis of organizational sophistication, clarity of objectives sought, wealth, size, and level and type of communication with government. Pross places groups on an institutional continuum, ranging from "institutionalized" to "mature" to "fledgling" to "issue-oriented" (Pross 1975, 10–15). Groups differ also in terms of membership eligibility, ranging from "fully open" to "interest-specific" to "role-based" (that is, membership is restricted to those who hold leadership positions in other related organizations) (Salisbury 1975, 188–89). Groups vary also with respect to patterns of participation. David Truman distinguishes between groups based on the "democratic mold" and those of a "corporate" type (Truman 1951, 129–55). The nature and level of participation in ethnic interest groups is also frequently affected by prevailing customs and traditions of that group. For example, Jews of European descent have a strong political tradition of "aristocratic republicanism" (that is, of communal leadership on the basis of scholarship, wealth, or social class). Great trust was placed in a principal actor, the *shtadlan*, who was assigned the task of representing the interests of the community before the non-Jewish powers-that-be (Elazar 1972, 1980; Waller 1981a). The extent to which the corporate style of Jewish political behavior melds with the political culture of North America remains a matter of some conjecture. A particularly important aspect of the organizational variable relates to the cohesion of the group. Interest group leaders have long recognized the legitimizing effect of (real or apparent) unity and often expend as much political energy in this regard as they do in the act of lobbying government and other groups (Bauer, Pool, and Dexter 1964, 349; Milbrath 1967, 243; Truman 1951, 112). Groups tend to differ in their achievement of these various organizational aspects. A particular group's organizational capacities may vary significantly over time and be reflected in varying levels of influence over the policy process.

3. *The structure of the state's foreign policy decision-making system, in particular the extent to which the state's decisional process and popular political culture are open and receptive to intervention by nongovernmental organizations, including organized ethnic interest groups.* The most important determinant of the influence of a pressure group "in any political system is the structure of the decision-making system which it seeks to influence" (Eckstein 1960, 16). Just as all interest groups are not equally endowed with political and organizational resources, so too not all political cultures and decision-making systems are equally receptive and responsive to interventions by nongovernmental organizations. Much of the current foreign policy literature focuses on the statist or

state-autonomy thesis (Krasner 1978; Nordlinger 1981; Nossal 1983–84, 1985, 1989). The statist thesis holds that the liberal democratic state has considerable autonomy from "civil society." The state, comprised of "those individuals who are endowed with society-wide decision-making authority" (Krasner 1978, 28), has its own vision of the national interest, policy preferences, and sources of power and authority. In the making of public policy, the state is insulated from the pressures of civil society. Certain societal elements may in fact gain entrée to the decisional process, but they do so at the discretion of the state.

Democratic states are said to be distinguishable on the basis of their adherence to the statist thesis; some states enjoy greater decisional autonomy than others. Many analysts offer a comparison of the United States and Canada as a case in point. Stephen Krasner describes the United States as "a strong society but a weak state" (Krasner 1978, 61). The central feature of the American policy process is its fragmentation and noncentralization of authority. By constitutional dictate and by cultural inclination, the American political system denies government the capacity to ignore the often competing demands and policy preferences of societal groups (Dahl 1967, 1976; Lindblom 1965). The constitutional balancing of powers between branches of the federal government, decentralized authority in Congress, an entrenched committee and subcommittee decisional process, and the seemingly constant preparation for elections, creates a distinct political environment in which private groups thrive. Such groups, operating as organized pressures or as political action committees, enjoy many opportunities for access and potential influence upon the makers of foreign policy of concern to them.

By contrast, Canada fits more closely the image of the statist foreign policy actor. Subject still to a certain residue of puritanism, conservatism, and deference to authority, Canada is generally defined as a weak society but a strong state (Clarke 1973; Lipset 1965; Presthus 1973). Foreign policy-making, with limited exception, remains the almost exclusive preserve of a handful of politicians, bureaucrats, and ex-officio players who, both by the rules of parliamentary procedure and by custom and tradition, are well insulated from the demands of civil society (Nossal 1983–84, 1985, 1989). Nevertheless, state autonomy is a relative concept; even the statist-like Canadian policy system is being increasingly "domesticated" (Kirton and Dimock 1983–84; Stairs 1977–78). Nongovernmental groups, including ethnic interest groups concerned with the Middle East, occasionally gain access to, and potential influence over, the makers of Canadian foreign policy (Taras and Goldberg 1989). The openness of the decision-making system remains an important factor explaining a nongovernmental group's potential influence over foreign policy.

4. *The domestic political environment, including such factors as the formal makers of decisions and their institutions, the media and other nongovernmental organizations, particularly "counterforce groups"; that is, organized nongovernmental groups pursuing foreign policy preferences that are considered by the principal ethnic group to be antithetical to its concerns.* Ethnic interest groups

acting alone usually have little chance of directly influencing public policy-making. They tend to be too small and lack the political resources required to independently influence government. Building coalitions with sympathetic government officials and other nongovernmental organizations then becomes an important vehicle for broadening the power base of the group and increasing its potential influence over policy. Coalitions will also be sought for the purpose of balancing the perceived or potential influence of counterforce groups.

5. *The international political environment, including the general international mood concerning the ethnic group's principal foreign policy concern, the nature of relations between that concern and the ethnic group's home government, and the extent to which the group can facilitate linkage between the foreign policy concern and the home government.* A positive relationship is assumed between the perceived independence of a domestic ethnic interest group from the object of its foreign affection and the group's ability to influence its own government's policy concerning that foreign concern. A group's degree of independence ranges from "fully autonomous" to "semiautonomous" to "related" to "dependent." The credibility and potential influence of an ethnic foreign policy interest group is also a function of the nature of relations between its home government and the group's foreign concern. There is much evidence to suggest that close interstate relationships are not guarantees of positive foreign policy decision-making (Kenen 1981; Pollock 1982; Safran 1981). However, it is logical to assume that the more amiable the relations between the governments of two countries, the greater the credibility and influence of the domestic ethnic group seeking to develop linkages between the countries.

6. *The policy issue, including the amount of attention a particular issue receives relative to other features of the ethnic group's foreign policy agenda, the extent to which the issue is considered to be a crisis for the group and its primary constituency, and the extent to which the group and its home government share the perception of crisis about that issue.* An underexamined determinant of an ethnic interest group's influence over foreign policy relates to the specific foreign policy concern confronting the group at any particular time. Contrary to a frequently held assumption, ethnic interest groups do not necessarily perceive all foreign policy issues to be of equal importance. Rather, there is a gradation of issues. These range from crisis issues (that is, situations in which the basic values of the group and its constituency are perceived to be at stake) to chronic issues (that is, noncrisis, routine matters of concern to the group). Obviously, the greater the perceived crisis, the more willing the group is to utilize scarce resources in seeking to have the government address its concerns. There are three basic problems associated with crisis policy issues. First, members of the ethnic group's active cadre may differ amongst themselves concerning the crisis nature of a particular issue or at least the strategy for responding to a situation that all agree constitutes a crisis. A second problem relates to the fact that the government and the leaders of other nongovernmental organizations may not share the ethnic group's sense of crisis vis-à-vis a particular issue. And, finally,

even if the group and the government agree that an issue constitutes a crisis for both, there is still no guarantee of group influence over policy made to address the situation. Indeed, the foreign policy literature suggests the existence of a curvilinear relationship between group influence and the intensity of perceived crises; the more the government perceives a situation as threatening to its basic values and concerns, the less likely the nongovernmental group is to have direct and immediate access to or influence over decision makers (Milbrath 1967, 249–50; Trice 1976b, 21). In recognition of this fact, the influence-seeking group will work to establish permanent networks of political association that will sustain the public salience of the group's core values and minimize the political damage to its credibility resulting from the occasional emergence of a crisis involving itself or its constituency, its central foreign concerns, and other actors in the domestic and international political environment.

A final note on the method of comparison relates to the matter of influence. The problem of discerning and attributing influence continues to bedevil students of politics. This is especially the case for foreign policy analysts and even more particularly for those seeking to understand the relationship between the goals articulated by an ethnic interest group and the actual decisions taken by foreign policy decision makers.

Contrary to the traditional "billiard ball" conception of the public policy process, wherein the demands of a single actor (conceivably including an ethnic interest group) directly determine the decisions of government, the pattern of influence in the real world of policy-making is far more complicated and mul-tifaceted. Given the number of players and the amount of interaction conceivably associated with any particular foreign policy issue, it is doubtful that a totally reliable direct line of causation can be drawn between an ethnic group's expressed interests and the government's policy behavior. In a sense, then, one cannot go much beyond making the most general of assertions (based more on inference and innuendo than solid fact) about an ethnic group's alleged influence over one decision or another. Such an approach may lead to fallacious conclusions con-cerning the power and influence of a group or to the problem of "parallelism" (that is, of attributing influence to a group based on a set of factors and influences unrelated to anything that group has or has not done).

Clearly, a preoccupation with a narrow conception of direct cause and effect will produce few or at best dubious generalizations about actual influence over policy-making. A great deal more insight is achieved if influence is conceived of as a continuum, what Samuel Eldersveld called "an index of power achieve-ment" based on "categories of differential influence" (Eldersveld 1958, 187).

With Eldersveld's comment in mind, I have chosen to conceive of the ethnic group-government policy relationship as a five-point "index of influence." At one end of the index (scoring 1) are situations in which the government adopts or maintains a foreign policy that is perceived as diametrically opposed to that advocated by the ethnic interest group. The policy is not only contrary to the concerns of the group, it may be perceived by the group as harmful to its foreign policy concerns. This represents a situation of "nil-low" group influence over policy. The next point on the scale (scoring 2) refers to a situation in which government policy is perceived as generally unsympathetic to the concerns of the ethnic interest group, although such is not reflected in explicitly nonsupportive government behavior. For example, the American or Canadian government may indicate a desire to cut back foreign aid allocations as part of a general program of fiscal austerity. Israel may not be the prime or even among the explicit targets of such cost cutting. However, the fact that the government appears willing to tamper with a principal feature of the North American Jewish value system is nonetheless felt to represent a circumstance of "low-marginal" group influence over government. Members of the ethnic group may feel that some of their interests have been ignored by the government and that the situation may require some type of political response. However, the situation is not perceived as a crisis for the group, which will likely conserve much of its political resources for another day and another issue.

The midpoint on the index of influence (scoring 3) reflects a condition of government indifference toward the foreign policy concerns of the ethnic interest group. The government's policy behavior toward a particular foreign policy issue area is essentially peripheral to the group's principal concerns. Nor does the government's action appear to benefit the interest of groups supporting concerns antithetical to those of the subject group. Under the circumstances, the group is considered to have "moderate" influence over government policy. The next point on the continuum (scoring 4) describes a situation of "moderate-high" group influence. The government adopts or maintains a foreign policy posture that is perceived as generally sympathetic to the interests of the ethnic group. Although there are elements of the policy that are still less than consistent with what the group prefers, some of the group's principal interests will have been addressed. Of equal importance, political advantage will have been denied to competing groups. At the far end of the continuum is a situation in which government follows a foreign policy line that is virtually indistinguishable from that sought by the ethnic interest group. The group is satisfied with government policy and is considered to have had "high" influence over the formulation (and implementation) of that policy (thereby scoring 5 on the index of influence). To be sure, there are still methodological and theoretical difficulties associated with my index of influence. For example, the situation of high influence suggests the previously discussed possibility of parallelism: how is one to know if the government's adoption of a policy consistent with that preferred by the ethnic interest group was a consequence of anything that group did or was due to a host of other unrelated pressures? In the zero-sum rationale that tends to prevail among analysts of group behavior, influence is attributed to the ethnic interest group whose articulated or inferred policy preferences most closely approximate those adopted by the government, whatever the group's actual role. Discerning and measuring influence is problematical and will likely remain so. The goal, as Avery Leiserson concluded, is to find "certain strategic, critical variables that will provide guides or indices to relevant facts'' (in Ehrmann 1958, 297). Designing a consistent method of measurement, rather than achieving absolute consensus among the experts, is the key to measuring ethnic group influence over governmental foreign policy.

CONCLUSION

This chapter has introduced many of the issues, both theoretical and practical, to be addressed in this book. To reiterate, the objective is to compare American and Canadian Jewish lobby groups and to use that comparison as the basis upon which to analyze the phenomenon of ethnic political behavior generally.

Subsequent chapters of the book are organized in the following way: Chapter 2 will briefly outline the history, mandate, and organizational structure of the American Israel Public Affairs Committee (AIPAC); chapter 3 will do the same for AIPAC's Canadian counterpart, the Canada-Israel Committee (CIC). Chapters 4 and 5, respectively, analyze the political behavior, institutional dynamic, and relative influence enjoyed by the organized American and Canadian Zionist lobbies from October 1973 until December 1988. The final chapter of the book provides a detailed comparison of AIPAC and the CIC on the basis of the six criteria of analysis outlined earlier in this chapter; it concludes with some general comments concerning ethnic interest groups and ethnicity as the basis for effectively comparing political systems.

NOTES

1. As several analysts have noted, philanthropy—rather than active immigration—has always represented the major thrust of North American Zionism. Naomi Cohen wrote, "For all practical purposes, Palestine was conceived as a refuge built by a vanguard of a few pioneering Jews, supported by the wealthy, but peopled largely by refugees. [American] Zionism affirmed a messianic goal, not unlike the messianism of the early American restorationists, but it did not exact a personal commitment to settle in Palestine" (Cohen 1975, 11). See also the insightful comments of Irving Howe in the May/June 1989 issue of *Tikkun*.

2. I am indebted to David Dewitt, director of the Center for International and Strategic Studies at York University (Toronto), for initially suggesting this problem to me.

3. These various factors and criteria have been accumulated through a detailed review of the relevant literature. The works of Robert H. Trice (1974, 1976a, 1976b, 1977b) were especially instructive in this regard.

2

The American Israel Public Affairs Committee: History, Mandate, and Organizational Structure

ORIGINS

The development of a united national American Zionist movement was slow and sporadic. This was partly a function of disputes inherent to all Jewish communities over level of religious adherence and the legitimate role of political Zionism as a vehicle for Jewish national regeneration and survival (Hertzberg 1979; Weizmann 1949). It was also attributable to certain factors distinct to American Jewry. Among these were: the Jew's long tenure in America, dating back to 1654; the different inclinations toward Zionism carried to the United States by various waves of Jewish immigrants throughout the nineteenth and twentieth centuries (Dawidowicz 1982; Elazar 1980, 38–42; Cohen 1975; Halperin 1961; Urofsky 1975, 1978); the sheer physical size and geographic distribution of American Jewry; and the elaborate network of national organizations and local federations that arose to service both the general and the specific interests of the community (Elazar 1980). A final factor contributing to the delayed evolution of American Zionism was the tendency on the part of many American Jews to view Zionism more as a philanthropic exercise than a personal pioneering endeavor (Cohen 1975, 11).

It was only with the course of historical events, most notably the European Holocaust and the post–World War Two international debate over the future of the Palestine Mandate and the struggle for Israel's creation, that American Zionism developed into an all-encompassing national Jewish cause. Zionism, which began as an ambiguous, quasi-spiritual philosophy of little relevance to the majority of American Jews, evolved into a series of decentralized groups "bedeviled by internal factionalism and public apathy" (Halperin 1961, 25).

During its most recent phase, Zionism has become a fairly cohesive movement of national scope and jurisdiction.

The American Israel Public Affairs Committee (AIPAC) represents only the most recent and enduring of American Jewish efforts at coordinating activities in support of Zionism and Israel. Earlier efforts in this regard, including a Provisional Executive Committee for Zionist Affairs organized during the First World War under the chairmanship of the respected jurist, Louis D. Brandeis, failed. Internal disputes within the Zionist movement and/or the active opposition or passive ambivalence of non-Zionist American Jews scuttled the earlier efforts (Cohen 1975; Halperin 1961).

The dramatic rise of state-sponsored violent antisemitism in Europe motivated American Zionists to greater unified political activism. In late 1939 the American Emergency Committee for Zionist Affairs (ECZA) was established (Cohen 1975, 63). Its goal was to spread the Zionist message equally to the non-Zionist majority of American Jews and to the non-Jewish general populace. Initially, ECZA suffered many of the same organizational maladies that weakened its institutional precursors. A reorganization of ECZA in August 1943 involved the broadening of the leadership core and the incorporation of a larger number of Zionist groups and unaffiliated American Jewish leaders. It was generally hoped that this would mitigate some of the organizational headaches and permit Zionist leaders to concentrate on the greater political goal of disseminating pro-Israel propaganda to the wider population. The reorganized group, called the Zionist Emergency Council, was in time succeeded by the American Zionist Council (AZC) as the national umbrella organization of American Zionism.

By the early 1950s, as the initial crisis over Israel's existence dissipated and was replaced by a no less dramatic need for assured American economic assistance, American Zionists recognized the need for an official, permanent American Jewish pro-Israel lobby in Washington (Kenen 1981). This realization led to the establishment, independent of the AZC, of the American Zionist Committee for Public Affairs (AZCPA) on March 22, 1954. The organization, to be renamed the American Israel Public Affairs Committee (AIPAC) in 1959, was assigned the task of "co-ordinating and directing public actions on behalf of the American Zionist movement, bearing upon relations with governmental authorities, with a view to maintaining the improving friendship and good will between the United States and Israel" (Windmueller 1973, 167). AZCPA was, and AIPAC remains, the only American-based agency registered with Congress for lobbying and disseminating propaganda in the field of American-Israeli relations.

The early days were not easy ones for AZCPA. Its founding director, I. L. ("Si") Kenen, found himself combating the efforts of "Arabists" and "Anglophiles" located throughout the American foreign policy bureaucracy. Kenen had to counter not only what he called the American "petro-diplomatic complex," but also the rabidly anti-Zionist activities of groups like Rabbi Elmer Berger's American Council for Judaism (Kenen 1981, 12, 114–115). Kenen also faced opposition from groups within the mainstream of American Judaism and

Zionism. These included the older, more established defense organizations (who tended to see the upstart AZCPA as a threat to their traditional leadership of American Zionism), and the Conference of Presidents of Major Jewish Organizations.

The Presidents Conference was established in 1954 to enlist the cooperation of influential leaders of Zionist and non-Zionist American Jewish organizations in support of Israel. Kenen claims to have had serious reservations from the outset about this body. He felt that the Presidents Conference was "undemocratic as well as impractical" because of the restriction of membership to organization heads. "It could not move on any issue unless it had a consensus" (Kenen 1981, 111; Kenen Interview). It also represented a formidable institutional rival to the incipient AZCPA. Relations between the Presidents Conference and AZCPA/ AIPAC improved markedly in response to the crisis and war of June 1967. In fact, AIPAC is now an integral part of the Presidents Conference. But, the potential for organizational rivalry within the upper echelon of American Zionism remains.

MANDATE AND ORGANIZATIONAL DYNAMIC

AIPAC's general mandate of maintaining and enhancing U.S.-Israeli relations is supplemented by a number of more specific responsibilities. AIPAC serves as a "force" between Washington and Jerusalem, keeping each informed of the moods, needs, and concerns of the other and lobbying each in order to coordinate activities between them. AIPAC also deals directly with the executive and congressional branches of the U.S. government for the purpose of facilitating granting of aid and other assistance to Israel. Through wide distribution of the *Near East Report* and other research papers and memoranda, AIPAC seeks to maintain its credibility as a source of accurate information and reasoned analysis of U.S. policy toward Israel, the Middle East, and the Arab-Israeli conflict. AIPAC also serves as the political eyes, ears, and mind of American pro-Israel groups, and as a political intelligence center and source of political education for American Jews. AIPAC acts as a conduit of information and attitudes between American Jewry, official Washington, and the broader American domestic political environment on matters of concern to its constituency (Dine Interview; Rosenbaum Interview).

In interviews with its lay and professional leadership, past and present, one point was consistently emphasized: AIPAC is not a foreign agent. It is described as an American organization working to facilitate relations between the peoples and governments of the United States and Israel. This requires that AIPAC represent not only the concerns of Israel and its natural ethnic constituency in the United States, but also the organization's conception of what is in the best interests of the United States. AIPAC activists operate not only in areas of dense Jewish population concentration, but also in regions of the country where few Jews are to be found (Amitay Interview; Dine Interview).

Organizationally, AIPAC approximates an institutionalized interest group. Membership is open to the general American Jewish community, although the leadership core is role-based. The organization is governed by a group of eighteen lay officers, the majority of whom are leaders of other related organizations. They are selected every two years by an executive committee of 150 representatives of some thirty-eight national and local organizations and federations. AIPAC is unquestionably elitist in orientation. The lay leadership tends to be self-perpetuating and self-selecting. It is comprised of the most affluent and powerful of Jewish community activists who gravitate to AIPAC due to its Jewish and Israeli context and the "sexiness of high politics" (Rosenbaum Interview).

The recruitment of professional staff and the utilization of an annual budget that reportedly exceeds $3 million (Rosenfeld 1983) is the exclusive responsibility of the executive director. AIPAC has a staff of approximately sixty-seven people, two-thirds of whom perform support duties. The median age of these professionals is twenty-six years; most are recruited from Capitol Hill and other locales of intense political activity. As the current executive director, Tom Dine, explains, in hiring professional staff AIPAC directors have an explicit bias for "experienced, quality, self-starters" (Dine Interview).

Organizationally, AIPAC is tightly centralized. Its activities are headquartered in Washington D.C., along with the offices of the *Near East Report* and AIPAC's research and information facilities. All day-to-day operational decisions are made from the Washington office, although there are also three offices, in New York City, San Francisco, and Austin, Texas, that coordinate regional political activities and fund-raising campaigns. The regional offices represent recent attempts to broaden AIPAC's base of support through stronger liaison with local federations and Jewish Community Relations Councils throughout the United States (Dine Interview; Kenen Interview).

AIPAC more closely fits the corporate than the democratic mold of participation. Given the highly specialized nature of their work, AIPAC professional staff members are generally granted wide decisional latitude. Democratic principles are sustained through a variety of mechanisms, the most notable of which is the annual policy conference. AIPAC's general constituency is invited to participate in seminars and in the articulation of the organization's general statement of policy. However, the corporate inclination is indisputable. The executive committee meets once a month to deal with specific issues of concern. Daily affairs and crisis situations are for the most part managed by the executive director, who is nonetheless "being constantly scrutinized" by the lay executive (Dine Interview). There also is an "invisible component of decision-making," composed of a cadre of legislative and administrative assistants, senators, and congressmen, who are "the holders of real information" and determine "what is and is not possible" for the committee to achieve (Rosenbaum Interview).

The relationship between lay leaders and professional staff is complicated by the nature of AIPAC's organizational structure. While AIPAC's specialized function tends to give predominance to the professional staff, AIPAC is also heavily dependent on individual financial contributors for much of its operating budget. As a registered lobby, AIPAC must solicit financial contributions that are not deductible from income tax—a fact that tends to increase the influence of wealthy laymen, who may in turn seek to involve themselves in the agency's decision-making activities.

INTRACOMMUNAL RELATIONS

Today AIPAC is generally acknowledged as the effective political arm of the organized American Zionist community. Although initially opposed by more traditional power bases, AIPAC has established fairly effective working relations with the broader Jewish community. Special consideration is given to the local federations: "for issues are won or lost at the grass roots" (Dine Interview). The diffusion of AIPAC's network of authority on a national basis was not easily achieved, either in terms of maintaining centralized decisional authority or winning over the support of local community power holders. Nevertheless, AIPAC leaders have been relatively successful in gradually co-opting local officialdom while maintaining effective hands-on control over most decision-making responsibilities.

As already noted, there has always been a certain ambivalence between AIPAC and other national Jewish organizations. The Presidents Conference is a case in point: despite strained beginnings, relations between AIPAC and the Presidents Conference have become more amiable and routine since the Six Day War. And yet a residue of antagonism remains. Some analysts see the Presidents Conference as essentially a figurehead agency heavily dependent on AIPAC both for expertise and political initiative. Tom Dine asserts that even during the height of crisis the Presidents Conference must still seek to achieve a consensus among its various member organizations. He suggests that in times of crisis attentive elements of American Jewry look to AIPAC for immediate and decisive leadership and direction (Dine Interview). Some analysts see an informal division of labor between AIPAC and the Presidents Conference in which the former deals with the legislative branch of government while the latter concentrates its efforts on the executive branch (Lanouette 1978a; Spiegel 1984, 9; Trice 1976b, 37–39; Trice 1977b, 117–19). Dine rejects this view. When pressed, he speaks rather disparagingly of the "actual" functions performed by members of the Presidents Conference in the active foreign policy arena (Dine Interview).

AIPAC officials similarly summarize as ineffective the role played by the various national Jewish defense organizations in support of U.S.-Israeli relations. The Washington representatives of the American Jewish Congress (AJC), the American Jewish Committee (AJCommittee), and the Anti-Defamation League of B'nai B'rith may become involved in specific aspects of the American Jewish agenda of concern to their respective constituencies. But most analysts agree that on most Israel-related matters the defense agencies permit AIPAC to exercise its primacy (Amitay Interview; Bookbinder Interview; Dine Interview).

As a result of traditional disputes with much of the American Zionist mainstream, the American Jewish Committee is not a member of the Presidents Conference (Cohen 1972; Halperin 1961, 127). And it is frequently individuals associated with the AJCommittee who stand at the vanguard of groups of Jewish Americans advocating policy postures on Israel independent from (though often parallel to) AIPAC's. Hyman Bookbinder, formerly Washington representative of the AJCommittee, describes his organization's functions as those of nonpartisan general advocacy and public education on a range of issues of concern to American Jewry. It is not a registered lobby; but with a national membership of over fifty thousand and an influential International Relations Commission it is perhaps inevitable that the AJCommittee should engage in a not "insubstantial amount of lobbying" with regard to Israel (Bookbinder Interview). Bookbinder claims that during his long tenure in Washington, a full seventy percent of his time was spent on Israel-related questions and that he often worked closely with AIPAC professionals (Bookbinder Interview).

Differences between AIPAC and other major national Zionist organizations are usually confined to matters of tactic or political style. For example, Hyman Bookbinder believes the AJCommittee's relations with the government are "tolerant" and "moderate" compared to those of AIPAC, which on occasion have been "overly forceful" and "narrow minded" in approach. Bookbinder cites the two organizations' different postlegislative interactions with U.S. senators who voted in favor of the 1981 AWACS sale as a case in point (Bookbinder Interview). Bookbinder further claims that the independent course followed frequently by the AJCommittee places it in a particularly strong position in support of Israel's interests: potential coalition partners who may be frightened off by the stridency of AIPAC and the high level of public exposure accorded to its lobbying activities may find in the AJCommittee's "quietist" approach a vehicle through which to support Israel without compromising other aspects of their political agendas (Bookbinder Interview).

Differences between these two groups over specific policies or issues may be intense. However, disputes between AIPAC, the Presidents Conference, the American Jewish Committee, and other mainstream American Zionist groups usually are confined to matters of tactic and style or may reflect traditional interorganizational rivalries. They do not place into doubt American Jewry's basic value commitment to the maintenance and security of the state of Israel.

INTRACOMMUNAL DISSENT

AIPAC representatives are quick to note that they are not simply handmaidens to the Israeli government. They point to the occasions when they have differed with Israel's policies and behavior and sought to transmit their concerns and criticisms to Jerusalem in a constructive manner (Dine Interview; Kenen 1981, 106–7). AIPAC has appeared, moreover, to have accepted that a certain amount of intracommunal debate of Israel-related issues is not only natural but also necessary for the psychological and spiritual well-being of American Jewry (Dine Interview; Elazar 1980, 315–19; Fein 1989).

There is, however, an implied range of permissible behavior relating to intracommunal dialogue and dissent. A distinction has tended to be drawn between constructive debate and perceived threats to communal solidarity on Israel. The occasions of outright dissension have been relatively rare. But when they have occurred the American Zionist community, led by AIPAC or its institutional precursors, has acted vigorously.

Before Israel was a state and during the early years of its existence as a state, the American Council for Judaism was avowedly anti-Zionist. American Zionists dealt with this threat to communal solidarity by initiating an aggressive counterpropaganda campaign (Halperin 1961; Kenen 1981, 11, 22).[1] While the campaign did not entirely eliminate the Jewish anti-Zionism of Rabbi Elmer Berger et al., it did have the effect of neutralizing much of that movement's fire and of delineating fairly clearly the line beyond which intracommunal criticism of Israel would not be tolerated.

The Six Day War had an integrating effect upon much of American Jewry, including elements that were traditionally critical of Zionism (Cohen 1975). The American Council for Judaism (and its institutional successor, American Jewish Alternatives to Zionism) continued to function following the war but only as a shell of its former self: "[it] . . . has [never] been able to recover the momentum that the anti-Zionist movement appeared to have prior to 1967" (Trice 1976b, 39).

Following the October 1973 Yom Kippur War, more significant threats developed to communal solidarity on Israel-related matters. An example was *Breira* (Hebrew for *alternative*). Formed by an element of the American Jewish students' counterculture movement, Breira rapidly became a national membership organization comprised of rabbis and intellectuals, with a paid professional staff and monthly newsletter. Its membership favored a more conciliatory Israeli stance toward relations with the Arab states and the Palestinian Arabs of the occupied territories. It also emphasized the need to end what it considered to be the stifling of "the creative viability and autonomy" of Jewish communities outside of Israel, especially in the United States (Waxman 1983, 222). Many of the movement's pronouncements were sharply critical of organized American Zionism, which it considered to be unquestioning in its support of Israel's behavior.

The proper handling of the Breira challenge represented a serious dilemma for much of American Zionism. On the one hand, it was generally agreed that an effort had to be made to constrain such sentiment before it became too popular. On the other hand, too harsh a line would perhaps inadvertently give credence to many of Breira's contentions concerning Israel's inflexibility and the lack of American Zionist independence (Isaac 1977). Many of these concerns became largely academic as active support of Breira began to wane. Despite its initial popularity, Breira began to gradually crack under the combined weight of internal and external strain. Many of its activities exposed Breira to attacks on its claim that it was "a Jewish organization dedicated to the well-being of Jews and Jewish communities, both in Israel and throughout the world" (Waxman 1983, 222). Its members' placards at the United Nations reading "Palestinians—Yes, Arafat—No," at the time of the Palestine Liberation Organizations (PLO) leader's 1974 address to the General Assembly was perceived by many to be an "example of a decent political sentiment vitiated by a miserable sense of timing" (Waxman 1983, 222). The credibility of the organization was made further suspect by charges of its having "gone to great lengths to court intellectuals who have hitherto had no connection with other Jewish causes" (Mintz 1976–77, 7). These internal factors weakened Breira's capacity to withstand strong criticism from outside of the movement. Such criticism came primarily from the mainstream of American Zionism, which reportedly "launched a powerful attack upon the organization and portrayed it as an enemy of Israel" (Waxman 1983, 223–24). Whatever their veracity, these allegations had the desired effect: given the priority of Israel in the American Jewish value system, Breira lost much of its initial support and credibility.

Individual and organized dissent from the communal standard is, nevertheless, still very much in evidence. Although dissent is occasionally aroused, it has not yet coalesced into an institutionalized movement of permanent internal opposition. Influential individual American Jewish voices arose in criticism of the 1982 Israeli siege of Beirut. Even louder and larger dissent was heard in response to the excesses taken by some Israeli soldiers with regard to the human rights of Palestinian Arabs suspected of participating in the disturbances of 1987–88. A particularly serious threat to communal solidarity occurred when a small group of influential American Jews, including the respected international lawyer Rita Hauser, met with PLO chairman Yasser Arafat at Stockholm, Sweden, in early December 1988.

The organized Zionist community chose to deal with these contemporary incidents of internal dissent less through condemnation and ostracism than through denial. The strategy was to deny that there was significant dissent within American Jewry on support of Israel (Berman 1984; Dine Interview; *Near East Report*, December 5, 1988; December 12, 1988). Such denials notwithstanding, there is evidence to suggest that even prominent American Zionists, including former AIPAC staffers, had begun to quietly dissociate themselves from the prevailing communal line on Israeli policy. While continuing to declare unyielding commitment to the safety and security of Israel, many prominent American Zionists had come out publicly in opposition to some of Jerusalem's more controversial policies by the late 1980s. The future of the occupied territories and relations with the Palestine Liberation Organization drew the greatest focus (Bookbinder Interview; Rosenbaum Interview).

This handling of intracommunal relations says a great deal about the relationship between American Jewry and Israel as well as about the handling of dissent within the American Zionist community. Differences of opinion over the specific policies of particular Israeli governments are generally accepted and perhaps even tacitly solicited by the organized community. However, when intracommunal dissent degenerates into a questioning of the very legitimacy of the Jewish state—as was clearly the case with the American Council for Judaism and also conceivably among elements within Breira—dissent is no longer tolerated. The organized community then employs all of its tangible resources and moral sanctioning capacity to reimpose cohesion and solidarity.

INTERCOMMUNAL RELATIONS

AIPAC officials employ a multitude of direct and indirect methods of interacting with important segments of the domestic political environment. They establish personal contacts with influential politicians, administrative assistants, advisers, and bureaucratic officials. They provide formal briefs and testimony before a vast array of congressional committees and subcommittees with jurisdiction over the Middle East and/or U.S.-Israeli relations. Such presentations are frequently supplemented by organized letter writing and other media-directed public relations campaigns.

Unlike many of its contemporaries, including the various pro-Israeli PACs that arose primarily in the early 1980s, AIPAC has traditionally followed a policy of official nonpartisanship (Bookbinder Interview; Fialka 1983; Findley 1985; O'Brien 1986). As I. L. Kenen wrote, "We [AIPAC] sought to unite Americans in support of Israel and to bring America and Israel closer together, never permitting Israel to become a partisan issue dividing the parties" (Kenen 1981, 108).

A technique employed successfully by Zionists in the past, and adopted with particular vigor by the current generation of AIPAC leaders, is that of full Jewish community activism in the American political process. By one account, ninety-two percent of Jews participate in American electoral politics (Waxman 1983, 147–51). Although there is no necessary correlation between Jewish political activity and progress on Israel-related issues, it is nonetheless understood that political involvement often increases the possibilities of government action. The domestic ethnic community that involves itself politically stands a better chance of achieving access to, and influence over, the makers of relevant foreign policy decisions than does the group that is only marginally active in domestic political affairs (Dine Interview; Dine 1981b, 1982a, 1983a, 1983e, 1983g, 1983h).

Zionists have also sought to influence the U.S. foreign policy process by forming alliances with influential non-Jewish segments of the general population. As early as the 1930s, American Zionists had achieved strong support from various non-Jewish individuals and groups. These included academics and Christian lay and clerical leaders (Halperin 1961, 177–88). Powerful domestic support for the Zionist movement and other Jewish-related matters was also formed through strong Jewish involvement in civil rights and civil liberties causes.

Alliances with nongovernmental groups have varied over time in strength and scope. For example, since June 1967 the traditionally strong ties between American Jewry and elements of both the Church and the new left have weakened. This is largely a result of differences over Israel's policies in the occupied territories (Hertzberg 1967; Isaac 1981; Liebman 1979). The significant working political alliance between Jews and Blacks also eroded during this time. This was a function of a variety of factors, mostly relating to domestic political affairs, many of which predated the Six Day War and were unrelated to events in the Middle East. But Jewish-Black tensions were seemingly aroused by Israel's political situation after June 1967, which some radical Black community activists considered fascist, militaristic, and racist (Geltman 1970; Tsukashima 1978). Jewish-Black relations have been strained in more recent years by the presidential campaigns of the controversial Reverend Jesse Jackson and the anti-Israel rhetoric of Nation of Islam leader and Jackson supporter Louis Farrakhan (Rosen and Abramowitz 1984, 2). Despite such strains, formal relations are maintained between leading institutions of the two communities: AIPAC, the Anti-Defamation League of B'nai B'rith (ADL) and the National Association for the Advancement of Colored People (NAACP) (Dine 1983g). Recent survey data also indicate that American Blacks remain generally supportive of Israel or neutral on the Arab-Israeli conflict. For example, one study indicated that "sixteen of the 21 members of the Black Congressional Caucus (an even higher percentage than their white colleagues), have consistently voted for foreign aid to Israel and against major arms sales to those Arab nations still not at peace with Israel" (Rosen and Abramowitz 1984, 1). Moreover, over the past decade, nonwhite to white support for Israel averaged about two-to-one (Rosen and Abramowitz 1984, 1, 12–13).

These statistics reflect an important feature of Israel's status in the American domestic political milieu. In their pleas on behalf of Israel, AIPAC officials have always benefited from the "positive emotional response" that Israel tends to arouse in the minds of many Americans (Cohen 1975, 97; Gilboa 1987).[2] Among the more prominent explanations for such pro-Israel popular sentiment are feelings of Christian guilt concerning the European Holocaust; the image of Israel's "David" to the Arab world's "Goliath"; and the similarity of Israel's pioneering spirit and religious heritage to that of the American frontier experience (Elazar 1980, 70–98; Feuerwerger 1979; Garnham 1977; Rosen and Abramowitz 1984, 3–4). The impact of Israel on the minds of Americans has elicited tremendous controversy and critical debate, especially in the latter half of the 1980s (Green 1984; Grose 1983; Tivnan 1987). Regardless of recent criticism, Israel continues to evoke the fascination of a large number of non-Jewish Americans, a factor that a politically astute pro-Israel lobby has often been able to use to its fullest advantage.

Another theme well exploited by American Zionists relates to Israel's status as a "sister democracy" and reliable strategic ally in the Middle East in defense of the security interests of the United States and the Western world (Safran 1969, 1981; Spiegel 1985, 1–15). The "strategic asset" argument indeed has become a linchpin of AIPAC's approach to the American domestic political environment

(Blair 1984; Carus 1983, 1984; Glick 1983; Indyk, Kupchan, and Rosen 1983; Rosen 1982).

The strong sympathy that the American public has traditionally demonstrated toward Israel has been "one of the most striking and consistent features of this nation's consensus on foreign policy for over three decades" (Rosen and Abramowitz 1984, 1). Some analysts have asserted that support for Israel has eroded recently, especially among certain key demographic sectors. This assumption is only partially borne out by empirical evidence. Even during the Lebanon War and the Palestinian disturbances, which must be seen as low points in Israel's international reputation, there was evidence supporting what Rosen and Abramowitz term "the extraordinary reservoir of sympathy" that exists for Israel in the United States (1984, 2; see also Gilboa 1989).

In addition to seeking to exploit persistent pro-Israeli sympathies within the general public, AIPAC also works to establish ties with selected influential nongovernmental organizations. Two particularly important sources of continued support for Israel throughout the 1970s and 1980s were leading elements of the organized labor movement and Christian fundamentalists. Although the course of events in the Middle East tempered attitudes among the rank and file of these two groups, each group's leadership expressed continued support of the state of Israel, if not the specific policies of the Israeli government of the day (*Near East Report*, November 28, 1988, 199). This continued support serves as a valuable political resource that AIPAC officials are quick to exploit in relations with Congress and the White House (Dine Interview).

The American media has played an interesting, if somewhat fickle, part in AIPAC's political activities. I. L. Kenen wrote that much of the early petro-diplomatic opposition to Israel in Washington was reinforced by the generally anti-Zionist editorial posture of the influential *New York Times* (Kenen 1981, 12, 114–15). Significant elements of the American Jewish mainstream criticized the media's coverage of Israeli actions in Lebanon and during the Palestinian disturbances as sensationalized, biased, and excessively fixated on Israel (See Karetzky and Goldman 1986). To many American Jews the print and electronic media seem "out to get" Israel. Scholars in the field of media and communications and practicing journalists alike tend to be of two minds on the issue: some concur with Jewry's criticism of elements within the media; others focus less upon any intrinsic journalistic bias against Israel than upon the "structural imperatives" of the North American communications industry itself (Taras and Gottlieb Taras 1986–87). The *Jerusalem Post*'s permanent correspondent in Washington, Wolf Blitzer, agrees that some elements of the American media may indeed be excessive and unfair in their coverage of Israel-related matters. However, he suggests that much of this bias is countered by a significant proportion of the media that remains relatively sympathetic toward Israel. He postulates further that the majority of the American media fall into a middle range of attitudes concerning Israel and the Arabs, indicating little or no overt sympathy or bias toward either side (Blitzer 1985).

Much of the American media's continued concentration on Israel reflects its audience's continued fascination with the Jewish state. Undoubtedly media coverage strongly critical of Israel must be harmful to the interests of the American Zionist lobby. Especially troubling was increased media focus, in the late 1980s, not upon Israel but rather upon the inner workings of American Zionism itself (*Near East Report*, October 31, 1988, 184). Although AIPAC has never been particularly shy about popular scrutiny of its activities (Dine Interview), its leaders expressed concern about media allusions to the alleged excessive influence of Zionist interests and to AIPAC's propensity toward "dual loyalty"; that is, a tendency on the part of the organized Jewish community to concern itself more with the interests of Israel than those of the United States (*Near East Report*, October 31, 1988, 184). Nevertheless, the media's opinion on Israel remains diverse and varied, and its need to cater to the public's basic sympathy toward Israel relative to the Arab world can conceivably be exploited by AIPAC activists.

CONCLUSION

This chapter concludes that the American Zionist community has been fairly complete in its organizational development. Although beginning with a rather disorganized and diffuse institutional base and a largely disinterested American Jewish constituency, AIPAC has evolved into a large, cohesive, and respected advocate of its constituency's concerns about U.S.-Israeli relations.

By the same token, AIPAC's organizational development is less than complete. It remains largely elitist, with a self-serving and self-perpetuating activist cadre. The organization's structural character also makes AIPAC's professional staff highly susceptible to the demands and policy preferences of large financial contributors. Moreover, American Zionism's handling of internal dissent on Israel is less than theoretically optimal. Although they usually co-opt and integrate critical voices, Zionist leaders have on at least two occasions taken a more heavy-handed approach. A Jewish "antiestablishment" on Israel-related matters does in fact exist, although it is generally weak and restricted to the periphery of the mainstream of organized American Jewry. One area of particular criticism centers on controversial aspects of Israel's political and military policies toward its Arab neighbors. Another is what critics perceive to be an unwillingness of American Zionist leaders to adopt a policy line that is both self-critical and independent of the Israeli government's policy.

In spite of its problems, AIPAC exhibits many of the qualities of an institutionalized domestic ethnic interest group. Its organizational sophistication is pronounced relative to its ethnic opposition in "the battle for Washington" (Barberis 1976; Speigel 1985). The organized American Arab community has tended to be plagued by disunity relating to a host of internal political, national, religious, and generational disputes (Abraham and Abraham 1981, 1983; Lanouette 1978b, 754; Orfalea 1988; Spiegel 1984, 1985; Trice, 1976b, 36–37, 52–

55). Despite significant organizational growth and domestic and international alliance-building during the period following the Six Day War and especially since the October 1973 Arab-Israeli War (Emerson 1985; Goot and Rosen 1983; Sander 1978c), the Arab American lobby remains objectively less well organized than its Jewish counterpart (Farrell 1983; Howe and Trott 1977, 271–361; Lanouette 1978b, 754).

Organizational sophistication, of course, is a relative concept and does not in any way guarantee ethnic group influence over governmental foreign policy decision-making. The extent to which AIPAC was able to exploit its organizational advantage over its ethnic Arab counterpart and transform this advantage into a consistent pattern of pro-Israeli U.S. government actions (or nonactions) during the 1973–88 period remains to be seen.

NOTES

1. For a description of the political program and behavior of significant elements of the Jewish anti-Zionist movement, see American Council for Judaism 1944a, 1944b, 1946. See also Berger 1942, 1945, 1951, 1957; Halperin 1961, 86–92, 281–292; and Lilienthal 1953, 1957, 1965, 1978.

2. **Table 1**

American Popular Sympathies for Jews/Israel and Arabs, 1947–1988

Date	Jews	Arabs	Both, Neither, Don't Know
November 1947	24%	12%	64%
June 1948	34%	12%	54%
April 1957	33%	17%	50%
June 7, 1967	56%	4%	40%
August 1970	47%	6%	47%
October 1973	39%	4%	56%
September 1978	42%	12%	46%
June 1982	39%	9%	52%
September 1982	32%	28%	40%
January 1988	47%	15%	38%
May 1988	44%	13%	43%

Source: Gilboa 1986, 1989.

3

The Canada-Israel Committee: History, Mandate, and Organizational Structure

THE DISTINCTIVE CANADIAN ZIONIST

Canadian Zionism, although operating from a much smaller population base, exhibits many of the same qualities as its American counterpart. As in the U.S., the Canadian Zionist community's evolution was adversely affected by intra-communal philosophical disputes and organizational rivalries (Kay 1978; Waller 1981b, 343–49). Also countering integrative tendencies was the growth of powerful local Jewish federations on the American model, especially in Montreal and Toronto, and the concomitant absence of a national body powerful enough to draw diverse and autonomous Zionist groups into a cohesive federation (Waller 1981b).

Despite these similarities, there are several factors that distinguish the Canadian Zionist experience. Many of these factors are cultural in origin. The staid and paternalistic Canadian political culture theoretically leaves little room for political self-expression by groups that do not comfortably conform to the prevailing socioeconomic elite portfolio, the so-called old boys' network (Presthus 1973). Although some Canadian Jews have been remarkably successful in the manufacturing sector and certain professions, the level of communal prosperity is mixed and has tended to limit widespread Zionist interaction with the effective public policymakers (Hayes 1966, 1979; Stanislawski 1981a, 397–400; Waller 1981a, 155–58). Additionally, the significant French Catholic minority in Canada is traditionally antithetical toward Judaism and Israel. Antisemitism is no less prevalent in the United States than in Canada. However, popular attitude in Canada toward Jews is intertwined with the French Catholic-English Protestant cultural bifurcation (Cohn 1979; Colter and Wisse 1977; Waller and Weinfeld 1981; Weinfeld 1980). Passive and overt antisemitism is not restricted to French

Catholic Canadians; witness its manifestation in various forms in Atlantic Canada, Ontario, and the Western provinces (Arnold 1981, 268–69; Ages 1981; Medjuck and Lazar 1981, 246).

The prevalence of social antisemitism in Canada has affected organized Jewry's lobbying efforts in the foreign policy-making process. A primary example is the exclusionist policy concerning Jewish refugees from Nazi Germany during the 1930s adopted by Prime Minister William Lyon Mackenzie King, his Quebec lieutenant, Ernest Lapointe, and the director of immigration, F. C. Blair (Abella and Troper 1982). The Canadian government's policy on the partitioning of Palestine and the granting of de facto and de jure recognition to the state of Israel in the late 1940s wedded latent Canadian antisemitism and Prime Minister Mackenzie King's unyielding determination to remain loyal to British policy on Palestine (Bercuson 1985; Kay 1978). In this complex intermingling of issues and considerations, Zionists were unable to influence Canadian policy on Palestine in a fashion generally attributed to them by their detractors.[1]

Executive dominance of the Canadian legislative process presents Zionists with a structural obstacle unmatched in the United States. Given the inherent statism of the Canadian foreign policy-making process, access for nongovernmental organizations (NGOs) is not assured. Even if by exploiting various political resources and personal contacts the NGO should achieve greater access to the locus of decision-making, there is no guarantee that influence over policy output will necessarily follow. As the political scientist Robert Presthus asserts, it is not only access into the system that presents the major problem for Canadians seeking to influence their government, it also is the difficulty of achieving their goals *despite* the opportunity to be heard (Presthus 1974b, 52). As less than completely assimilated Canadians, Jews in particular have experienced this phenomenon in their Zionist lobbying activities.

ORIGIN

Jewish immigrants to Canada, just as those to the United States, tended to carry diverse Zionist ideals with them. Various independent Zionist groups arose in Canada during the last decades of the nineteenth century. By the 1890s the first attempts were made to consolidate them (Kay 1978; Sack 1965, 220–59). Many of these early organizational efforts foundered on the rocks of intracommunal dispute. As a community, Canadian Jews were "emphatically Zionist in their folk aspirations" (Rosenberg 1970–71, 16) and were always among the highest per capita contributors of money to Zionist causes in the world (Gottesman 1964, 89). However, their principal affiliations were to specific Zionist parties, "each of which operated independently on a national basis with international connections and strong local chapters" (Waller 1981b, 347).

It was only with the end of the Second World War and the subsequent placing of the British Mandate for Palestine at the top of the international political agenda that Canadian Zionists began to seriously consider the need for greater unity (Kay 1978, 88). Although Canadian Zionists were ineffective in influencing the Mackenzie King government on that issue, they acquired some valuable political lessons from the Palestine debate of the late 1940s. Principal among these was recognition of the need to set aside their partisan differences and strive for greater communal solidarity on Israel-related matters. The organizational character and political behavior of Canadian Zionism during subsequent decades were a direct consequence of the experiences of the 1947–49 period (Waller 1981b, 348).

Between 1949 and 1967 Canadian Jewry in general and Canadian Zionism specifically became more centralized (Waller 1981b, 348). By the early 1960s a Zionist Public Affairs Committee had been established, involving many community leaders and notables. Although this particular exercise was short-lived, it is no coincidence that many of the same individuals were among the principals in the formation of the Canada-Israel Committee nearly a decade later. Centralizing tendencies experienced throughout the 1960s were significantly enhanced by the Six Day War. In response to impending hostilities, a Co-ordinating Committee for Emergency Aid to Israel was established. It was formally dissolved once the immediate crisis had passed, but the momentum it created gave rise to a second group that met throughout the war and continued to meet on an ad hoc basis in the days and weeks following the termination of hostilities. The Joint Public Relations Committee was cosponsored by the Canadian Jewish Congress (CJC) and the Zionist Organization of Canada (ZOC), which became the Canadian Zionist Federation (CZF) in 1970.

The Joint Public Relations Committee was slow to develop into a viable ethnic foreign policy lobby. It remained largely ad hoc in organizational character and lacked both the professional sophistication and internal cohesion required to effectively represent Canada-Israel interests in the political domain on a permanent basis. In late 1967 the committee was transformed into the Canada-Israel Committee (CIC), and was mandated to serve as the formal liaison between the Canadian Jewish community and Ottawa as well as Israel's advocate before the Canadian media and public.

Despite its more formalized mandate, the CIC's organizational structure remained fluid. Indeed, the committee was briefly dissolved in 1971 when its cosponsors, the CJC and CZF, were unable to agree on a common political agenda (Bick Interview; May Interview; Plaut Interview). The CIC was formally reconstituted in late 1971 with the B'nai B'rith as a full sponsoring partner and under the professional direction of Montreal lawyer Myer Bick. Initially operating only out of Montreal, Bick surrounded himself with a small coterie of young and aggressive individuals. But the operation remained small and the professional staff politically untested.

The watershed in the CIC's development was the October 1973 Yom Kippur War. It was this event that certified the Canada-Israel Committee as the principal representative of Jewish pro-Israel interests in Canada (Cotler 1974a; Hayes 1974). Prior to the war, the CIC had only a staff of three or four at its Montreal office and no permanent representation in Ottawa. Following the war, the committee expanded its operation dramatically. It established a permanent Ottawa office and acquired a larger permanent professional staff and a budget appropriate to its expanded responsibilities (Bick Interview). The CIC also expanded its Montreal office, establishing a French-speaking adjunct (the Comité Quebec-Israel), and in 1975 opened a Toronto office housing its research and communications facilities.

Membership in the Canada-Israel Committee is exclusively role-based. Its three main sponsors, the Canadian Jewish Congress, the Canadian Zionist Federation, and B'nai B'rith each have representation on the committee's board of directors. In an effort to broaden the constituency, as part of a general recent process of Canadian Jewish democratization (Plaut Interview), representatives of other major national Jewish organizations and of the major Jewish communities throughout the country also now sit on the committee's governing body. Past presidents and executive directors of the CIC and other community notables are also included among the committee's leadership. The board of directors meets on a quarterly basis, at which time general policy guidelines are discussed and established. The executive committee, the size of which varies between nine and twelve members, meets informally on shorter notice and acts with considerable discretionary authority during crises.

The management of an estimated annual budget of $900,000 is the direct responsibility of the national executive director (Abugov Interview; Willmot Interview). Most CIC professionals feel that they operate in a fairly autonomous structural framework, despite the existence of a lay leadership of ultimate authority (Bessin Interview; Resnick Interview). Day-to-day administration is generally left to the professional staff. However, the interaction between lay leaders and professionals tends to be rather complex and very dependent on the personalities of the individuals involved. As a past CIC national executive director said, while usually given more than adequate decisional autonomy, "I am [was] still responsible to the board of directors" (Resnick Interview).

The Canada-Israel Committee tends strongly toward the corporate mold of organizational structure. Membership is not only role-based; it is also dominated by many of the financial and political elites of Canadian Jewry (Waller 1981a). The group's lay leadership is self-perpetuating. The national chairman is selected by formal ballot, but this tends to be a perfunctory affirmation of decisions already made on the basis of informal negotiations and brokering among communal elites.

The group shows democratic accountability in various ways. The general Canadian Jewish community is kept abreast of CIC concerns and activities through reports in the Jewish press and various Canadian Zionist in-house publications. The *Canadian Middle-East Digest* and the CIC's various special research handbooks and memoranda are disseminated widely throughout the Jewish community. CIC leaders also seek to co-opt influential segments of the formally unaffiliated Jewish community. For example, "upwardly mobile" Jewish businessmen and professionals are invited to participate in periodic leadership seminars, and Jewish academics and political activists are made part of an informal resource network. Finally, the Canada-Israel Committee convenes an annual policy conference to which all of Canadian Jewry is invited to interact with communal leaders and politicians and thereby become more actively involved in the performance of the committee's lobbying activities.

Even this degree of democratization tends to be more apparent than real. Communal involvement in the CIC is usually interest- or issue-specific, reserved to those with specialized backgrounds and career interests or who are motivated by specific issues on the Canada-Israel agenda. And while the annual conference often concludes with a plenary vote on general resolutions, this vote usually represents perfunctory affirmation of a silent communal consensus that does not significantly restrict the decisional latitude of the CIC elites in responding to more specific issues of concern to the organization.

Another concern relates to the amount of institutional latitude granted to the Canada-Israel Committee by its unique organizational characteristics. The CIC is "devoted to the promotion of increased understanding between the peoples of Canada and Israel. . . . It speaks and acts on behalf of the Canadian Jewish community on all matters relating to Canada-Israel affairs" (CIC 1977). As a former national executive director of the CIC succinctly puts it, "the Jewish community is our constituency" (Resnick Interview).

The exclusivity of the CIC's mandate is generally acknowledged. However, the committee is the child of a marriage of various national organizations and local federations. The CIC does not formally have its own constituency; a politically attentive Canadian Jew cannot "join" the national Canada-Israel Committee in the way that he or she can join various membership-based community groups. This organizational non-independence affects the CIC in a variety of ways, most notably in the areas of funding and policy-making. Without an independent membership base, the CIC does not have an independent source of financing. Its budget is established by the National Budgeting Conference (NBC) on the basis of the overall contributions made by affiliate organizations and federations and the overall needs of the community as a whole. Canadian Jews value Israel highly so the CIC's budget is usually given high priority; nevertheless, nothing is sacrosanct: the NBC's budgetary allocation is still subject to the varying needs of other communal agencies, constituent organizations, and federations (Abugov Interview; Bessin Interview; Willmot Interview).

Its lack of an independent base of support also tends to affect the CIC's independence in regard to policy-making and agenda-setting. Given the unique nature of its sponsorship, the CIC faces the problem of having too many masters to answer to simultaneously. The problem is exacerbated when representatives of the various constituent agencies disagree on the Canadian Israeli agenda or on the proper political course the CIC should adopt. When lay leaders disagree, the professional staff is left either unclear as to the appropriate policy direction or so preoccupied with reaching an intraorganizational consensus as to severely restrict the fulfillment of the committee's mandate to lobby government and the Canadian public (Bessin Interview; Willmot Interview).

The organizational structure of the Canada-Israel Committee is itself somewhat problematical. The CIC is formally a centralized operation. Although offices are located in Toronto and Montreal and volunteer support committees are found in Jewish communities throughout the country, most major decisions emanate from the Ottawa office. The centralization of CIC activities seems reasonable given the small population size of the Canadian Jewish community and its concentration in two or three cities. The dominance of the federal government in the foreign policy-making process lends further credence to a centralized lobbying effort. And yet two factors constrain this centralizing tendency. First, the political and financial power of large local federations, especially those in Toronto and Montreal and the concern that the committee not alienate smaller Jewish communities outside of the metropolitan regions requires that the CIC devolve some of its central authority and expend considerable energy integrating representatives from across the country into the decisional framework (Bessin Interview; Willmot Interview).

The second factor relates to Le Fait Francais. Given the exigencies unique to Canadian federal politics and the existence of a large and influential Jewish population in Montreal, the Canada-Israel Committee has established a separate French-speaking adjunct to its English-speaking Montreal office. The Comité Quebec-Israel, while still very much within the CIC's general framework of activities, nevertheless gives the impression of quasi independence. And it does indeed deal with a range of Canada-Israel issues alien to much of the rest of Canadian Jewry, especially the strange blend of antisemitism and anti-Zionism common to French Roman Catholicism and disseminated in recent years by some Quebec union leaders and nationalists (Cohn 1979; Cotler and Wisse 1977; Waller 1981b, 355–56; Waller and Weinfeld 1981; Weinfeld 1980). Although integration of the French-language bureau into the mainstream of Canadian Jewish affairs has been attempted, the Comité Quebec-Israel remains a partially autonomous element of the national operation, a structural factor that to some extent inhibits the CIC's agenda-setting and representativeness.

INTRACOMMUNAL RELATIONS

Many of the Canada-Israel Committee's organizational idiosyncracies also impact directly upon its relations with its broader Jewish constituency and with other local and national Jewish and Zionist organizations. Two issues are particularly worthy of note: relations between the Canada-Israel Committee and dissenting communal elements, and relations among the committee's three principal national constituent units.

Canadian Jewry has no organization comparable to the anti-Zionist American Council for Judaism (Waller 1981b, 355). To be sure, some individuals within the Jewish community, including notable rabbis and academics, have been critical of either the behavior of the government of Israel or the way in which the organized Jewish community operated in support of Israel. These critical voices were most pronounced during Israel's 1982 misadventure in Lebanon (*Montreal Gazette*, October 2, 1982, B8; *Toronto Star* August 22, 1982, A33). However, critics remained for the most part on the periphery of the Jewish community during the Lebanon War and did not constitute an organized or serious challenge to the communal power structure or to the prevailing consensus on Israel-related questions.

The Palestinian disturbances of 1987–88 caused further dissent to emerge within Canadian Zionism. Controversies produced by the disturbances, including the active debate in Israel about the future of the occupied territories, affected the mainstream of Canadian Jewry. Articulate elements within the community were divided by the issues. The CIC attempted to conciliate the diverse groups and in the process was condemned by virtually everyone. It was criticized by elements of the center-left, organizing themselves for the most part under the banner of "Peace Now," as too conservative, too quick to defend Israel's policies in the territories, and exclusivist in its orientation and policy-making. Elements of the center-right criticized the CIC for not being forthright enough in its support of the state of Israel in its hour of need (Waller 1988).[2] The opinions of the vast majority of Canadian Jews fell somewhere between the two poles, and these Jews lamented the CIC's inability to somehow unite everyone in support of Israel. The goal of unifying a small, yet highly diverse and opinionated, Jewish community was made all but impossible given the course of developments in Israel and the occupied territories and the Arafat "peace offensive" of late 1988 (Willmot Interview). Yet, the sense that the CIC had somehow failed to do its job was prevalent and in a way understandable. The center-left coalition that arose out of the Palestinian disturbances, although representing only a small segment of Canadian Jewry, presented a potential challenge to the communal consensus on Israel-related matters that the Canada-Israel Committee had long sought to achieve and maintain.

A more enduring threat to communal solidarity results from policy differences among mainstream leaders themselves, particularly those constituting the Canada-Israel Committee's inner circle of volunteers. Two historical examples will suffice. The first example has already been cited: in 1971 the activities of the CIC were brought to a halt temporarily when delegates from the Canadian Jewish Congress and the Canadian Zionist Federation could not agree on the appropriate strategy for the committee to adopt. The second example of intraorganizational dispute relates to former Progressive Conservative party leader Joe Clark's 1979 pledge to transfer the Canadian embassy in Israel from Tel Aviv to Jerusalem. Although largely tactical in nature, the differences in opinion over the embassy issue were reportedly strong enough to threaten the very existence of the Canada-Israel Committee.

The war in Lebanon and the Palestinian disturbances did not appear to produce severe differences among the CIC's inner circle. A former member of the committee's staff candidly suggests, however, that at the time of the latter incidents there were some "pragmatists" among the CIC's lay leadership as well as some "who are still living in the ghetto" (confidential interview with CIC official).

The fact that the Canada-Israel Committee has been able to maintain a sense of cohesion and unity of purpose even when faced with communal dissenters and intraorganizational disputes speaks of the basic unity that has traditionally prevailed within Canadian Jewry on Israel-related matters. Although there may be "occasional breaches of community solidarity," these usually are confined to intraorganizational rivalries and/or differences over political style (Bick Interview). Notwithstanding organizational parochialism and the occasional emergence of intracommunal dissent, Canadian Jewry as a whole remains fairly disciplined in its commitment to the survival and security of the state of Israel (Bick Interview; Plaut Interview).

INTERCOMMUNAL RELATIONS

The CIC employs various strategies in the fulfillment of its mandate as the exclusive representative of Canadian Jewry on matters relating to Israel and Canada-Israel relations. At a general level, the CIC keeps the Jewish and non-Jewish public informed of Israel's concerns through a sophisticated process of written and oral communication. Through such activities, the CIC aspires to maintain the saliency of Israel's interests within a general populace often preoccupied with domestic political and economic concerns.

The CIC seeks to represent Israel's interests and affect the general course of Canada-Israel relations by establishing "political relations with the body politic" (Resnick Interview). All members of Parliament (MPs) receive copies of the *Canadian Middle-East Digest* and other CIC research material. The CIC does not aim to inundate the already overworked MP with pro-Israel literature but rather to serve a vital "information-processing function" in the Canadian policy process (Resnick Interview). The rationale is straightforward: the average Canadian parliamentarian is far too much a generalist and far too busy to do extensive research on the vast number of issues confronting him or her on a daily basis. If the first piece of information the parliamentarian receives on an issue concerning the Middle East (and having nothing whatsoever to do with Israel) has been professionally prepared by the Canada-Israel Committee, then the MP will be more likely to adopt a pro-Israel perspective on subsequent issues (Bick Interview; Resnick Interview).

Proper performance of the information-processing function also involves presenting briefs and testimony before parliamentary committees and subcommittees and royal commissions of inquiry. Although CIC leaders acknowledge the limited role such bodies usually have in the Canadian foreign policy decisional process, if one is to play the game of influence-peddling then one must play it fully. The failure to make representations before relevant parliamentary committees could very well be construed as a group's indifference towards a particular issue, thereby giving unwarranted political advantage to competing groups that go to the trouble of making representations (Resnick Interview).

Another principal area of CIC activity involves establishing meaningful relations with newly elected MPs and incumbent backbenchers of all parties. CIC activists seek to explain Israel's position when controversies arise in the Middle East. MPs are invited to meet with Israeli officials, participate in study missions to Israel and attend the CIC's annual parliamentary dinner. The purpose of these contacts is to stimulate policy debate within the three federal party caucuses and to cultivate pro-Israeli sympathies among the next generation of Canadian political leaders. In the Canadian parliamentary system of government, today's backbencher may be tomorrow's cabinet minister.

A principal tenet of the CIC's lobbying strategy has always been to relate to federal politicians on a nonpartisan basis. (The one serious deviation from this strategy—Joe Clark's Jerusalem Embassy pledge—produced less than satisfactory results for Canadian Jewry's leaders). The CIC's strategy is to tailor its approach so as to appeal to the ideological dispositions of all parliamentarians: to members of the New Democratic Party, Israel's social-democratic roots are emphasized; to those of the ideological right, Israel's strong anticommunism and antiterrorism credentials will be cited; and to parliamentarians disposed toward Christian fundamentalism, the religious significance of Israel as the Holy Land and the freedom of worship guaranteed by Israeli law is stressed (Bick Interview; Taras 1983, 304).

In deference to the statist quality of foreign policy-making in Canada, CIC activists concentrate a good part of their energies on achieving institutionalized relations with the federal cabinet and senior bureaucracy. Delegations from the Canada-Israel Committee meet formally with the Secretary of State for External Affairs (SSEA) at least three or four times a year. Less formal interactions may occur on a more frequent basis, depending on the objective circumstances in the Middle East as well as the predisposition of the SSEA and his or her senior bureaucratic and political advisers (Bick Interview; Resnick Interview).[3]

The CIC makes formal representations before various cabinet committees and, when possible, before the prime minister. As the essential gatekeepers in the Canadian policy process, officials in both the Privy Council Office (PCO) and the Prime Minister's Office (PMO) have increasingly become formal and informal routes through which the CIC seeks access to, and influence over, the makers of decisions in Canadian foreign policy.

The professional foreign service officer plays an important role in advising cabinet members on foreign policy issues. The CIC maintains extensive ongoing relations with officials in the Department of External Affairs and other bureaus and agencies of government with potential impact upon Canadian-Israeli bilateral relations and Canada's policy toward the Arab-Israeli conflict. Traditionally, the CIC was perceived by many at External Affairs as the most knowledgeable source in Ottawa of reliable information on Israel and the Middle East (Bick Interview; Former Member of the Middle East Division, Department of External

Affairs Interview). Although the Ottawa "marketplace" on Middle East-related issues has become much more crowded of late (Taras and Goldberg 1989), the CIC is still a respected source of credible information and analysis on current developments in Israel and the Middle East of concern to Canada (Bessin Interview; Willmot Interview; Former official of the Middle East Division, Department of External Affairs Interview).

Jewish community leaders counseled the CIC to work within the parameters of the prevailing Canadian foreign policy-making process. The key to effective interest group intervention in the Canadian process, unlike in the competitive American system, tends to be accommodation and compromise in the pursuit of that which is achievable (Rose n.d., 5–6). Myer Bick, former CIC national executive director, summarizes the Canadian approach to ethnic interest group lobbying in the following way: "You can get things done with an element of pleasantness. . . . Don't be heavy all the time. . . . We live in a democracy; if you are good enough and are serious enough . . . and are pleasant in your relations with government . . . you can get things done" (Bick Interview).

Although the Canadian foreign policy decisional process approximates the statist model, even the prime minister is not entirely immune to changes in public opinion or the pressures of significant coalitions of nongovernmental groups. Consequently, the Canada-Israel Committee seeks to complement its lobbying of government with appeals to Canadian public opinion and influential NGOs. In such interactions, the CIC has frequently avoided advocating a distinctly "Jewish" or "Israeli" posture. The practice of soft-pedaling Zionism permits the CIC to appeal to more universal principles, values, and norms prevalent throughout much of Canadian society. A former CIC national executive director expresses this philosophy simply: "To be a good advocate for Israel, be a good Canadian" (Bessin Interview).

As do their counterparts in the United States, Canadian Jews have long-standing affiliation with liberal and civil rights causes. The organized Jewish community also has traditional ties with the United Church of Canada. Relations with the United Church became strained in the post–1967 period because of the church's criticism of Israel's relations with the Palestinian Arabs (Plaut 1981b; Slonim 1976; Taras 1989). The intifada exacerbated relations between Canadian Jewry and the United Church and various other Christian denominations.[4]

Canadian Zionists have traditionally enjoyed fairly friendly relations with organized labor. Much of this resulted from solidarity with Israel's *Histadrut* labor movement and the social democratic roots of Israel's political culture. While such sympathy has sometimes been translated into general political advantage for Zionists, more often Canadian labor's affection toward Israel has remained symbolic rather than tangible. Canada's policy in the Middle East is not a major item on labor's political agenda. As the 1980s progressed, even organized labor's general sympathy with Israel was showing signs of strain. The 1982 Lebanon War produced differences between the Ontario Federation of Labour (OFL) and the umbrella Canadian Labour Congress (CLC) over the former's condemnation of Israel. In May 1988 the CLC plenary in Vancouver adopted a resolution strongly critical of Israel's handling of the Palestinian disturbances (Ferman 1988, 12). Individual Canadian unionists may remain sympathetically disposed toward the state of Israel; however, as a corporate entity, Canadian labor has joined the growing number of domestic NGOs critical of Israeli policy.

The media, electronic and print, serve as important conduits of information and opinion in Canada. However, the media's coverage of Canadian foreign policy has traditionally been "highly fragmented, superficial, and given an extremely low profile" (Taras 1983, 247). As the noted Canadian journalist Robert Fulford writes, "In the Press Gallery in Ottawa there are 175 reporters, but I don't believe there is one of them who could be called an expert on foreign policy" (In Stanbury 1978, 197).

The Middle East and the Arab-Israeli conflict have always drawn interest from significant portions of the Canadian media (Dewitt and Kirton 1983b; Kay 1962–63). There has, however, been no consistent pattern either with regard to the scope or the editorial slant of the coverage. For example, the political scientist Peyton V. Lyon has long charged that Canadian policy in the Middle East is tilted overwhelmingly in favor of the Israeli posture and attributes this, among other things, to a de facto political alliance between important segments of the media and Canadian Jewry (1982a, 1982b). Dewitt and Kirton (1984, 1989), Kirton, Barei, and Smokum (1985), and Keenleyside, Soderlund, and Burton (1985) all have put Lyon's allegation to empirical examination but have arrived at contrary conclusions.

The only real consistency in the relationship between Israel and the Canadian media appears to rest with the French-language press in Quebec, which traditionally has been critical of Israel. Increasingly, the francophone media's coverage of the Middle East has included explicit references to Canadian Jewry's alleged dual loyalty vis-à-vis Canadian policy towards Israel and the Arab-Israeli conflict (Kirton, Barei, and Smokum 1985; La Presse, March 12, 1988, 7). The Palestinian disturbances sparked the extension of such editorial comment into much of the influential English-language Canadian print media (Aikenhead 1988, 13–14; Calgary Herald, February 18, 1988, 5; Ottawa Citizen, March 11, 1988, A1, A7; Toronto Star, March 12, 1988, A1, A11).

The CIC's greatest successes in forming alliances with the media have tended to be with specific newspapers and in reference to specific issues (e.g., the Globe and Mail in the antiboycott campaign). But these successes are few. Several other events during 1973–88—including the Jerusalem embassy affair, the Lebanon War, and the Palestinian disturbances—resulted in widespread media criticism of Israel. In response to media criticism during the Lebanon War and the intifada, leading Canadian Jews charged that the media were either inexplicably fixated with Israel-related issues or deliberately anti-Zionist in orientation (Abella 1988a; Aikenhead 1988; Zerker 1988). Research suggests that such alleged media malice toward Israel may be more the exception than the rule

Table 2
Canadian Sympathies for Israel and Arabs

Date	Pro-Israel	Pro-Arab	No Sympathy/Opinion
1958	14%	5%	81%
1969	26%	9%	65%
Dec/1973	22%	5%	73%
1978	23%	13%	64%
Nov/1982	17%	13%	70%
Mar/1988	23%	14%	63%

Source: Canadian Institute of Public Opinion/Gallup Poll. Globe and Mail/Environics Survey   March 30, 1989

(Taras and Gottlieb Taras 1986–87): it is ambivalence that most typifies media concern with the Middle East; and it is this ambivalence that constrains Zionist efforts to institutionalize relations with the Canadian media.

For some analysts, the media's ambivalence toward the Middle East reflects a broader traditional Canadian popular indifference towards the region and its conflicts. As the political scientist James Eayrs wrote in the late 1950s, "The Middle East is not a part of the world in which the Canadian people and their governments have tended to take much interest" (1959, 252–53). Eayrs's assertion is borne out by public opinion poll data (table 2).

Poll data also suggest that popular support for Israel tends to vary between regions and ethnocultural/linguistic groups, the most telling of such variance being the low support for Israel among French-speaking Quebeckers (Benesh 1979; Cohn 1979).

Variance on the basis of region and ethnicity/mother tongue notwithstanding, the most distinctive factor about Canadian popular opinion on the Middle East remains the consistently high rate of indifference. For the most part, attentive Canadians have been supportive of the state of Israel since at least 1956. However, the proportion of Canadians indicating interest in the Middle East is so small as to adversely affect the CIC's attempts to establish reliable coalition ties with influential segments of the domestic political environment.

Despite the limited Canadian popular concern with the Middle East, fairly strong pro-Israeli sympathies have traditionally prevailed among Canadian parliamentarians. The reasons for this are similar to those used to explain support for Israel in the U.S. Senate. There is an electoral dimension; the Canadian electoral system is constructed in such a way as to accentuate well-represented interests in individual constituencies. The Canadian Jewish community is concentrated in perhaps six electoral ridings nationally that can make or break a party's electoral fortunes. The potential electoral sanctioning or supporting capacity of Canadian Jews is especially pronounced when contrasted to that of Arab Canadians, who constitute barely one-third the size of their Jewish counterparts and tend to be more disparate, both geographically and politically (Abu-Laban 1980, 1988). Also prompting pro-Israeli sentiment among politicians is the extent to which a handful of influential Jews have integrated into the mainstream of Canadian political life. Although some analysts and practitioners suggest that the community sometimes harms itself with the stridency of its presentation (Former Assistance to the SSEA, Interview; Official of DEA, Interview; Stanfield Interview), its political activists, operating mainly through the Canada-Israel Committee, have successfully established a network of contacts and alliances that span the Canadian political spectrum. The sophistication of the Jewish community's coalition building, and its integration into the Canadian political milieu, again compare favorably to that of its Arab Canadian counterpart (Abu-Laban 1980, 1988). In the late 1980s there was a significant narrowing of the gap between the two ethnic communities in this regard (Abu-Laban 1988; Resnick Interview).

There is also a generational factor that contributes to the CIC's relatively successful interactions with Canadian parliamentarians. Organized pro-Israeli activities in Canada began seriously during the late 1960s, coinciding with a climate of good will towards Israel enhanced by Israel's widely perceived status as "David" to the Arab world's "Goliath." The passing of the generation of Canadian politicians with personal memory of the Nazi Holocaust and the altered international perception of Israel and the Arabs have significantly changed the parliamentary mood concerning Israel and the Middle East. There is some evidence of a residue of pro-Israeli sentiment in the Canadian House of Commons. But, there is also a new generation of parliamentarians unaffected by an earlier generation's inherent sympathy toward Israel, who tend to either find favor with the Palestinian cause or be more open in their criticism of Israel (Willmot Interview).

CONCLUSION

This chapter has outlined the history, mandate, and organizational dynamic of the Canada-Israel Committee and has placed the CIC and its ethnic political lobbying within the context of the Canadian foreign policy-making process. The Canada-Israel Committee does not meet all of the criteria of an institutionalized ethnic interest group. It is lacking in terms of accountability and representativeness. Although the participatory base of the organization has been broadened, the CIC stands at least once removed from the majority of Canadian Jews. The committee remains fundamentally corporate and elitist in nature, comprised of (and dominated by) a small group of the most wealthy and well-placed members of the Canadian Jewish community.

The Canada-Israel Committee is also somewhat deficient with respect to intracommunal and intraorganizational cohesion. Canadian Jewry has always been characterized by a widely held general consensus on Israel-related questions. This appears to remain in place. However, events in the latter part of the 1973–88 period—most notably, the Lebanon War and the Palestinian disturbances—witnessed the emergence of fairly strong intracommunal dissent, which could conceivably threaten the internal cohesion (and hence the political effectiveness) of the Canada-Israel Committee.

This chapter has also suggested that disputes internal to the CIC's leadership core have threatened its organizational integrity. Philosophical disputes and intraorganizational rivalries are common to Zionism and Judaism generally. These impact most severely upon the Canada-Israel Committee because of its status as the child of several parents. Group cohesion is a relative concept. Internal disputes within the Canada-Israel Committee are mostly over political style rather than policy substance. Disputes are usually resolved through accommodation and brokering among communal elites. Compared to its traditionally disparate Arab ethnic counterpart (Abu-Laban 1980, 1989), the Canada-Israel Committee remains a fairly cohesive, if somewhat nondemocratic, entity.

To their credit, the leaders of Canadian Zionism make no pretense of fulfilling optimal democratic ideals (Bessin Interview; May Interview). They hold firmly to a narrower conception of communal advocacy and representation. This view is consistent with both the aristocratic republicanism of Jewish political tradition and the statism and accommodation of elites that prevails in the Canadian foreign policy-making process.

Although there are certainly no guarantees in this regard, the fact that Canadian foreign policymakers and Canadian Zionists share a tendency toward making decisions on the basis of private interactions among elites should theoretically provide an advantage to the Canada-Israel Committee in its lobbying activities. The extent to which this similarity was converted into a pattern of Jewish community influence over Canadian foreign policy on Israel and the Arab-Israeli conflict during the period from October 1973 to December 1988 is addressed in chapter 5 of this book.

NOTES

1. David Bercuson (1985, 1989), Anne Trowell Hillmer (1989), and Zachariah Kay (1978) dispel much of the conventional thinking (see Ismael 1973, 1976, 1984; Lyon 1982b; Massoud 1976) concerning the factors contributing to Canada's participation in the United Nation's Palestine debate in 1947 and the formation of Resolution 181 (the plan to partition the Palestine Mandate into separate Arab and Jewish states with an economic union linking them and much of Jerusalem as an internationalized corpus separatum). Canadian participation in the partition debate was delayed, mainly due to Prime Minister Mackenzie King's reluctance to have Canada dragged into the Middle East quagmire. And when Canada did become involved, it did so not out of any meaningful interest in the Middle East per se but in order to achieve a compromise between Washington

and London, whose divergent perspectives on the future of Palestine threatened to crack the incipient Western alliance. Bercuson and Kay both indicate further that, although Canada was party to the United Nations Special Committee on Palestine's (UNSCOP) majority report favoring partition, Canada was still reluctant to recognize the state of Israel. It did not follow the American lead in granting immediate de facto recognition to the Jewish state in May 1948 (this did not come until late December 1948). Canada abstained on Israel's first, unsuccessful, attempt to gain admission to the United Nations and did not grant de jure recognition to Israel until July 1949.

2. Much of the intracommunal dissent during the December 1987–December 1988 period focused on the Jewish community's involvement in the Montebello Conference. The conference, organized in late April 1988 at a luxurious resort outside of Ottawa by the government-sponsored Canadian Institute for International Peace and Security on behalf of the Department of External Affairs, brought together 30 influential Canadian Arabs and Jews to discuss the Middle East conflict and Canada's contribution to peace-making in the region (Waller 1988). Dissent rested primarily on the alleged secrecy of the conference and the way in which Jewish representatives to the conference were selected (the center-right charging that the conference organizers—and the Canadian Jewish Establishment—demonstrated an explicit bias towards "moderates") (Waller 1988).

3. One Secretary of State for External Affairs was renowned for his receptivity to Jews and Zionism, resulting both from electoral considerations and his "Old Testament" sensitivities towards the Holy Land. His immediate successor at the Department of External Affairs, unaffected by similar electoral or biblical considerations, proved to be far less receptive to the advances of the CIC (Former Assistant to the Secretary of State for External Affairs Interview).

4. The Canadian Council of Churches, including the United Church, although always concerned with the situation in the Middle East, had traditionally sought to maintain a balanced, nonpartisan posture on the Arab-Israeli conflict. However, in May 1988 the council's annual plenary adopted a strongly worded resolution critical of Israel's handling of the Palestinian disturbances. In January 1989, the council presented a controversial brief critical of Israel (prepared by its Middle East Working Group in coordination with the council's Consultative Committee on Human Rights) to a meeting of nongovernmental organizations with the Department of External Affairs. Similar sentiments were formally expressed by the Council of Canadian Catholic Bishops in June 1989. The Canadian Jewish community considered such criticism of Israel to be biased, unfair, and historically inaccurate (*Canadian Jewish News*, June 8, 1989, 3).

4

AIPAC and U.S. Middle East Policy: October 1973– December 1988

THE ARAB-ISRAELI WAR OF OCTOBER 1973

Overview

In the immediate aftermath of the Egyptian-Syrian joint surprise attack on Israel on the morning of October 6, 1973, AIPAC's primary concern was to ensure congressional support for Israel (Kenen 1981, 300; *Near East Report*, October 10, 1973). The morning following the attack, AIPAC director I. L. Kenen invited thirty Jewish community leaders, sympathetic politicians, and legislative assistants to his office. Operating under the assumption that Israeli forces would quickly prevail, Kenen wanted this group to draft statements urging congressional support of Israel at the end of the hostilities. Strongly worded statements of support for Israel followed from this and other meetings. Many of these statements drew analogies between the Arab attack on the morning of Yom Kippur and the Japanese attack on Pearl Harbor. They were signed by a group of influential senators, including Edward Kennedy, George McGovern, Walter Mondale, Claiborne Pell, and John Tunney (Kenen 1981, 301; *Near East Report*, October 10, 1973).

It was four days into the war before the full gravity of the initial Arab advances upon Israeli positions became known. At this point, AIPAC's concern became Israel's desperate need for weapons and replacement parts, to be fulfilled by an American airlift of arms and material (Kenen 1981, 302–3). Regardless of Jerusalem's and AIPAC's pleadings, the Nixon administration did not implement such an airlift until October 13. The reasons for the delay remain a source of conflict between Washington, AIPAC, and Jerusalem (Kissinger 1982, 497; Quandt 1977, 171, 183–87; Spiegel 1985, 250–52).

Once the U.S. airlift was deployed and the situation on the battlefield had turned in Israel's favor, AIPAC focused its attention on swift congressional passage of the Nixon administration's proposed $2.2 billion arms and aid package to Israel (Kenen 1981, 305; *Near East Report*, October 31, 1973). Concurrent resolutions supporting this proposal were presented to the House of Representatives and the Senate in late October and received overwhelming endorsement. The full appropriation was approved by Congress and the White House in early December 1973.

Conceptual Analysis

AIPAC's behavior during the war was a virtual textbook example of how an ethnic interest group lobbies the American foreign policy-making process. The committee was constantly active, and its level and scope of activity rose in response to the perceived threat posed to its constituency's core values (especially regarding the survival and security of the state of Israel). AIPAC's policy objectives were advocative; it sought to conserve Washington's traditional support for Israel and to stress evidence of Soviet aggressiveness in the Middle East. In altering its objectives during the war—that is, from airlift to aid—AIPAC also showed itself to be highly adaptive to changing circumstances, an essential feature of an institutionalized ethnic interest group.

AIPAC's director, I. L. Kenen, and his staff behaved in a formulative manner with regard to both the airlift and aid proposals. AIPAC officials concentrated throughout the war on the legislative branch of government, not only because of the isolated character of a White House increasingly besieged by Watergate allegations, but also because, constitutionally, all aid appropriations must be approved by Congress. AIPAC staffers used both direct and indirect approaches to influence the government. Kenen brought together key congressional players, orchestrated the introduction of pro-Israeli resolutions into both houses of Congress, and testified before the Appropriations and Foreign Affairs committees of each. AIPAC also directed massive telegraph and letter-writing campaigns and purchased advertising space in major newspapers throughout the United States.

AIPAC also exhibited advanced organizational traits. It did not seek to dominate all aspects of American Jewry's communal response to the Yom Kippur War. Fundraising was handled jointly by the United Jewish and United Israel Appeals, the Israel Bonds office, and the local federations, all of whom had become significantly more proficient in crisis mobilization since the 1967 Six Day War (Elazar 1980, 343–55). Similarly, AIPAC shared some lobbying responsibilities with other national organizations, most notably the Presidents Conference. But Kenen was, nonetheless, authorized to speak publicly on behalf of all constituent members of the conference (Kenen 1981, 300–351).

AIPAC remained highly corporate in nature during the crisis. Kenen and some lay leaders, operating through AIPAC, took upon themselves the responsibility of defining and articulating the concerns of all of organized American Jewry about U.S. support of Israel in its time of need. As the crisis in the Middle East escalated, AIPAC's decisional network was expanded laterally to incorporate a wider range of sympathetic politicians, administrative assistants, bureaucrats, and Jewish communal leaders. However, there is little evidence of any serious attempt on the part of AIPAC to broaden the organization's base to the grass roots level. Such expansion was essentially unnecessary, given the unifying effect of the crisis upon virtually all of American Jewry (Davis 1974). It was only in the aftermath of the war that AIPAC and the American Zionist mainstream were confronted with significant intracommunal dissent on Israel-related matters.

The nature of the American foreign policy-making system during the war affected AIPAC's lobbying activities both positively and negatively. On the one hand, AIPAC's lobbying activities during the war were perceived by the general public as well within the permissible range of political behavior by nongovernmental organizations (Bookbinder Interview; Kenen Interview). On the other hand, the way in which the governmental decision-making system structured itself in response to the war was less than conducive to AIPAC's influence. Decisional authority was concentrated in crisis-management teams, the most prominent being the Washington Special Actions Group (WSAG) under the direction of Secretary of State Henry Kissinger. These crisis-management teams were isolated from virtually all nonexecutive parts of the government and all nongovernmental groups. Attempts by the latter, including AIPAC, to influence U.S. policy were severely restricted as long as effective decisional authority was concentrated in the hands of Kissinger's crisis-management teams on behalf of the increasingly isolated White House (Spiegel 1985, 235).

Nevertheless, AIPAC's interactions in the domestic political environment were fairly effective. American public opinion supported Israel throughout the Yom Kippur War (Rosen and Abramowitz 1984, 6), and this support was reinforced by AIPAC's exploitation of the Pear Harbor analogy (*Near East Report*, October 10, 1973; November 7, 1973). Pro-Israeli popular sentiment suffered somewhat as the objective reality of the war became entangled in the international economic crisis arising from the embargo imposed upon the United States by the Organization of Petroleum Exporting Countries (OPEC) (Garnham 1976). The American public exhibited no particular sympathy toward the multinational oil corporations or the Arab oil producers. But the energy crisis, artificial or real, sensitized significant portions of the American public to the political demands of the moderate Arab states at the expense of Israel (Kenen 1981, 311–13; Sherbiny and Tessler 1976; Spiegel 1985, 220–22).

During the war AIPAC received valuable political support from the American media, large segments of which concentrated on the Pearl Harbor analogy and Soviet interventionism in the Middle East. However, an element of the media, especially reporters of a liberal-left perspective, focused on what it perceived to be Israeli "provocations" leading to the Egyptian-Syrian attack. The Palestinian Arab issue was raised for the first time as an independent issue on the U.S.-Middle East agenda (Kenen 1981, 305–7; Ghareeb 1977).

AIPAC's success in achieving its goals during the war underscores the value of domestic coalition-building in the American policy process. AIPAC attempted to collect virtually all of its political debts during the war. Although there were some exceptions, most representatives and senators responded positively to AIPAC's plea for support of Israel. AIPAC also received important moral and political support from organized labor and other nongovernmental groups (Blitzer 1985, 180–81; Rosen and Abramowitz 1984, 16–17).

AIPAC also suffered some strategic losses in the domestic political environment. Losses sustained by the Israel Defense Forces (IDF) in the initial stages of the war underminded the level of confidence American Jews felt when building pro-Israel domestic political coalitions (Rosenbaum Interview). Israel's military losses also seriously weakened pro-Israeli sentiment within the Pentagon. Already burdened by the imminent collapse of American military efforts in Southeast Asia and desperately looking for a strong military ally, the Pentagon was disillusioned by Israel's inability to repel the initial Arab attack (Spiegel 1985, 221).[1] The reduced credibility of Israel within the U.S. defense bureaucracy is perhaps best illustrated by the explicitly anti-Israel and anti-Jewish comments made by Chairman of the Joint Chiefs of Staff General George Brown at an address to Duke University in October 1974 (*Near East Report*, November 10, 1974, 243–44). General Brown called upon the U.S. government to "get tough-minded enough to set down the Jewish influence in this country and break that lobby. . . . It's so strong you wouldn't believe now. . . . They own, you know, the banks in this country, the newspapers. . . . You just look at where the Jewish money is in this country" (cited in *Washington Post*, November 13, 1974, A9). Although the general's retraction was immediately forthcoming, the fact that a high-ranking military official made such critical public comments reflects the extent to which Israel's and AIPAC's influence had been weakened in a traditionally sympathetic segment of the U.S. foreign policy community (Spiegel 1985, 221–23).

The international political dimension also sheds important light on AIPAC's influence during the October 1973 period. AIPAC is formally autonomous of the Israeli government. Nevertheless, a generally perceived unofficial deference to Jerusalem harmed AIPAC's credibility during the war and immediately thereafter (Kenen Interview). In the initial hours and days of the war, AIPAC adopted a cautiously optimistic wait-and-see posture based primarily on information transmitted from the Israeli embassy: "I was assured by the embassy that 20 planes would be chartered [to carry weapons to Israel]; presumably, the crisis was over. . . . I had been led to believe by the embassy that [an official American airlift] would not be necessary" (Kenen 1981, 302). In retrospect, such optimism was unfounded. Jewish community leaders acknowledge that because AIPAC officials had to shift courses in midstream and pursue an airlift—after assuring their congressional allies that an airlift was not required—the committee's credibility and effectiveness were seriously compromised (Amitay Interview; Bookbinder Interview; Kenen Interview; Rosenbaum Interview).

Communication between AIPAC and Israeli officials during the war was far from ideal. This was in part a consequence of what the political scientist Michael Brecher calls "crisis-induced communications deficiencies" (Brecher 1980, 10, 21–23). It was also a result of an explicit request from Jerusalem that American Jewry engage in a low-key campaign during the war (Elazar 1980, 360–61). Analysts differ on the rationale for this request. William Quandt suggests that Secretary of State Kissinger had "skillfully persuaded the Israeli ambassador not to 'unleash' Israel's supporters" (1977, 203). Others, including Kissinger himself, suggest that Jerusalem was, perhaps, attempting to disguise the true extent of Israel's initial military losses so as to reduce U.S. pressure for an early cease-fire (Kissinger 1982, 491–504). Whatever the reason, the poor state of communication between Israeli officials and AIPAC during at least the early part of the war temporarily weakened the American Jewish lobby's status as a reliable source of accurate information about events in the Middle East (Amitay Interview; Kenen 1981, 300–303; Rosenbaum Interview). AIPAC was only partially able to act as a link between Washington and Jerusalem.

AIPAC's relative lack of effectiveness as an intermediary is, in part, explained by the unique quality of relations that prevailed between Israel and the United States during the Nixon years. Under Nixon and Kissinger, relations between the two governments—especially in the strategic/regional security domain—were institutionalized to the point of making much of AIPAC's linkage efforts during the war superfluous. Washington and Jerusalem may not have agreed with each other on long-term goals, but each had a fairly good idea of what the other wanted to achieve once the initial shock of the Arab attack wore off.

The extent of AIPAC's influence over U.S. policy was also related to the nature of the issues at stake. AIPAC officials perceived the war as a threat to their constituency's core values, as a crisis in the purest sense. The problem for AIPAC, from a strategic perspective, was the fact that Washington gradually came to share this perception, especially after the initiation of the Soviet airlift to Egypt and Syria and most definitely after the superpower nuclear alert of October 24–25 (Kissinger 1982, 497). Ironically, this sharing of perceptions restricted AIPAC's influence over the U.S. policy process. Prior to Soviet intervention in the war, the Nixon administration had consuled fairly consistently with congressional leaders and selected nongovernmental groups, including AIPAC. The administration's increased sense of crisis resulting from Soviet "adventurism" caused a significant narrowing of the decisional forum; Congress was less informed of developments and, by extension, AIPAC was less able to access and influence the policymakers (Spiegel 1985, 255–57). As the crisis subsided, the influence of AIPAC and its congressional allies again grew. This is confirmed by the swift passage of the unprecedented $2.2 billion postwar aid package to Israel.

AIPAC's influence over American policy during the Yom Kippur War was indirect but nevertheless great. Despite considerable frustration over the delayed implementation of the airlift and an inability to access key decision makers during the period of highest crisis, the results of U.S. policy on the war paralleled those sought by AIPAC and much of its primary constituency within the American Jewish community.

Kissinger and others argue that the pro-Israeli posture adopted by the Nixon administration during the war was more a response to geostrategic considerations than domestic political pressures (Kissinger 1982, 468, 496, 575–91; Quandt 1977, 203–6; Spiegel 1985, 256–57). This may very well be true; surely AIPAC did not enjoy the type of access to policymakers at the height of the crisis that it would have liked. However, parallelism is an important aspect of the definition of influence being used in this study. The unqualified American support for Israel throughout the war, including the airlift and the granting of massive amounts of economic assistance, must be considered indicators of AIPAC's ability to help influence, if somewhat indirectly, decisions taken in the American foreign policy-making process.

POST–OCTOBER 1973 DIPLOMACY

Overview

AIPAC officials were generally satisfied with the results of their efforts during the Yom Kippur War. Although troubled by what appeared to them to be a deliberate delaying of the airlift, they were pleased with the aid the Nixon administration granted to Israel. Given the administration's proven support for Israel, much of American Jewry viewed favorably the intense commitment to Middle East conflict resolution that directed American strategic thinking after October 1973 (See Quandt 1977, chs. 7 & 8; Spiegel 1985, 223–28; Steinberg 1983b). However, it was not long before America's efforts in the peace process clashed with American Zionist policy preferences, contributing ultimately to direct confrontations with the White House over a variety of issues.

Many of these differences resulted from Secretary of State Henry Kissinger's attempts to orchestrate regional stability from the uncertain military conclusions of the Yom Kippur War. The Israelis and much of American Jewry became increasingly irritated by virtually every aspect of Kissinger's diplomatic strategy. Given its domestic political status, AIPAC would not be expected to play an up-front role in the diplomatic process. It became directly involved as a consequence of Kissinger's practice of employing foreign aid as a principal tool of diplomacy (Pollock 1982). In April 1974, on the eve of Kissinger's first Middle East shuttle, Nixon announced that he had unilaterally waived repayment of $1 billion of the $2.2 billion allocated to Israel in the previous December. This seemed a generous move on the part of the White House until it became apparent that when the aid package had been initially appropriated Congress had intended $1.5 billion to be in grants and the balance to be in credits at concessionary rates. Nixon's offer, then, represented a $500 million *loss* in grants to Israel (*Near East Report*, April 10, 1974, 103). Moreover, the administration appropriated only $350 million in aid for fiscal 1975, $300 million in military credits and $50 million in support assistance (Kenen 1981, 317). AIPAC felt that the administration's initial aid appropriations were kept deliberately low by Kissinger to elicit a more conciliatory response from Israel to his diplomatic initiatives (*Near East Report*, May 1, 1974, 113; *Near East Report*, May 8, 1974, 117; Pollock 1982, 180).

Kenen and AIPAC lobbied aggressively for increases in aid. In testimony before the Senate Appropriations Committee, Kenen submitted an elaborate memorandum that included a lengthy citation from an editorial in the *New York Times* counseling continued assistance to Israel (Kenen 1981, 317). Kenen also implied that AIPAC's call for increased assistance to Israel had the support of hundreds of thousands of American Jews. The implicit threat of electoral sanctions was not lost on the senators; in December 1974 the Senate and House Conference Committee approved an aid package with $324.5 million for fiscal 1975 (*Near East Report*, December 11, 1974, 253–55).

Although economic matters were seemingly under control, Secretary Kissinger's credibility with Israel and AIPAC was deteriorating rapidly. The tension was greatly exacerbated in May 1974 when Israeli prime minister Golda Meir received a letter from Kissinger suggesting that a "reexamination" and "reassessment" of U.S. Middle East policy would be forthcoming if Jerusalem were to take actions that might jeopardize what Kissinger called "favorable diplomatic trends" (Quandt 1977, 240). Later in May 1974 President Nixon publicly requested a list of all military and economic aid promised to Israel *as well as the total amount of domestic tax-free private contributions to the Jewish state*. The carrot-and-stick strategy for dealing with Israel was now well in place.

Relations between AIPAC and Gerald Ford were even more strained. The new president, a neophyte on foreign affairs, was almost totally reliant on Kissinger, who was becoming increasingly frustrated by what he considered to be Israeli intransigence over the Middle East peace process (Golan 1976; Kissinger 1982, 1038–42, 1079–89). Kissinger ended an unsuccessful phase of his Middle East diplomatic shuttle on March 23, 1975: on March 24 President Ford announced the formal implementation of a reassessment of U.S. policy in the Middle East, "including our relations with Israel" (*New York Times*, March 27, 1975, A1).[2]

Israeli and AIPAC officials were concerned about the possible long-term effects of any significant alteration in America's policy toward Israel. They were equally concerned that Israel's enemies might take reassessment as a sign of a weakened Israel and, hence, an opportunity for renewed hostilities (*Near East Report*, April 30, 1975, 77; Rabin 1979, 204, 256).

On May 22, 1975, a letter, signed by seventy-six U.S. senators, was sent to President Ford, demanding that the White House halt its threatened reassessment of relations with Israel.[3] The so-called Letter of 76, and several subsequent statements by influential senators and congressmen, severely undercut the entire thrust of the Ford administration's proposed reassessment of Middle East policy.

Conceptual Analysis

The behavior of AIPAC throughout the post–Yom Kippur War diplomatic period was consistent with much of the assumptions of an influential ethnic foreign policy lobby group. Its level of activity and its interactions with key decision makers were consistently high. AIPAC's policy objectives were largely advocative; it called for the maintenance of the traditional heavy flow of economic and military assistance to Israel. The emphasis was on the positive; aid to America's "proven" Arab allies—if such could be found—would not be vigorously opposed as long as Israeli security was not compromised and Jerusalem continued to receive its fair share of foreign assistance (Amitay Interview; Kenen 1981, 316–20). With respect to Ford's policy reassessment, however, AIPAC's objectives were more overtly antagonistic; the goal was to force the president to end the reassessment or face the political consequences.

The timing of AIPAC's actions during the postwar period was somewhat less than perfect. On the aid issue, AIPAC focused on the formulative stage of policy development. In his testimony before various congressional committees, Kenen successfully pleaded AIPAC's case for aid totals consistently greater than those recommended by the White House. AIPAC's timing on the proposed policy reassessment was necessarily reactive. Obviously, it could not act until the reassessment was formally announced by President Ford; once the reassessment was initiated, AIPAC shifted to a formulative strategy by forcing the issue in Congress.

Its choice of targets and strategy during this period indicates the full extent of AIPAC's comprehension of the U.S. policy process. During deliberations of both aid and reassessment, AIPAC concentrated on the legislative branch, especially the Senate. This focus was, in part, a result of the fact that the animosity associated with Kissinger's diplomatic strategy had diminished AIPAC's access to the executive branch. However, it was also a consequence of AIPAC's realization that all aid appropriations and arms sales must ultimately be approved by Congress. AIPAC also used its reservoir of congressional support as an independent source of pressure upon the White House. The May 1975 Letter of 76 had the desired effect of causing the Ford administration to retract any plan to seriously alter the prevailing pattern of U.S.-Israeli relations.

AIPAC's organizational capacities were fully demonstrated in the immediate post–1973 period. The crisis of the Yom Kippur War generated significantly greater communal awareness, wealth, and active membership for AIPAC. These tendencies were sustained in the period following the war (Amitay Interview). In retrospect, intracommunal cohesion was not a particularly serious problem during this period. To be sure, there were some people in the community, especially those associated with Breira, who perhaps agreed with the Nixon and Ford administrations that aid should be used as a means of eliciting Jerusalem's increased diplomatic flexibility. However, overt expression of such sentiments were, for the most part, confined to the communal periphery or supplanted by an aggressive counterpropaganda campaign.

A more serious challenge to communal solidarity on Israel-related issues arose from the evolving atmosphere of confrontation between AIPAC and the White House. Although most American Zionists agreed that aid to Israel had to be protected, some expressed concern about the potential long-term ramifications of AIPAC's seemingly constant confrontation with the White House (Bookbinder Interview; Rosenbaum Interview). Such fears were not without foundation. For example, some analysts speculate that the Ford administration's decision, made during the summer of 1975, to sell mobile HAWK antiaircraft missiles to Jordan was in part a consequence of Ford and Kissinger's growing annoyance with American Jewry's lobbying activities (Bookbinder Interview; Spiegel 1985, 303–4).

Intracommunal differences remained essentially stylistic. Some leading American Jews were concerned with the stridency of AIPAC's style (Bookbinder Interview; Rosenbaum Interview); however, few actively opposed AIPAC's stance in favor of increased aid for Israel or against policy reassessment.

The structure of the American decisional process assisted AIPAC's active defense of Israel's aid requirements. Nixon, Ford, and Kissinger clearly did not appreciate the various domestic political embarrassments, such as the letter of the senators, many of which they attributed to AIPAC and its aggressive new executive director, Morris Amitay (working in close association with powerful congressional allies) (Ford 1979, 287–88; Kissinger 1982, 1143–51, 1205). However, the American foreign policy-making system is so constructed that AIPAC was able to effectively circumvent the executive branch. For the Nixon and Ford administrations to avoid total foreign policy legislative stalemate, they had to deal with pro-Israeli forces in Congress. And it was through such interactions that AIPAC maintained a degree of indirect influence over the policy process and its output.

The domestic political environment was also fairly conducive to AIPAC's influence-seeking. A January 1975 public opinion poll found that Americans with an opinion on the Middle East favored Israel over the Arabs by a margin of forty-four to eight percent (Rosen and Abramowitz 1984, 6). Despite the rapid ascendance of the Palestinian issue internationally and the continued demands of the Arab oil producers upon Washington for increased diplomatic pressure on Jerusalem, American popular opinion remained overwhelmingly supportive of Israel. The Nixon and Ford administrations' confrontations with Israel and AIPAC were not widely supported by the majority of Americans.

The media were an important source of influence for AIPAC. The Jewish lobby publicized its differences with the White House through advertisements taken out in the *New York Times* and other major newspapers throughout the country. The media's coverage of PLO leader Arafat's controversial first visit to the United Nations in November 1974 also strengthened AIPAC's posture.

In reporting the event, many of the media, with some exceptions, concentrated on the PLO's record on terrorism (*Near East Report*, December 18, 1974). This served to indirectly benefit AIPAC's lobbying strategy (Kenen 1981, 322–28).

In its lobbying efforts on both aid and reassessment, AIPAC benefitted from coalitions with important elements of the domestic political environment. Israel's support in Congress was overwhelming. On both the reassessment and HAWK missile issues, AIPAC was able to help draw together a bipartisan congressional alliance powerful enough to cause the White House to initiate compromises satisfactory to Jerusalem (*Near East Report*, May 21, 1975; October 1, 1975; November 26, 1975; Spiegel 1985, 303–10; Steinberg 1983b, 127).

Given the level of congressional support for Israel in this period, AIPAC did not have to focus much attention on relations with other nongovernmental groups. However, significant anti-Israeli social and political coalitions began to emerge in response to the legislative controversies. The opposition became particularly active in support of the proposed sale of Hercules transport jets to Egypt and SIDEWINDER air-to-air missiles, MAVERICK air-to-surface missiles, and TOW antitank missiles to Saudi Arabia (*Near East Report*, July 9, 1975; Spiegel 1985, 308–10; Steinberg 1983b, 127). Although some compromises were forced upon the White House on these various sales, in the final analysis the political influence of the pro-Arab coalition was greater than that of the congressional-AIPAC opposition (Sampson 1977). This represented a harbinger of the future difficulties to be encountered by AIPAC and its congressional supporters in protecting Israel's qualitative military advantage.

AIPAC found itself deeply involved with the Israeli government over the American practice of linking aid to diplomacy. However, rather than Jerusalem guiding AIPAC, it appears that AIPAC was helping to steer the Israeli government through the treacherous waters of U.S. domestic politics (Amitay Interview; Bookbinder Interview; Rosenbaum Interview).

Differences between AIPAC and the executive branch were exacerbated by differing perceptions of the policy issues at stake. AIPAC officials saw the proposed reduction of aid to Israel and the proposed reassessment of U.S. Middle East policy as a crisis of the first order. The Nixon and Ford administrations also viewed the Middle East as high priority, but for very different reasons. Kissinger perceived progress on the diplomatic front (that is, the satisfaction of the Arab oil producers' demands for Israeli territorial concessions) as essential to America's long-term strategic concerns, both diplomatic and economic (Kissinger 1982, 614–66).

AIPAC and the White House, then, both perceived the Middle East as a crisis for their particular interests. This is one of the rare instances in which the inverse relationship between a government's sense of crisis over a policy issue and an interest group's level of direct influence over that policy does not hold. Regardless of the White House's perception of crisis, the domestic pro-Israeli forces, led by AIPAC, were able to undermine any proposed adjustments to the U.S.-Israeli relationship and force compromises on arms sales to the Arab world. The determining factor in the equation was the continued strong support for Israel in Congress and the willingness of influential congressmen and senators to do battle with the White House over Israel-related matters.

AIPAC, then, was quite successful in its defense of Israel's economic and military aid interests during the post–Yom Kippur War period. Aid to Israel was consistently increased, and Ford's reassessment of America's policy in the Middle East was concluded without any permanent damage to Israel's interests.

Influence, of course, is a relative concept. AIPAC was able to protect and indeed increase aid appropriations; but it was not able to inhibit the White House from pushing through Congress, with some modification, proposed arms sales to moderate Arab states such as Egypt, Jordan and Saudi Arabia (Pollock 1982). Paradoxically, this failure is an illustration of AIPAC's status as an institutionalized ethnic interest group. AIPAC activists acknowledge that they lived in an imperfect world; they reasoned that it was better to concentrate on political certainties and near certainties (i.e., congressional support for aid to Israel) than to possibly compromise the organization's carefully constructed credibility by "going to the wall" over less secure policy issues (including weapons sales to the Arab world) (Amitay Interview; Bookbinder Interview; Rosenbaum Interview).

CONFRONTING THE ARAB BOYCOTT OF ISRAEL

Overview

The Arab economic boycott of Israel and related discriminatory Arab visa practices[4] have been a constant source of concern to American Jewry (Kenen 1981, 159, 185–87; *Near East Report*, June 17, 1957; Teslik 1982, 13–18, 53–54). However, it was only in the late 1950s and early 1960s that AIPAC was able to marshall enough political support for a meaningful legislative response to these challenges. Even then, the response was limited: the Arab boycott of Israel was not an issue of concern to the American populace or its elected representatives (*Near East Report*, Special Issue, May 1965; Teslik 1982, 55–60).

The altered international economic situation resulting from the events of 1973–74 significantly increased popular interest in the boycott. This interest was reinforced by the evidence of American corporate collusion with Arab oil producing states made public in the Senate Foreign Relations Committee's Subcommittee on Multinational Corporations, chaired by Senator Frank Church (See *Near East Report*, February 27, 1974; August 21, 1974; Teslik 1982, 78–82).

The Ford White House appeared reluctant to move rapidly on growing demands for federal antiboycott legislation. The initiative was taken up by Congress. By the end of 1975 over a dozen congressional bills, amendments, and initiatives had been introduced that in one way or another addressed the Arab boycott of Israel. It became an important issue in the Carter-Ford presidential campaign;

both candidates pledged immediate postelection action on the boycott (*Near East Report*, October 13, 1976). As the campaign dragged on, active consideration of antiboycott legislation was transferred to the private sector. A group of major corporate executives (including members of *Fortune 500*) known as "The Business Roundtable" began to meet first informally and then formally with a triumvirate of representatives of the American Jewish Congress, American Jewish Committee, and Anti-Defamation League of B'nai B'rith. The goal was to negotiate a workable compromise that would establish the basis for substantive federal antiboycott legislation. Such a compromise was reached in late April 1977 and served as the basis for congressional approval, in conference committee, of antiboycott legislation that was formally enacted by President Jimmy Carter on June 22, 1977. The Export Administration Amendments, while still subject to legalistic loopholes and the exigencies of bureaucratic interpretation and application, were the most stringent national response to the Arab boycott of Israel and of firms and individuals doing business with the Jewish state (Amitay Interview; Bookbinder Interview).

Conceptual Analysis

AIPAC's involvement in the antiboycott legislative debate meets many of the criteria of an influential ethnic foreign policy lobby. AIPAC's formal activity was moderate; it allowed the three national Jewish defense organizations to take the lead role. However, AIPAC was involved behind the scenes in creating and sustaining congressional coalitions supporting antiboycott legislation (Amitay Interview; Bookbinder Interview; Kenen 1981, 185–87). AIPAC's substantial political muscle also was applied when, in the opinion of its leaders, the Jewish organizations were being "manhandled" by the corporate sector (Amitay Interview; Rosenbaum Interview).

AIPAC's objectives on the issue were advocative; the primary goal was to alter prevailing American official ambivalence concerning the discriminatory practices of the Arab states. The objective was institutionalized; that is, the boycott was presented as but one of many interests championed by American Jewry.

The organization's timing on the boycott was purely formulative. Much of the action of the late 1970s was based on groundwork laid by AIPAC in the 1960s and on initiatives taken by AIPAC and other Jewish organizations in cooperation with congressional allies in the preformulative phase of the current policy process.

Jewish leaders lobbied government officials and corporate executives in the attempt to influence passage of antiboycott legislation. The American Jewish Congress launched a shareholders' proxy campaign to discourage corporate compliance with the boycott (Teslik 1982, 126–27). Anti-Defamation League (ADL) officials publicly charged that two government agencies, the Overseas Private Investment Corporation and the Army Corps of Engineers, in collaboration with six major corporations were knowingly discriminating against Jews by refusing to do business with Israel (Teslik 1982, 75). The ADL also filed a lawsuit alleging that the U.S. Commerce Department was "cooperating and assisting" in boycott operations by "disseminating boycott-tainted trade opportunities"; a similar suit was filed by twenty-five members of Congress with the assistance of the American Jewish Congress (Teslik 1982, 103). The Jewish organizations followed through on the law suits, maintained close contacts with leading congressmen and senators, testified before congressional hearings, worked in support of state antiboycott legislation, interacted frequently with corporate spokesmen, and publicized the alleged boycott-related "misdeeds" of governmental agencies and private firms (Teslik 1982, 128).

One of the most interesting aspects of the antiboycott campaign is the relative noninvolvement of AIPAC. The organization's low profile contrasts sharply with its leadership on previous antiboycott efforts and most other Israel-related issues. There are a number of plausible explanations for AIPAC's reduced level of activity. These range from a deliberate decision to domesticize and secularize the boycott issue, to a specific request from Jerusalem to allow the domestic Jewish defense organizations to handle the issue, to AIPAC's underestimating the chances of the antiboycott effort succeeding (Teslik 1982, 91). AIPAC's relative quiescence was probably based on a conscious decision to allow others to take the lead and to concentrate on other more pressing aspects of U.S. Middle East policy. AIPAC's primary role was to serve as the unofficial coordinator of communal activities and mobilize congressional alliances in order to expedite the legislative process. Nevertheless, on more than one occasion the new AIPAC director, Morris Amitay, reportedly had to be reminded of his organization's support function in the antiboycott struggle (Bookbinder Interview; Howe and Trott 1977, 276, 315–18; Teslik 1982, 44).

Jewish community participation throughout the boycott campaign was role-based and predominantly corporate. Although American Jewry's general interest in the boycott issue was enhanced by widespread media coverage, there is little evidence of attempts by community leaders to popularize the prolegislation campaign. Communal cohesion was maintained by the fact that distaste for the Arab boycott was an issue about which few American Jews disagreed.

The structure of the formal decision-making system was not particularly conducive to the rapid achievement of antiboycott legislation. The Ford administration's preoccupation with the energy crisis and fear of a renewal of the Arab oil embargo infringed significantly upon its serious consideration of antiboycott legislation (Teslik 1982, 98–108). The White House was quite happy to allow the volatile issue to be handled through interactions among private constituencies. What makes this case so interesting is the considerable latitude granted to two private concerns, The Business Roundtable and the Jewish organizations, to formulate the basis for a piece of legislation with potentially significant impact on U.S. economic and strategic interests in the Middle East.

The antiboycott campaign was fostered by various aspects of the domestic political environment. Public opinion supported the prolegislation position. A January 1977 Louis Harris survey found that seventy-one percent of the respondents disapproved of the Arab refusal to do business with U.S. companies that deal with Israel; only six percent approved. There was also strong support for antiboycott legislation: forty-four percent of the respondents favored imposing tax penalties against private firms that adhered to the Arab boycott (*Near East Report*, February 9, 1977). These poll results clearly strengthened the hand of the prolegislation forces by reminding the public sector and business community that they "should work for a compromise settlement while the opportunity existed" (Teslik 1982, 177).

The media became an important vehicle through which popular opposition to the Arab boycott was transformed into effective pressure for antiboycott legislation. Beginning in the spring of 1975, the boycott received almost daily coverage by major outlets of the national print and electronic media. Jewish organizations were quick to exploit this media attention (Teslik 1982, 74–75). The media were crucial in establishing a solidly prolegislation environment on the boycott issue.

Jewish organizations benefited significantly from their political contacts in Congress and among congressional aides and advisers. In large part, this was because the boycott issue had been effectively secularized; politicians with little sympathy toward Israel supported antiboycott legislation on the basis of human rights, religious nondiscrimination, and/or distaste for the growing power of the petro-corporate complex. A powerful coalition, involving Jewish organizations, a significant number of congressmen and senators, and nongovernmental groups was eventually formed in active support of antiboycott legislation.

During the 1975–77 antiboycott debate, a powerful domestic counteralliance also emerged. Among the principals to this alliance were influential elements of the American corporate community (especially the multinational oil companies), politicians and foreign service officers sympathetic to Arab or corporate interests, and domestic Arab groups. The activities of this alliance were particularly noticeable given their relative quiescence during previous antiboycott debates in the United States (Teslik 1982, 60).

Opposition to antiboycott legislation was spearheaded by Washington-based business lobbies such as the Emergency Committee for American Trade (ECAT), the U.S. Chamber of Commerce, the Associated General Contractors of America, and Charles E. Walker Associates. They were actively supported by other groups, such as Caterpillar Tractor Company, Bechtel Corporation, the National Association of Manufacturers, and the member companies of the U.S.-Arab Chamber of Commerce (Teslik 1982, 146). The president of EXXON reportedly wired all members of the House of Representatives urging rejection of antiboycott legislation, and Mobil Oil ran advertisements against the passage of strong restrictions (Teslik 1982, 146–47). Such powerful corporate lobbying coincided with the first evidence of political maturation on the part of the Arab American ethnic constituency. Arab American groups became actively involved in the boycott debate: publishing a newsletter addressing the boycott issue from the Arab perspective; sending telegrams to the president, vice-president, and all 535 members of Congress urging resistance to antiboycott legislation; and purchasing advertising space opposing legislative initiatives in major national newspapers (Teslik 1982, 147). James Abourezk, a U.S. Senator of Lebanese descent and cofounder, in 1980, of the American-Arab Anti-Discrimination Committee, was one of the principal congressional opponents of antiboycott legislation. He was supported in this effort by a small but influential group of congressmen and senators (Teslik 1982, 148–53).

The activity of the domestic antilegislation forces was considerable, but their effectiveness was diminished by a lack of unity and coordination. Significant elements of the corporate community were reportedly uncomfortable with the stridency of the Arab groups; American businesses sought to oppose antiboycott legislation "without appearing to take positions that could be condemned as antisemitic or seen as caving in to the formidable financial pressure of the Arab nations" (Teslik 1982, 189). Although its effect was somewhat hindered by such considerations, the coalition of business and pro-Arab groups nonetheless represented a formidable opponent to prolegislation forces.

The boycott debate gives strong evidence of Israel's role as an important extraneous dimension of American domestic political affairs. Jerusalem had originally sought to downplay the impact of the Arab boycott on Israel. Though frequently discussed by the two nations, the Arab boycott was not an essential component of the U.S.-Israeli agenda (Turck 1977, 472). However, as the domestic antiboycott campaign intensified in the mid–1970s, Jerusalem became more explicit in its support of prolegislation forces. A Special Cabinet Adviser on Economic Warfare was established, as was an Economic Warfare Authority of the Israeli Finance Ministry. The Israelis also sought, unsuccessfully, to link a formal end to Egyptian acquiescence to the boycott to the 1975 negotiation of the second Egyptian-Israeli military disengagement in the Sinai Desert (Safran 1981, 554–60; Spiegel 1985, 283–305).

American Jewry's influence over the boycott debate was affected, both adversely and positively, by relations between Jerusalem and Washington. The boycott issue became entangled with broader aspects of the interstate relationship, particularly those relating to Kissinger's diplomatic strategy and Ford's March 1975 proposed policy reassessment. The greater the animosity between Jerusalem and the White House over Kissinger's aggressive diplomacy in the Middle East, the greater American Jewry's determination to press for antiboycott legislation (Amitay Interview; Teslik 1982, 89, 128–31). This appears to support the theoretical assumptions concerning a group's influence and the broadness of its contacts in the decision-making process (in this case, with Congress).

Analysis of the antiboycott debate also appears to support the assumption that ethnic interest groups have more potential influence on issues that they and the government do not deem to be crises. Neither American Jewry nor the Ford administration viewed the boycott issue as a crisis for their respective interests.

The principal American Jewish foreign policy lobby group, AIPAC, took only a secondary formal role in the debate. At no time did the boycott represent the only (or even the primary) item on the American Jewish foreign policy agenda. The Arab boycott of Israel was anything but a crisis for the Ford administration; Ford and Kissinger did their best to bury it. The level of crisis grew slightly for the administration when it feared Arab economic sanctions in retaliation for the implementation of strong antiboycott measures; hence, Ford's implied threat to veto any legislation that was deemed excessively harsh. The administration's reluctance to deal with the boycott issue allowed the initiative to fall to Congress, which afforded AIPAC lobbyists and other American Jewish operatives and allies greater leverage and opportunity. The boycott was never a crisis for the Carter administration. Indeed, during the 1976 presidential campaign, Carter was able to use the issue to attack Ford. Immediately upon taking office, Carter took the somewhat unprecedented step of privatizing negotiations toward a compromise on antiboycott legislation. This corresponded to his administration's perception of the boycott as a noncrisis.

The outcome of the 1975–77 antiboycott debate was an indisputable victory for the American Zionist community. The Export Administration Amendments (1977) were based almost entirely on compromises thrashed out by the major national Jewish organizations in direct negotiations with some of America's most powerful corporate giants. And although the provisions of the law are subject to administrative discretion, the legislation parallels almost completely the policy objectives that American Jewry could have reasonably expected to achieve (Bookbinder Interview; Amitay Interview; Rosenbaum Interview).

From an institutional perspective, the potential influence of the American Israel Public Affairs Committee was strengthened by the debate's outcome. Its role was formally restricted to a support function; yet AIPAC's status as the preeminent representative of American Jewry on all Israel-related matters was enhanced by the victory of the community as a whole on the boycott issue (Amitay Interview; Bookbinder Interview; Dine Interview; Kenen Interview).

JIMMY CARTER'S MIDDLE EAST DIPLOMACY

Overview

American Jews supported the Democratic party and its presidential candidate, Jimmy Carter, in the November 1976 elections. They anticipated four years of relative tranquility between the United States, Israel, and American Jewry (*Near East Report*, November 10, 1976; January 12, 1977).

This expectation was rapidly tempered by a strong dose of political realism. The Carter administration, as no other U.S. presidency before it, was preoccupied with problems relating to energy and felt that it must do all in its power to prevent major oil production cutbacks and price increases. This meant, ultimately, pressuring Israel toward acquiescence to the political demands of moderate Arab oil producing states, especially Saudi Arabia. The confrontations between the White House and AIPAC were unprecedented.

Relations between the Carter administration and American Zionists foundered on two aspects of the president's Middle East policy: diplomacy and arms transfers. Jimmy Carter entered the White House with a vague conception of what he wished to accomplish in the Middle East, based primarily on his association with members of the Brookings Institution (Carter 1982, 51–52). A 1975 Brookings study group proposed an end to Kissinger-style step-by-step diplomacy and a return to the search for a more comprehensive resolution to the Arab-Israeli conflict (Brookings Institution 1975). Carter's image of such a resolution rested on two core components: permanent, secure, and recognized borders between Israel and its Arab neighbors (with substantial Israeli withdrawals from the occupied territories and minor adjustments to the pre-1967 lines) and the establishment of a Palestinian homeland or "entity" in the territories that would meet the legitimate interests of the Palestinian people (Brzezinski 1983, 85–91; Carter 1982, 274–77; Vance 1983, 163–73).

It was on the matter of the Palestinian Arab homeland that Carter encountered significant difficulties. Previous administrations had made quiet overtures toward the "legitimate political aspirations" of the Palestinians (Kissinger 1982, 624–29). But Carter's approach was distinct because it was so much more explicit. At a March 1977 town meeting in Clinton, Massachusetts, President Carter announced that the United States now favored the creation of a Palestinian homeland (Carter 1982, 279–81; *New York Times*, March 18, 1977, A10).

The administration's prerequisites for peace in the Middle East, resting largely upon alterations in the Israeli political and psychological makeup, were perceived to have taken a giant leap backwards with the May 17, 1977, election of Menachem Begin (Carter 1982, 279–88; Vance 1983, 163–86). Begin's Likud coalition was committed to maintaining Israeli sovereignty over the territories where the new Palestinian homeland was presumably to be established (Brzezinski 1983, 95–101; Carter 1982, 288; Vance 1983, 179–84).

The Camp David Accords of September 17, 1978, brought a temporary respite to the straining of relations between Washington and Jerusalem. However, it was not long before differences arose again, primarily over divergent interpretations of the Accords' provisions relating to the building of new Israeli settlements in the occupied territories and implementation there of the plan for Palestinian autonomy (Carter 1982, 405–7; Vance 1983, 229). A major diplomatic dispute between Washington and Jerusalem arose over the meeting, in mid-August 1979, between United Nations Ambassador Andrew Young and the PLO's permanent representative to the UN, Zehdi Labib Terzi. This meeting was a formal violation of Washington's commitment to Israel: no negotiations were supposed to take place with the PLO until it renounced terrorism and recognized Israel's right to exist. Tensions were exacerbated by the March 1980 U.S. vacillation on a United Nations resolution linking Israeli settlement policy in the occupied territories and the status of the city of Jerusalem (Brzezinski

1983, 441–43; Carter 1982, 492–94; *New York Times*, March 5, 1980). As Carter lamented, the two issues "proved highly damaging to me among American Jews throughout the country for the remainder of the election year. . . . A mountain was made of a mole hill–another indication of the politically charged character of the Middle East dispute" (Carter 1982, 491, 493–94). Carter's statement is also indicative of the antagonism felt by Israel, the White House, and American Jewry over Carter's approach to Middle East peacemaking.

Conceptual Analysis

AIPAC's response to Carter's diplomatic efforts corresponded only partially to the behavior anticipated of an influential ethnic interest group. AIPAC's level of political activity was high; it mobilized the congressional pro-Israel coalition and sought, wherever possible, to initiate and sustain a dialogue with the White House. However, the committee's policy objectives were antagonistic: the primary goal was to put a stop to a perceived drift in U.S. policy toward an Arab-defined posture. AIPAC did not appear to offer a constructive alternate policy; it simply wanted to reverse the trend in favor of the Palestinians. This adversely affected the organization's influence over Carter's evolving diplomatic strategy.

Carter's diplomatic initiatives were essentially nonlegislative in character; that is, appropriations were not yet requested and there were no treaties to be ratified. This mitigated much of the influence of AIPAC's congressional alliances. AIPAC's access to the White House was circumscribed by the organization's increasing opposition to issues concerning the Palestinian Arabs and the absence of strong pro-Israeli sympathies among the administration's inner circle.

Organizationally, AIPAC was in full control of American Jewry's organized response to Carter's diplomacy. Representatives of other groups were perhaps consulted, but AIPAC's leadership went basically unquestioned. Communal cohesion on the issues was fairly high. There were some intracommunal differences over specific Israeli policies, especially relating to Begin's building of settlements in the territories (Rosenbaum Interview). However, major American Jewish groups found themselves defending Jerusalem, right or wrong, because of "the administration's heavy-handedness toward Israel" (Spiegel 1985, 317).

The nature of the American decisional structure was not conducive to AIPAC's attempts to influence Carter's diplomatic strategy. Perhaps the most revealing characteristic of the Carter foreign policy team was its lack of connection to, or understanding of, the American Jewish community. Coming from the Deep South and from beyond the mainstream of the Democratic party, Carter did not appear to fully comprehend the American Jewish value system or the basis of Jewry's support for the state of Israel (Carter 1982, 273–82). Moreover, with the possible exception of Vice-President Walter Mondale, many of the key makers of foreign policy within the administration, including the secretary of state and the national security adviser, appeared philosophically inclined toward the Arab perspective. Simply put, "there was no one in the administration to challenge or augment the shared policy assumptions about the Middle East that prevailed at the White House and the State Department'' (Spiegel 1985, 327).

Significant aspects of the domestic political environment also restricted AIPAC's capacity to influence the drift in U.S. Middle East policy. Public opinion was generally supportive of Israel, although there was some discernible tempering of this sentiment on specific issues, including fear of a renewed oil boycott and the Begin government's building of settlements in the occupied territories (*Louis Harris Survey*, September 1980 and *Gallup Report*, 1977, as cited in Rosen and Abramowitz 1982, 32–33).

The American media were not demonstrably sympathetic toward Israel's opposition to Carter's diplomacy. With the election of Begin and differences between Carter and Begin after Camp David, much of the media's attention shifted directly to the occupied territories and Israeli policy there. AIPAC officials acknowledge having had some difficulty dealing with Israel's policy in the occupied territories, which, while not necessarily indefensible, was well beyond the organization's capacity to control (Amitay Interview; Dine Interview; Rosenbaum Interview). More debilitating still was the media's favorable impression of Egyptian president Anwar Sadat; Israel's Begin did not fare well by comparison. In this sense, the American media, with some notable exceptions, must be seen as detracting from AIPAC's ability to effectively influence Carter's diplomatic strategy.

AIPAC mobilized most of its congressional allies in response to Carter's diplomatic initiatives. However, primarily because of the nonlegislative character of international diplomacy, the AIPAC-Congress coalition was relatively ineffective in obstructing Carter's perceived drift toward the Palestinian Arabs.

AIPAC's influence was also mitigated by a number of international political factors. Menachem Begin's declining popularity and the simultaneous ascendance of Anwar Sadat undermined AIPAC's efforts to sustain a pro-Israel mood in the United States populace. Moreover, AIPAC's performance of its role as an intermediary between Washington and Jerusalem became increasingly difficult as the differences between Begin and Carter became more acute.

In an interesting twist, the Carter administration attempted at one point to enlist the American Jewish community as an independent source of pressure upon Begin (Spiegel 1985, 316–17; Spiegel 1977). The White House anticipated that some influential American Jews would be uncomfortable with aspects of the Likud's platform. It was Carter's hope that such people might employ their unique access to Jerusalem in order to press for Israeli diplomatic moderation (Carter 1982, 268–87). The Carter strategy was correct in principle; some American Jewish leaders, mostly connected to the Israeli Labor party, were troubled by the stridency of Begin's policies and political style (Bookbinder Interview; Rosenbaum Interview). This did not, however, result in the type of Jewish pressure upon Jerusalem that Carter had hoped for. The plan failed, primarily because Carter's open flirtation with a broader conception of Palestinian political rights was still well beyond the American Jewish value system and had the effect of drawing together the vast majority of American Jews in support of Israel, regardless of differences over Begin and Likud.

A final conceptual variable also adversely affected AIPAC's influence over Carter's diplomacy. AIPAC officials perceived Carter's support for a Palestinian homeland to be a crisis for Israel and American Jewry in the sense of potentially compromising cherished values. The Carter administration also viewed its Middle East policy as essential, but for very different reasons. The president and his key advisers saw oil and assured American and Western access to it as a crisis for U.S. foreign policy in the late 1970s. Carter and National Security Adviser Brzezinski viewed Israel as but one pawn in the oil resource game, as a vehicle through which to pacify the key player, Saudi Arabia. The administration's rapidly evolving "Saudiphilic" foreign policy limited the diplomatic options available to the White House; this in turn severely restricted American Jewry's influence over the policy process (Emerson 1985; Rosenbaum 1981).

Despite AIPAC's aggressive opposition (reinforced by the mobilization of the congressional pro-Israel coalition), the Carter administration held firmly to a conception of Middle East diplomacy that was generally unsympathetic (if not diametrically opposed) to the policy preferences articulated by AIPAC and much of American Jewry. (The one redeeming factor was the inability of Carter to implement his image of Middle East peace.) Regardless of AIPAC's abject displeasure, the Administration continued criticizing the Begin government and speaking of Palestinian political rights and a Palestinian homeland. The ability of a determined American president to prevail over even the most well organized domestic foreign policy opposition became a theme that repeated itself for AIPAC throughout the remainder of the Carter administration and well into the subsequent Reagan years.

CARTER AND ARMS TRANSFERS: THE F-15 CONTROVERSY

Overview

American Jewry's relations with the Carter White House, already strained by the president's diplomatic strategy, were exacerbated by the administration's policy on arms transfers and the use of arms sales as diplomatic leverage against Israel and the American Jewish lobby. Much of the community's concern focused on the White House's intention, announced in February 1978, to sell sixty F-15 jet interceptor aircraft to Saudi Arabia, as part of a package sale of fifty F-5Es to Egypt and fifteen F-15s and seventy-five F-16s to Israel (*New York Times*, February 15, 1978, A1).

The government of Israel and its American supporters were initially taken aback by the $4.8 billion proposed arms sale. Concern arose not so much because of the inclusion of arms to Saudi Arabia and Egypt, for this had been occurring on an increasingly frequent scale for a number of years (Pollock 1982; Steinberg

1983b, 124–29), but because the inclusion of the sophisticated aircraft ticketed for Saudi Arabia might disrupt Israel's qualitative edge in the Middle East arms race (Safran 1969, 143–204).

The Carter administration fought vigorously for congressional passage of the arms package. White House lobbyists concentrated on isolating Israel's most consistent allies in Congress. Former AIPAC officials suggest that Carter's staff misled congressional leaders, such as Senators Abraham Ribicoff, Frank Church, and Jacob Javits. Reportedly, the three politicians were led to believe that Carter was willing to work toward a compromise on the Saudi portion of the sale—the president's actual intention was to force a direct confrontation with AIPAC and pro-Israeli forces in the Senate (Amitay Interview; Rosenbaum Interview).

The political debate over the Saudi F-15s continued throughout the spring of 1978 and became entangled with Washington's criticism of Israel's mini-invasion of southern Lebanon ("Operation Litani") and Jerusalem's alleged violation of end-use restrictions on U.S.-built weapons (*New York Times*, April 6, 1978, A1; *New York Times*, April 8, 1978, A1; Vance 1983, 208–11). The legislative debate was finally resolved in mid-May 1978. Some last minute sweeteners, in the form of twenty additional F-15s to Israel, were tacked on to the package in order to win the support of pro-Israeli senators. As further mollification, Secretary of Defense Harold Brown wrote to Senator John Sparkman, chairman of the Senate Foreign Relations Committee, promising that the Saudis would not receive from the United States external fuel tanks, refueling air tankers, bomb racks, or other equipment designed to enhance the offensive capabilities of the F-15s (*Near East Report*, May 17, 1978). By a vote of fifty-four to forty-four, the Senate approved of the tripartite arms transfer on May 16, 1978.[5]

Conceptual Analysis

AIPAC's participation in the F-15 debate is consistent with some but not all of the criteria usually associated with an effective ethnic lobby group. The organization's level of activity and access to key decision makers were relatively great. However, the committee's policy objectives were perceived as essentially antagonistic, diffuse, and unconstructive; the principal goal was to eliminate the Saudi portion of the proposed arms deal. AIPAC's arguments against the sale were based on a number of central themes. The organization argued that in the hands of the Saudis the sophisticated F-15 posed an immediate threat to the security of the state of Israel. Another argument focused on the Middle East regional domain: because of its refusal to actively support the U.S.-sponsored Middle East peace process, its participation in the 1973–74 oil embargo, and the apparent instability of the regime, Saudi Arabia was an undeserving and unreliable recipient of such considerable American largess (Amitay Interview; Rosenbaum, 1981, 118; Rosenbaum Interview).

The problem with AIPAC's arguments opposing the arms sale was that, in the short term, at least, "the planes did not seem threatening to Israel"; after all, they were not even to be delivered for three or four years (Spiegel 1985, 349). Moreover, arguments premised on the Saudi's unreliability had the distinct disadvantage of being purely negative (Spiegel 1985, 349). Proponents of the sale argued in a positive manner. Delivery of the F-15s, they said, would increase Saudi Arabia's security, thereby contributing to greater confidence in the United States, greater participation in the peace process, and the freezing of oil prices (Spiegel 1985, 349). The apparent negativism of its policy objectives had a debilitating effect upon AIPAC's ability to influence the outcome of the F-15 debate.

AIPAC's timing on the debate was reactive. There is no evidence of Israeli or AIPAC officials or sympathetic members of Congress having been given advanced notice of the proposed sale (although, given the pattern of U.S. arms sales during the latter part of the 1970s, such a sale might well have been anticipated).

Despite its less than perfect timing, AIPAC's selection of targets and strategies appears appropriate for the task at hand. Its lobbyists concentrated on influencing rejection of the Saudi portion of the sale by Congress, primarily the Senate. This was a reasonable strategy, given the need for Congress's concurrent rejection of all U.S. arms sales. AIPAC officials sought access to the Carter administration in the hope of formulating a compromise (Rosenbaum Interview). However, the internal discipline of the foreign policy-making core on this issue was so complete and the growing mutual antagonism between the White House and the anti-F-15 forces so great, as to severely restrict AIPAC's effective targeting of the White House.

AIPAC was the principal organizational opponent to the F-15 sale. The committee's professional staff worked to coordinate congressional allies and legislative procedures. The same team represented American Jewry officially in all substantive deliberations. The Presidents Conference and its chairman, Rabbi Alexander Schindler, also were deeply involved in the lobbying process but seemed to be taking much of their lead from AIPAC (Bookbinder Interview; Dine Interview).

Intracommunal cohesion on the arms sale package was less than complete. Some members of the organized Jewish community, while not necessarily denying the strategic impact of Saudi Arabia's acquisition of the F-15s, remained confident of Israel's capacity to defend itself against any threat posed by the arms sale. Some members also expressed concern about the possible long-term implications of AIPAC's engaging the White House in open confrontation over the issue (Bookbinder Interview; *New York Magazine*, April 24, 1978; Rosenbaum Interview). Others raised quiet concerns about the wisdom of AIPAC director Morris Amitay's apparent determination to sacrifice generous arms provisions to Israel in order to defeat the Saudi portion of the package (Bookbinder Interview; *Near East Report*, May 24, 1978). In the final analysis, the Carter administration acquiesced to pressure to divide the package and gave Israel additional squadrons of F-15s. It is conceivable that AIPAC's Amitay had been working privately toward just such a compromise from the beginning. However, his stridency throughout the debate caused some further cracking of a communal consensus already strained by differences over Menachem Begin's policies toward the West Bank settlements and the peace process generally.

The structure of the decision-making system affected AIPAC's lobbying effort both positively and negatively. The fact that President Carter had to formally submit the proposed sale to Congress permitted AIPAC to mobilize its influential alliances in both houses. However, AIPAC's influence was reduced by executive control of the legislative initiative. The White House presented the proposed arms sales to Saudi Arabia, Egypt, and Israel as a package; defeat of Saudi Arabia's portion of the arms sale would also mean defeat of Israel's portion. This arrangement had a significant constraining effect upon AIPAC and many of its congressional allies (Rosenbaum Interview).

AIPAC's influence was also constrained by the unity of the administration's key decision makers on the F-15 issue. President Carter "let it be known that he would brook no internal opposition" on the Saudi portion of the package; few inside the White House dared to voice opposition to the sale (Spiegel 1985, 320–29, 347–49). Some degree of consultation with congressional opponents to the sale was inevitable; however, such consultations usually entailed a polite warning not to obstruct the president on the issue (Brzezinski 1983, 247–52; Vance 1983, 205–7). Moreover, a deliberate attempt was made to isolate pro-Israeli congressional leaders—including Senators Church, Ribicoff, and Javits—by disguising the administration's true intentions (Amitay Interview; Rosenbaum 1981, 118).

Various elements of the domestic political environment affected AIPAC's influence over the F-15 debate both positively and negatively. AIPAC was joined in opposition to the sale by a number of influential nongovernmental organizations. These included a nationwide interfaith group of religious and lay leaders (*Near East Report*, May 3, 1978); George Meany, president of the powerful AFL-CIO labor movement; and a variety of ad hoc groups, such as The Emergency Committee for Middle East Peace and Christians Concerned for Israel (*Near East Report*, May 17, 1978). By a four-to-one ratio, American popular opinion opposed the sale of F-15s to Saudi Arabia (*The Harris Survey*, April 1978, as cited in Rosen and Abramowitz 1984, 24–25). However, popular support for Israel had begun to wane because of other aspects of U.S.-Israeli relations, especially the Begin government's alleged intransigence on Middle East peace negotiations and Jewish settlements. This weakened to some extent popular support for the anti-F-15 forces. Active popular opposition to the F-15 sale also may have been weakened by the confused nature of the actual threat to Israeli security posed by aircraft that would not be delivered to Saudi Arabia for three or four years. The implied promise of Saudi moderation on the energy issue and the peace process may also have contributed to wider popular acceptance of the F-15 sale (Spiegel 1985, 349).

The F-15 debate was significantly affected by the emergence of a strong domestic political-corporate counterforce coalition. This coalition—a loose federation of major American and American-based multinational oil and aeronautics manufacturers, bureaucrats and politicians, and Arab-American groups—initiated a highly sophisticated prosale campaign. Its most successful strategy was to domesticize the issue by concentrating on the energy and employment benefits of enhanced U.S.-Saudi relations and significantly deemphasizing the military-strategic aspects of the proposed sale (Emerson 1985, 174–75; Lanouette 1978b, 754; Roberts 1978, 4; Sander 1978c; Spiegel 1985, 349; Teslik 1982, 48–49).

The American media had a mixed impact upon the F–15 opposition. Some elements remained strongly supportive of Israel's concerns. They emphasized the Israeli security imperative and the precarious Middle East arms balance, both of which would conceivably be compromised by the sale of highly sophisticated weaponry to Saudi Arabia (*New York Times*, May 16, 1978, A1). Others, however, granted either tacit or explicit support to the prosale argument by selling advertising space to influential segments of the corporate community and printing editorials denying the threat to Israeli security or emphasizing the dramatic domestic economic benefits to accrue from satisfying Riyadh (*Christian Science Monitor*, May 22, 1978; *Economist*, January 28, 1978, 58; *Economist*, February 18, 1978, 44; *Economist*, April 29, 1978, 47–48; *New York Magazine*, April 24, 1978; *Time*, May 15, 1978).

Through such diverse coverage the American media became important participants in the F-15 debate. The extent to which the media supported or hindered AIPAC's influence over the debate is less than certain.

Crucial aspects of the international political environment significantly hindered AIPAC's capacity to influence the F-15 debate. Most notable in this regard were the responses of the governments of Israel and Saudi Arabia. The Israelis initially appeared confused as to the appropriate response to the F-15 issue. Within the cabinet, Foreign Minister Moshe Dayan presented a hard line. Israel, he argued, must vigorously oppose the F-15 sale in order to maintain credibility with regard to Washington and the Arab states. If this meant sacrificing the Israeli portion of the $4.8 billion arms deal, such were the wages of statecraft. Defense Minister Ezer Weizman, by contrast, maintained that the overriding consideration must be to secure Israel's part of the deal and to then lobby for additional arms and incentives (Weizman 1981, 233–48). Also part of the cabinet's consideration was the suggestion—made to Dayan by Brzezinski in the early spring of 1978—that Israel and American Jewry's adoption of a low-key response to the Saudi F-15s would result in Washington's looking with favor upon a proposed U.S.-Israel bilateral security arrangement (Brzezinski 1983, 248–49). Prime Minister Begin, for his part, vacillated between the moderate and hard-line postures, initially supporting Weizman's position but later recommending that the U.S. Senate reject the entire arms package (Weizman 1981, 248).

The Saudi Arabians also played an important part in the F-15 controversy. They intimated to Carter administration officials the direct relationship they perceived between oil supplies and the successful passage of the F-15 deal (*Near*

East Report, April 19, 1978; May 10, 1978). And they publicly declared their intention to purchase arms from America's allies (or adversaries) if the U.S. deal were not promptly approved (Brzezinski 1983, 247–52). The Saudis also activated their long-standing relations with large segments of the American corporate community, as well as with influential politicians and foreign service officers (Emerson 1982a, 1982b, 1982c, 1985; Roberts 1978; Sander 1978c). For example, Frederick Dutton, former aide to John Kennedy, employed by Riyadh as its Washington lobbyist, was among the most active proponents of the F-15 sale (Emerson 1982c, 18–23).

AIPAC officials perceived the proposed sale of the F-15s to Saudi Arabia as a threat to both Israel's security and its valued qualitative edge in the Middle East arms race. America's commitment to regional peace and stability, as conceived of by the Jewish lobby, was equally threatened. By contrast, the Carter administration viewed the failure to complete the Saudi sale as a threat to America's national interests, especially as they related to assured access to oil. The greater the administration's perceived stake in the F-15 sale, the greater its determination to isolate and limit the influence of its opponents. The group affected most unfavorably by this sentiment was AIPAC, which spearheaded the anti-F-15 campaign.

Ultimately, it is difficult to understand how a compromise that saw the transfer to Israel of over 100 of America's most sophisticated fighter jets, worth more than $2 billion, could represent a political defeat for AIPAC and the American Zionist lobby. And yet there is virtual unanimity among analysts and practitioners that the U.S. Senate's May 1978 approval of the Carter administration's proposed $4.8 billion arms package to Israel, Egypt, and Saudi Arabia was an example of AIPAC's having minimal-low influence over the American foreign policy-making process (Amitay Interview; Rosenbaum 1981, 118; Spiegel 1985, 346–53).

These confusing assertions are reconciled by examining once again AIPAC's principal objective on the issue. From the outset AIPAC's goal was to defeat the administration's proposed sale of sixty F-15s to Saudi Arabia. AIPAC's director, Morris Amitay, considered such a defeat imperative. Defeat of the Saudi deal would protect Israel's qualitative edge in the Middle East arms race and effectively derail the increasingly Saudiphilic tendencies of the U.S. foreign policy-making establishment (Amitay Interview; Rosenbaum Interview).

There were many factors that impeded AIPAC's success in this endeavor. Principal among these was the determination of the White House to expend all of the presidency's formal and informal political resources to assure congressional approval of the Saudi deal. Despite the powerful anti-F-15 lobbying campaign, involving the mobilization of important societal and governmental actors, AIPAC was unable to overcome the combined weight of the powerful competing interests, led by President Carter himself, working for the sale's approval. In the final analysis, the lesson to be learned from the F-15 debate is that an ethnic foreign policy interest group, regardless of how well situated and well represented in a diversified decision-making process, is still hard-pressed to influence the outcome of a policy championed (in an opposite direction) by a fully committed president.

THE AWACS DEBATE

Overview

The American Jewish community viewed optimistically the election of Ronald Reagan as president in November 1980. Reagan's frequent condemnation of the PLO, his criticism of Carter's Middle East diplomatic strategy, and his apparently sincere affinity toward Israel all contributed to the community's positive attitude about U.S.-Israeli relations under Reagan (Kenen 1981, 331–32; *Near East Report*, July 25, 1980; November 7, 1980; December 26, 1980; January 16, 1981; *Washington Post*, April 15, 1979, A25; Spiegel 1985, 406).

This optimism was rapidly muted by the tone and substance of the new administration's approach to the Middle East. Reagan soon found himself embroiled in the same types of regional controversies that had plagued Jimmy Carter. Most prominent of these was the need to reconcile two competing core national concerns: the achievement of improved relations with the moderate Arab world and the maintenance of America's long-standing commitment to the state of Israel (Tucker 1981a).

The Reagan administration was quickly drawn into the quagmire of arms sales to Saudi Arabia. Regardless of Defense Secretary Brown's May 1978 assurance, the Carter administration was, by early 1980, considering the sale of enhancement equipment for the F-15s to Saudi Arabia (Brzezinski 1983, 449–53). In mid-1980 a letter opposing such a sale, and bearing the signatures of sixty-eight U.S. senators, was sent to President Carter. The Carter reelection team needed little further cause to reconsider; Saudi Arabia was informed that no formal decision could be taken on the enhancements until after the November 1980 presidential election (Brzezinski 1983, 452–53; Carter 1982, 577–80, 591–92).

In late January 1981 the Reagan administration took up consideration of the Saudi request. Perceiving Riyadh's cooperation as essential to the creation of a pro-Western strategic alliance in the Middle East, the administration announced in late February 1981 its intention to sell F-15 enhancements to the Saudis (*New York Times*, March 8, 1981, A4).

Israeli officials and leaders of the American Zionist community immediately criticized the proposed sale, presenting essentially the same arguments used against the original F-15 sale in 1978 (Rosenbaum 1981). In addition, they argued that the security of Israel was now even more compromised by the proposed enhanced offensive capacity of the F-15s. They suggested that events in the Middle East since 1978—the fall of the Shah of Iran, the radicalization of the Persian Gulf, and the Soviet invasion of Afghanistan—diminished the Saudi regime's credentials as a secure recipient of sophisticated American weaponry (*Jerusalem Post (International Edition)*, February 20, 1981, 1; *Near East Report*, February 13, 1981; February 27, 1981; March 6, 1981; March 13, 1981; March 27, 1981).

The Reagan administration chose to ignore all such arguments. The Saudis would be sold the F-15 enhancements and Israel would be offered compensation in the form of another squadron of F-15s and increased military and economic assistance (reportedly amounting to some $600 million) (Pollock 1982, 277).

The proposed F-15 enhancement sale sent disturbing signals to Jerusalem and much of American Jewry. The sense of crisis was significantly heightened by the Reagan administration's announcement in April 1981 of its intention to include five Airborne Warning and Command System (AWACS) jet aircraft in the arms sale to Saudi Arabia (thereby increasing the value of the proposed package to a staggering $8.5 billion) (*New York Times*, April 22, 1981, A1).

The Israelis and their American Jewish supporters were collectively "horrified that such an advanced intelligence tool with a possible combat role would be placed under Saudi control" (Spiegel 1985, 408). The inclusion of the AWACS was perceived as an open provocation to political battle (*Near East Report*, April 10, 1981; April 17, 1981; April 24, 1981; May 1, 1981).

As described by AIPAC's director at that time, Tom Dine, the subsequent debate over the AWACS was a ten-month marathon lasting from December 1980 until October 28, 1981. It was a vigorous battle, waged inside Congress as well as in the print media and on the airwaves. The 1978 F-15 debate seems pale by comparison. The anti-AWACS coalition worked through the provisions of the Arms Export Control Act, which stipulated Congress's concurrent rejection of all proposed arms transfers. This strategy succeeded at obstructing the AWACS sale at every legislative step except the last: the final vote in the full Senate.[6] On October 28, 1981, the Senate, by a margin of fifty-two to forty-eight, voted to defeat the anti-AWACS resolution thereby approving the arms sales package (*New York Times*, October 29, 1981, A1).[7]

Conceptual Analysis

AIPAC spearheaded the campaign opposing congressional approval of the F-15 enhancement and AWACS sale to Saudi Arabia. Although it ultimately failed to achieve its objectives, the committee's involvement in the AWACS debate holds fairly consistently to the type of involvement anticipated for an influential ethnic foreign policy interest group.

AIPAC's level of lobbying activity was extremely high throughout the debate, up to and including the final vote on the Senate floor. AIPAC was the undisputed leader of both Jewish and non-Jewish opposition to the AWACS. Its policy objectives were both antagonistic and advocative. The primary goal was to influence the rejection of the Saudi sale. There was, however, also a more constructive dimension to AIPAC's program: to lay bare the "errors of Arabism"; that is, to demonstrate that Arabist and Saudiphilic tendencies prevalent in U.S. Middle East policy since October 1973 had not contributed significantly to the broader national interests of the United States and that such interests were better served through a policy more sensitive to Israel's concerns (Amitay Interview; Dine Interview; Dine 1983b, 1984a; *Near East Report*, March 27, 1981; April 3, 1981; April 10, 1981; Rosenbaum 1981, 14–15; Rosenbaum Interview).

AIPAC's timing on the AWACS issue was necessarily reactive. AIPAC, of course, lobbied constantly against arms transfers to the Arab world. However, although pro-Israel congressional actors received prior consultation on the F-15 enhancement plan and AIPAC officials were seemingly well aware of the support within the administration for continued military support to Riyadh, they could not respond to the specific issue of AWACS until it was formally announced by the White House in April 1981 (*Near East Report*, January 23, 1981; Rosenbaum 1981, 13–14). Once confronted with this challenge, AIPAC officials concentrated on targeting the congressional-legislative phase of the decisional process. Recognizing the unlikelihood of persuading the Reagan administration to voluntarily withdraw the AWACS proposal, AIPAC sought its concurrent rejection in the two legislative chambers. AIPAC lobbyists focused much of their attention on the Senate.

Many of the arguments and alliances employed in the 1978 F-15 debate were reactivated in 1981. Direct appeals made to politicians and NGOs presented in dramatic and graphic detail the threat to Israeli security and regional stability posed by the Saudi arms sale. A constant flow of letters and resolutions sensitized Congress and the media "to both the issue at hand and the weakness of the President's case" (Rosenbaum 1981, 18). Rosenbaum asserts that the anti-AWACS coalition's strategy of direct and constant pressure made it easier to attract and hold support in Congress for the resolution of disapproval initiated by Senator Robert Packwood (Rosenbaum 1981). AIPAC activities worked the media through formal policy statements, selective leaks of information, and orchestrated demonstrations of "popular" concern about the AWACS sale (Blitzer 1981a). Taken together, these strategies resulted in significant pressure upon government officials and NGOs to declare their opposition to the AWACS sale.

The one serious flaw in an otherwise efficient lobbying effort was the tendency on the part of some elements within the national Jewish community to concentrate exclusively on the Israeli dimension of the AWACS controversy in their lobbying activities, thereby compromising the opportunity of drawing non-Jewish societal elements into a broader anti-AWACS coalition. Aaron Rosenbaum, a former AIPAC research director, suggests that this strategic error was committed mainly by Jewish leaders in smaller and more remote communities, where "too many Jews vitiated their impact by not following AIPAC's lead, instead talking only about Israel" (Blitzer 1981b, 18). This assertion undoubtedly has an element of truth to it. However, the fault may lie less with the local Jewish community leaders, who were lobbying on the basis of the only political strategies they knew, than with AIPAC for failing to integrate them effectively into the national network of information and political education (Rosenbaum Interview).

From an organizational perspective, its participation in the AWACS debate reinforced AIPAC's status as an institutionalized ethnic lobby. It was the undisputed spearhead of the anti-AWACS campaign, drawing to it numerous non-Jewish politicians and NGOs, who often opposed the AWACS sale for reasons different from those of the Jewish community (Blitzer 1981a).

Throughout the AWACS debate, AIPAC remained centralized and corporate in structure. Jewish community notables were consulted and frequently integrated into a broadened informal decisional and consultative network. However, AIPAC professionals were firmly in control of the communal response to the AWACS controversy. In one sense, such centralization of communal authority was productive; administration officials and sympathetic legislators knew with whom to interact. However, a political price was paid for AIPAC's not having effectively extended its intracommunal lines of communication and education.

Agreement was high among American Jews concerning the arms sale to Saudi Arabia. However, communal cohesion was still less than complete. Differences prevailed over the tactical response to the issue. Some important members of the American Jewish decisional core held that the selection of lobbying techniques had to be based on consideration of the entirety of U.S.-Israeli relations, as well as the community's goal of maintaining institutionalized influence over the making of America's Middle East policy. They agreed that the AWACS sale had to be vigorously opposed. But, it was not the only issue on the U.S.-Israeli agenda, nor was it likely to be the last crisis American Jewry would face in its defense of Israel's interests. While opposing the sale of the AWACS, the community had to be careful not to burn its bridges; it had to conserve a base for interacting with Congress and the executive branch on a host of other future issues, regardless of the outcome of the AWACS debate. Individuals articulating this view suggested that the stridency with which AIPAC's new director, Tom Dine, pursued the AWACS question—including making a senator's vote on the issue a litmus test of his or her support for Israel generally—would have the effect of weakening American Jewry's credibility in the long-term policy process (Bookbinder Interview; Rosenbaum Interview; Rosenbaum 1981, 58). Although many of these concerns were voiced only retrospectively, there appears to be a certain merit to them. Evidence suggests that tactical differences of this type may have weakened AIPAC's internal cohesion, and hence, its potential influence over the AWACS debate (Rosenbaum 1981, 58).

The structure of the formal decision-making system associated with the AWACS debate was in some important ways similar to that relating to the previous F-15 legislative controversy. Common to both was the White House's control of the legislative initiative and the perception of Saudi Arabia as a key international ally whose confidence had to be secured through generous arms transfers. There was, however, something unique about the Reagan administration's handling of the 1981 issue. In 1978 Carter had presented to Congress a virtual fait accompli, in the form of a tripartite arms sale package, and had rejected until the eleventh hour demands to divide the package and negotiate compromises on its constituent parts. Reagan's approach to the AWACS issue was seemingly more open ended and conciliatory. Unlike Carter, Reagan attempted to avoid both political confrontation and legislative stalemate. Compensations to Israel were included in the original draft legislation, and the door was conceivably left open to further economic and military inducements if Israel and its domestic supporters acquiesced to unimpeded congressional approval of the sale of the F-15 enhancements and the AWACS. To be sure, the Reagan administration's ultimate strategy was probably not much different from Carter's: to isolate and defeat the pro-Israel coalition's opposition to U.S. arms sales to Saudi Arabia and other Arab moderates. However, Reagan's style was different from Carter's intense combativeness. Even at the height of the legislative battle, when the AWACS proposal was put in doubt primarily by AIPAC's lobbying efforts, access to the White House was never denied to AIPAC in the way it had been throughout much of the F–15 debate (Dine Interview).

The domestic political environment provided less than optimal conditions through which AIPAC attempted to influence a defeat of the AWACS deal. In October 1981 a public opinion survey commissioned by the *Los Angeles Times* discerned a two-to-one ratio of opposition to the AWACS sale, down from the four-to-one ratio of popular disapproval of the 1978 F-15 sale (Harris Survey, April 1978, as cited in Rosen and Abramowitz 1984, 24–25). This suggested a moderation in the American public's traditionally strong aversion to weapon sales to Arab states (Gallup Organization, October 1973, as cited in Rosen and Abramowitz 1984, 24–25). Obviously, this worked against the interests of AIPAC and the anti-AWACS forces.

The American media became acutely interested in the AWACS debate. However, unlike in the 1978 case when the media remained somewhat divided, a more definitive prosale consensus emerged. Some commentators, focusing on the technical aspects of the argument, found themselves debating AIPAC's charge that the enhanced F-15s and AWACS represented a direct and immediate threat to Israeli security (*Aviation Week*, October 26, 1981, 20–21; *Newsweek*, May 4, 1981, 24; *New York Times*, April 20, 1981, A7; *U.S. News and World Report*, May 4, 1981, 12; *U.S. News and World Report*, September 7, 1981, 25–26; *U.S. News and World Report*, October 12, 1981, 25). Others demonstrated prosale tendencies explicitly through editorials or implicitly (as in the case of the *New York Times* and *Wall Street Journal*), by agreeing to publish a series of advertisements purchased by Mobil Oil praising the multiple virtues of strong U.S.-Saudi relations (see Spiegel 1981, 1–2). Former Secretary of State Alexander Haig asserts that when the Saudis wished to publicly voice their support for the AWACS sale, they spoke directly to members of the editorial board at the *New York Times* (Haig 1984, 192).

Many of the American media focused less on the substantive aspects of the

AWACS debate than on the personalities involved. The activist role adopted by President Ronald Reagan and the "Reagan or Begin" theme (attributed to Riyadh's Washington lobbyist, Frederick Dutton) was emphasized by many of the media (Spiegel 1985, 409). Charges of American Jewish dual loyalty, raised implicitly by some members of the administration (and more explicitly by others), were picked up by large segments of the American media (*New York Times*, October 2, 1981, A1; Friedman 1981, 1982; Lipset 1981; *Nation*, December 12, 1981, 633–35). Alexander Haig defends the role of the media in this regard, asserting that the media "did itself proud" in not permitting antisemitism to become a dominant feature of the AWACS debate (Haig 1984, 192–93).

AIPAC and the anti-AWACS coalition were not without supporters within the media. The *New Republic* and the syndicated columnist William Safire were among the most virulent opponents of the AWACS sale (*New Republic*, May 9, 1981, 12; *New Republic*, October 7, 1981, 5; Tucker 1981b; *New York Times*, March 12, 1981, A28). Alexander Haig claims that when the Israelis and AIPAC wished to make a point plainly to the White House, "they would consult a friendly columnist on the *Washington Post*" (Haig 1984, 192). Some elements of the media were critical of the administration's handling of the AWACS affair (*Newsweek*, September 28, 1981, 100; *Time*, May 4, 1981, 14–16; *Time*, September 7, 1981, 10–11); others, of the increasingly overt lobbying practices of the Saudis and other elements of the petro-diplomatic complex (Emerson 1982a, 1982b, 1982c, 1985; *Newsweek*, November 2, 1981, 42).

Although a certain amount of diversity was still apparent in the media's coverage of the AWACS issue, a certain prosale—or, perhaps more correctly, pro-Reagan—consensus was manifested in many of the American media. In the final analysis, media coverage probably worked against AIPAC's attempt to influence defeat of the popular new president's arms sale proposal.

In its anti-AWACS campaign, AIPAC received tremendous support from influential congressional actors. Although their motivations varied (ranging from concern for Israel's security, to fear of Jewish electoral sanction, to dissatisfaction with Saudi Arabia's performance as an American strategic asset, to distaste for overt efforts on the part of the Saudis to intervene in the American policy process), numerous congressmen and senators provided a secure base from which AIPAC could launch forceful legislative opposition to the AWACS sale.

The AWACS debate also led AIPAC to attempt to mobilize (and remobilize) coalitions with influential segments of the domestic political environment. These included American labor, religious groups (such as the rapidly ascending Moral Majority and ad hoc alliances such as Churches United For American Security and the Christian Leadership Conference For Israel), and elements of the general population concerned with national security or unconvinced of Saudi Arabia's strategic reliability (Rosenbaum 1981, 57).

The organized Jewish community's relations with the Reagan administration, even at the height of the AWACS debate, were significantly better than they were with the Carter administration at the best of times. However, relations with the Reagan team were never strong enough to affect reversal of its determination to implement the controversial AWACS sale. The limited quality of AIPAC's interactions with the Reagan White House was not based on the latter's inexperience with Jewish issues (as was in part the case with Carter). Rather, it had much to do with the White House's bias in favor of the Arab perspective. None of Reagan's principal advisers, upon whom he was by inclination so dependent, had particularly close ties to Israel or previous foreign policy experience (Biggart 1981; Dine Interview; *Time*, December 13, 1982, 10–17). More importantly, many had strong previous business experience with American and multinational corporations with ties to the Arab world (Spiegel 1985, 405).

AIPAC and its congressional allies were initially able to influence a stalemate on the F-15 enhancements by exploiting the personal and political rivalries within the Reagan Administration: primarily between Reagan's inner circle of personal advisers and National Security Adviser Richard Allen, and between Secretary of State Haig and Defense Secretary Caspar Weinberger (Haig 1984, 175–82; Rosenbaum 1981, 13–14). However, the pro-Saudi sentiment within the foreign policy-making core and the White House gatekeepers was so great as to undermine Haig's initial reluctance to support the inclusion of the AWACS in the arms package (Haig 1984, 175). There was no significant counterweight—with the exception of Secretary of State Haig and Reagan's first UN ambassador, Jeanne Kirkpatrick—to the administration's determination to sell the F-15 enhancements and AWACS to Saudi Arabia.

The 1981 AWACS debate witnessed the coalescence of a pro-Arab domestic lobby of unprecedented political influence. This was comprised of essentially three complexes—the military-industrial, the petro-dollar, and the industrial-political. Former state department officials, former secretaries of state and defense (notably Henry Kissinger, Cyrus Vance, and James Schlesinger), and three former presidents of the United States (Nixon, Ford, and Carter), also publicly aligned themselves with the pro-AWACS camp (Emerson 1985; Rosenbaum 1981, 16–17). The prosale coalition was led by such American corporate giants as Boeing (the main contractor for the AWACS), General Electric, United Technologies, AMOCO, Transworld Airlines, Intercontinental Hotels, Ford, Trans-America Corporation, and Kellogg. In a series of advertisements that appeared in the *Wall Street Journal* and the *New York Times*, Mobil Corporation expressed the widely held view of the importance of Saudi Arabia to America's future corporate, employment, and energy interests (Spiegel 1981, 1–2).

The convergence of this powerful pro-Saudi coalition on Capitol Hill countered the influence of the anti-AWACS forces. It also provided a forum for many of the more virulent critics of Israel and American Jewish foreign policy activism (Blitzer 1985, 134–35; Findley 1985, 50–59, 104–9; Mathias 1981).

Key administration officials, including NSC Adviser Richard Allen and White House Chief of Staff James Baker, were assisted in their pro-AWACS congressional lobbying by several influential senators, including Majority Leader Howard Baker, Charles Percy, and Jesse Helms. This group exerted considerable pressure upon senatorial colleagues to fall into line behind the president on the AWACS issue. AIPAC activists acknowledge that the turning point of the entire AWACS debate may have been when Iowa Senator Robert Jepson publicly renounced six months of vigorous opposition to the AWACS sale after a brief meeting with Ronald Reagan (*Near East Report*, June 5, 1981; *New York Times*, October 28, 1981, A14; Rosenbaum 1981, 18–19). The "defections" of Jewish senators Warren Rudman and Edward Zorinsky were damaging to AIPAC's efforts, as was that of Senator William Cohen of Maine, who obliquely raised the fear of increased domestic antisemitism if the AWACS legislation was defeated (Rosenbaum 1981, 19–20).

Regardless of the influence of the prosale coalition, most analysts agree that it was Ronald Reagan who made the difference: "The scales were tipped in favor of the AWACS sale by the President's forceful intervention. Without him, opponents of the sale would certainly have won" (Spiegel 1985, 398).

Elements of the international political environment also restricted AIPAC's influence over the AWACS issue. The Iran-Iraq War and the radicalization of the Persian Gulf caused many American officials to support the need for the increased security of Saudi Arabia and to deemphasize Israel's importance (Haig 1984, 169). Similarly, the October 6, 1981, assassination of Egyptian President Anwar Sadat strengthened the Reagan administration's resolve to demonstrate America's commitment to the security of its moderate Arab state allies (Haig 1984, 322–28). The June 7, 1981, Israeli air strike upon the Iraqi nuclear reactor at Osirak—however justified from a strategic perspective—weakened AIPAC's capacity to influence the AWACS debate (*Jerusalem Post [International Edition]*, June 14–20, 1981, 1; *Near East Report*, June 12, 1981; June 26, 1981). Riyadh alleged that Israel's overflight of Saudi airspace on the way to Baghdad indicated Saudi Arabia's dramatic need for increased defensive capabilities, such as those provided by the AWACS. Alexander Haig suggests that his effort to downplay the significance of the AWACS in the Arab-Israeli conflict became a principal casualty of the Osirak raid (Haig 1984, 184). AIPAC officials are reticent to acknowledge a direct causal relationship between the Osirak raid and the July 17, 1981, air strike on PLO headquarters in Beirut and the legislative defeat of the anti-AWACS resolution the following October. They do acknowledge, however, that those events caused AIPAC and the pro-Israeli congressional coalition to divert their attention temporarily from the AWACS debate (Dine Interview; Rosenbaum Interview).

The governments of Saudi Arabia and Israel each lobbied extensively in support of their respective interests concerning the AWACS sale. As it had in the 1978 arms sale, Riyadh declared the sale of the AWACS to be a litmus test of U.S.-Saudi relations. It also made clear that if the AWACS proposal were defeated, it would not hesitate to deal for arms elsewhere (*Aviation Week*, October 26, 1981, 20–21; *Newsweek*, November 21, 1981, 42).

The Israeli government was no less animated on the AWACS issue. Alexander Haig recounts an official visit to the United States in September 1981 of Prime

Minister Begin and Defense Minister Ariel Sharon. Although careful not to violate the hospitality of the U.S. government, Begin and Sharon, when asked, made known their serious reservations about the proposed Saudi arms deal (Haig 1984, 186–88).

Nevertheless, AIPAC's campaign in opposition to the AWACS was, in part, inhibited by a degree of uncertainty among Israel's leaders about the appropriate response to the issue. The Israelis were reportedly of two minds on the initial plan to sell the F-15 enhancements to the Saudis. Although obviously troubled by it, they needed the economic and military compensation offered by the Reagan administration; they also sought to avoid initiating confrontation with the new U.S. president. Although much of their initial ambivalence evaporated with the inclusion of the AWACS in the sale, many Israelis were still less than confident about the wisdom of doing political battle with an apparent friend in the White House. There is indeed evidence to suggest that Begin's ultimate decision to continue opposing the AWACS sale was strongly influenced by the urgings of AIPAC's leaders. Executive Director Tom Dine reportedly informed Begin that any easing of Israel's posture would damage Jerusalem's and the Jewish lobby's credibility on Capitol Hill: "Many members had gone out on a limb against the sale largely because of their concern over the potential threat to Israeli security. . . . They did not want to see the rug pulled out from under their feet" (Blitzer 1985, 139). In the final analysis, Begin maintained his opposition to the AWACS sale. The influence of Dine's urgings upon Begin's decision-making is an unanticipated twist to the assumed relationship between a domestic ethnic interest group and a foreign government.

American Jewish leaders perceived the sale of the F-15 enhancements and AWACS to Saudi Arabia as a grave threat to core values (*Near East Report*, April 3, 1981; April 24, 1981; May 1, 1981; Rosenbaum 1981, 14–15). AIPAC officials considered opposition to the sale a moral imperative: "To refuse to join the fray would be the surest way to encourage even greater aggressiveness among the Arabists, the bureaucratic opponents of Israel and the corporate advocates of the politics of oil" (Rosenbaum 1981, 14). Based on such a rationale, AIPAC became the undisputed leader of the national anti-AWACS campaign, surpassing, by a considerable margin, the opposition presented by the Israelis themselves.

The final outcome of the AWACS debate illustrates the theoretical assumption concerning the shared perceptions of crisis and the level of a group's influence over government policy. The high priority accorded to the AWACS issue by the Reagan administration countered all of AIPAC's lobbying efforts. Ronald Reagan and his key advisers saw a confident and well-armed Saudi Arabia as an essential counterforce to the regional instability caused by the radicalization of Iran and the Soviet invasion of Afghanistan (Haig 1984, 168–69). Although not preoccupied with the issue (as had been its immediate predecessor), the Reagan administration also perceived a direct linkage between Saudi Arabia's enhanced sense of security and Western access to affordable supplies of oil (Haig 1984,

170–71). A basic truism of American political life is again confirmed: If the president of the United States is ready and willing to commit all of his political resources to a preferred conclusion to a particular policy issue, the influence of domestic forces seeking alternate conclusions is severely diminished.

The Senate's vote of October 28, 1981, narrowly rejecting the concurrent resolution of disapproval of the sale of the F-15 enhancements and AWACS, represents an indisputable defeat for AIPAC. To be sure, the anti-AWACS coalition took the White House "to the wall" on the issue and won considerable compensation for Israel, leading some to view the AWACS debate as "a victory on the merits" and "a good fight . . . not quite a defeat" (Dine Interview; Rosenbaum 1981, 57). Regardless, former AIPAC director Morris Amitay declares that "there is no such thing as a moral victory in politics" (Amitay Interview). AIPAC had set as its principal objective congressional passage of the resolution of disapproval: the failure to achieve this goal was a major defeat for the American Zionist movement (approximating a situation of least influence for AIPAC). It was also a clear and unambiguous message to American Jewry that "victory is no longer automatic when it comes to maintaining U.S. support for Israel" (Blitzer 1985, 126).

LEBANON WAR OF 1982

Overview

The AWACS debate appeared to produce a series of new "irritants" in U.S.-Israeli relations, and hence, in the relationship between the U.S. government and its Jewish and pro-Israel constituencies. These irritants included official Israeli opposition to Western European participation in the multinational observer force slated for the Sinai Desert following the April 1982 Israeli withdrawal (*Jerusalem Post [International Edition]*, December 6–12, 1981, 1; *Near East Report*, December 11, 1981); tacit U.S. support for the Saudi Arabian proposal for Middle East peace (the so-called Fahd Plan); and the December 14, 1981, Knesset decision to extend Israeli jurisdiction over the disputed Golan Heights (*New York Times*, December 15, 1981, A1).

Increasingly, the U.S.-Israel dialogue focused on the rapidly deteriorating situation in Lebanon. Under considerable pressure from Washington, the Begin government had exhibited restraint in its "miniwar of attrition" with the PLO in the spring of 1981 and during Syria's deployment of Soviet-supplied surface-to-air missile (SAM) systems in Lebanon's Bekaa Valley. Jerusalem also took the unprecedented step in July 1981 of agreeing to a de facto cease-fire with the PLO negotiated by U.S. Special Ambassador Philip Habib. Throughout the latter half of 1981 and early 1982, American officials counseled Jerusalem to continue its restraint, although Secretary of State Alexander Haig acknowledged by early May 1982 "that the U.S. would probably not be able to stop Israel from attacking'' southern Lebanese bases of the Palestine Liberation Organization (1984, 335).

The Reagan administration was not surprised by the invasion of southern Lebanon launched by the Israel Defense Forces (IDF) on June 6, 1982. Although White House officials may not have been privy to the specifics of the Begin government's "grand design" for Lebanon, they were well aware of the plan to attack and had reportedly granted their tacit approval (Schiff 1983; Schiff and Ya'ari 1984, 31–44, 62–72). Washington's "green light" to Israel is suggested by the White House's relatively benign official response to the initial invasion and Israel's establishment of a forty kilometer cordon sanitaire north of the Israeli border. Jerusalem's goal of forcing the PLO from the southern half of Lebanon was compatible with the Reagan administration's goal of expediting the withdrawal of all foreign military forces from Lebanon and restoring the authority of the central government (Haig 1984, 317–18).

Washington's unofficial acquiescence to Israel's intervention in Lebanon, however, diminished markedly. A small group of decision makers in Jerusalem, reportedly under the direct control of Defense Minister Sharon and operating independently of the prime minister and cabinet, extended Israel's military objective beyond the limited cordon sanitaire to include the complete eradication of the PLO's and Syria's military presence in Lebanon. The swift Israeli destruction, three days into the fighting, of the Syrian SAM emplacements in the Bekaa Valley, greatly disturbed the Reagan administration. Washington saw this action as a source of potential escalation of an otherwise limited conflict into an open Israeli-Syrian war (with the attendant possibility of Soviet intervention in support of Damascus) (Haig 1984, 343; Spiegel 1985, 415). The IDF's siege of Beirut and the seemingly indiscriminate daily shelling of its Muslim-dominated western neighborhoods (reportedly housing the PLO headquarters), was initiated on June 11 and sustained throughout the summer months. This exacerbated American frustration with the government of Menachem Begin (Blitzer 1985, 111; Haig 1984, 347; Rosen and Abramowitz 1984, 2–3).

The final evacuation of PLO forces from southern Lebanon, negotiated through Habib and begun on August 21, 1982, came as something of an anticlimax after the events of the previous two months. Seeking to capitalize on the limited diplomatic momentum generated by the pullout, Reagan, on September 1, announced a series of proposals for the achievement of a broader resolution of the Arab-Israeli dispute (*New York Times*, September 2, 1981, A1). The "Reagan Plan" involved the U.S. becoming an active participant in the pursuit of Middle East peace and was premised on some form of Palestinian Arab limited self-rule on the West Bank and Gaza in association with Jordan. Reagan's plan was ignored by the Arab League, meeting in mid-September at Fez, Morocco and outrightly rejected by Menachem Begin's ruling Likud coalition government in Israel (*Jerusalem Post [International Edition]*, September 5–11, 1982, 1; *New York Times*, September 10, 1982, A1).

U.S.-Israeli relations, already strained, were further damaged by events resulting from the September 14, 1982, assassination (by Muslim forces) of Christian Phalange leader and Lebanese president-elect, Bashir Gemayal. Immediately following Gemayal's death, Israeli forces were ordered into West Beirut, ostensibly to capture and destroy arms depots held by the two thousand PLO fighters suspected of having remained behind in Beirut after the evacuation (*New York Times*, September 16, 1982, A1, 12; Schiff and Ya'ari 1984, 250–53). Through what an official Israeli commission of inquiry, headed by Supreme Court Chief Justice Yitzhak Kahan, later called indirect complicity on the part of Israel's highest military and political leaders, Christian Phalangist forces seeking revenge for the assassination of Gemayal were permitted by Israeli soldiers to enter the West Beirut Palestinian refugee camps of Sabra and Shatila (Reich 1985, 74; Schiff and Ya'ari 1984, 250–85). Hundreds of unarmed Palestinians were viciously massacred. Menachem Begin's initial refusal to acknowledge any Israeli involvement in the incidents precipitated a severe deterioration in relations between Washington and Jerusalem.

Conceptual Analysis

AIPAC responded to the Lebanon War in a fashion generally expected of an influential ethnic foreign policy interest group. However, it was less than effective in influencing U.S. policy on the issue.

Before, during, and after the Lebanon invasion, AIPAC's level of lobbying activity was extremely high. The committee's policy objective, however, was antagonistic; it aimed to end the perceived pro-Arab drift in U.S.-Israeli relations resulting from the Iraqi nuclear raid, the bombing of PLO headquarters, the Golan law, and finally the Lebanon invasion and the subsequent siege of Beirut.

Beyond this essentially negative goal, however, AIPAC officials also sought to add a positive dimension to their objectives. They attempted to keep the various factors at dispute in their proper perspective. Whenever possible, they diverted attention to less controversial and more positive aspects of the U.S.-Israeli relationship (*Near East Report*, June 18, 1982; June 20, 1982; July 2, 1982; July 16, 1982). For example, the Lebanon invasion was explained in terms of Israel's legitimate concern for the safety of its northern settlements, whose security was threatened by PLO terrorists operating from bases in southern Lebanon. AIPAC's defense of the invasion as a strike against international terrorism was given added credence by the discovery of irrefutable evidence of Lebanon's status as a major training center for international terrorists (*Near East Report*, June 18, 1982; June 25, 1982; July 2, 1982; July 16, 1982).

AIPAC's targeting of its lobbying efforts to key individuals was appropriate under the circumstance. Because he remained emphatically more sensitive to Israeli concerns than many of his cabinet colleagues, Secretary of State Haig was a principal target of AIPAC's appeals. AIPAC also targeted Congress and the general public. The goal was not simply to defend Israel's actions in Lebanon, but to protect against any attempt to impose economic or military sanctions against Israel in reaction to the invasion. Although both strategies succeeded in eliciting some support, the controversial nature of some of Israel's military behavior forced AIPAC into an unenviable, increasingly defensive posture (Bookbinder Interview; Rosenbaum Interview).

AIPAC remained well organized throughout the Lebanon War. Virtually all of the criteria of an institutionalized ethnic interest group were met. Just prior to the Lebanon conflict, AIPAC found itself in its strongest position from an organizational perspective. Increased financial support and membership resulting from the "AWACS aftermath" brought renewed strength to the organization (Blitzer 1985, 121–22; Dine Interview). Although AIPAC officials had begun a process of gradual decentralization and broadening of the consultative network, the committee remained essentially corporate (Dine Interview; Kenen Interview). AIPAC was in full control of American Jewry's lobbying effort throughout the Lebanon War. Virtually all important decisions emanated from or were affirmed by AIPAC's Washington offices. Participation in the committee remained essentially role-based, although there was some evidence of spontaneous demonstrations in support of Israel in Jewish communities throughout the United States (Blitzer 1985, 148–49).

AIPAC's effectiveness was, however, inhibited by a fairly high degree of intracommunal dissent about the Lebanon War. Support for the initial Israeli incursion into southern Lebanon was relatively high; it was explained and generally accepted as an act of legitimate self-defense. The siege of Beirut and the developments that followed from it were far less well received by significant elements within the Jewish community's mainstream. Some American Jews were disturbed by the seemingly indiscriminate shelling of a foreign capital by the Israeli military. Others worried that the Lebanon exercise appeared to represent a radical departure from a long-established Israeli security doctrine stating "that the Israel Defense Forces were mandated only to defend Israel and were not to be used for the sake of installing or toppling governments in neighboring countries" (Schiff and Ya'ari 1984, 43). Still other American Jews were disturbed by what they perceived to be an excessive personalization of the war; that is, a few leaders were seen to be conducting the war "as if they existed in a vacuum, untouched by any political constraints and oblivious to the danger of causing a rift in the nation" (Schiff and Ya'ari 1984, 43).

The task of maintaining communal solidarity was made significantly more difficult by the Sabra and Shatila refugee camp massacres; community leaders acknowledge that allegations of Israeli involvement led many American Jews to begin to reevaluate their automatic defense of Israel's behavior, right or wrong (Dine Interview; Bookbinder Interview; Halperin 1982; Rosenbaum Interview).

There was, of course, precious little AIPAC could do about how the Israelis conducted their war in Lebanon. What AIPAC officials sought to do was to explain to their constituents the multiple causes of the Lebanese conflict and the extent to which Israel's original goal of removing the PLO from southern Lebanon was consistent with American policy (*Near East Report*, June 11, 1982; Dine

1983f, 1984a). When all else failed, AIPAC officials tried to contain intracommunal dissent by stressing the need for solidarity with the people of Israel in their time of crisis (Berman 1984, 17; Blitzer 1985, 148–49; *New York Times*, September 22, 1982, A16; Rosenbaum Interview).

The process of decision-making within the Reagan administration inhibited AIPAC's capacity to influence a pro-Israeli American conception of events in Lebanon. The AWACS debate and various regional developments during 1981 and early 1982 had caused temporary, yet tangible, rifts in the official U.S.-Israeli relationship. The invasion of Lebanon, and particularly the siege of Beirut, intensified ongoing disputes within the executive branch concerning America's proper handling of the Begin government, Israel, and the American Jewish lobby. By June of 1982 Alexander Haig stood virtually alone in opposing the growing support within the Reagan administration for specific sanctions against Israel (Haig 1984, 343–48; Spiegel 1985, 415–16). Obviously, this sentiment had a detrimental effect upon AIPAC's ability to influence America's immediate response to the Lebanese War.

AIPAC's influence over policy was further constrained by the postures adopted by significant segments of the domestic political environment. Public opinion fluctuated somewhat on the Lebanon issue. Popular support for Israel actually increased slightly at the outset of the war (Gallup Poll, June 11–14, 1982, as cited in Rosen and Abramowitz 1984, 2–3); however, by late September popular sympathy for Israel had eroded substantially (Rosen and Abramowitz 1984, 3; Rosenfield, 1982). AIPAC was generally perceived as defending an unpopular cause (Bookbinder Interview; Dine Interview; Rosenbaum Interview). This perception was reflected in AIPAC's temporarily diminished status in the domestic political environment.

Wolf Blitzer of the *Jerusalem Post* asserted that the American media's coverage of the Lebanon War gave full evidence to the fact that "Israel's honeymoon with the American news media, if there ever really was one, is clearly over" (1985, 159). Israeli media analyst Ze'ev Chafets charges that (with only rare exceptions) his country received "devastatingly bad press" throughout the war (Chafets 1985, 297). Chafets perceives the occurrence of a "melodramatic and sometimes vitriolic press campaign which was aided and abetted by Israel's own conduct, both of the War and its press relations" (1985, 297). According to Chafets, the media's coverage of the war "graphically exhibited the uneven quality of Middle East reporting. Expert journalists worked side by side with neophyte reporters who lost their poise in the confusion and destruction; old Middle East hands' by-lines appeared alongside those of correspondents who couldn't tell Druze from Druids" (1985, 299).

Errors of fact and errors of bias were committed by the American media, both of which adversely affected AIPAC's ability to explain Israel's conduct during the war to an increasingly skeptical American government and public.[8] Exaggerated casualty reports and sensationalized media descriptions are the accompaniment of any modern military conflict. However, Chafets argues, in the

Lebanon War such reporting errors tended to have a common underlying theme: "the inhumanity of Israel's attack against civilians" (Chafets 1985, 303). Chafets hypothesizes a direct causal linkage between the alleged inaccuracies and biased media reporting of the Lebanon War and American Jewry's difficulty defending Israel's actions within the American domestic political environment: such distorted reports were "the raw material with which American opinion makers fashioned a picture of cruel and unusual behavior by the Israeli army" (Chafets 1985, 303).

Blitzer divided media coverage of the Lebanon War into three broad categories: critics, middle ground, and supporters (1985, 166–70). Some of the press, such as the *Washington Post* and *Newsweek*, appeared overtly critical of Israeli behavior. By contrast, the *New Republic* and *Wall Street Journal* and syndicated columnists George Will and William Safire strongly defended Israel's goal of eliminating the PLO and Syrian military presence in Lebanon, and cautioned the Reagan administration to resist the call for sanctioning Israel.

Blitzer claimed that many of the American media occupied a middle ground on the Lebanon War. Among the most notable in this regard was the influential *New York Times*. Its greatest contribution to the Lebanon debate was the extent of its experienced coverage of the Middle East. The trio of Thomas Friedman, Bernard Gwertzman, and David Shipler "developed a well-earned reputation as being by far the most informed and most reliable when it came to understanding the nuances of the region" (Blitzer 1985, 170).

Israel, then, was not totally abandoned by the American media during the Lebanon War. However, a combination of factors—including the inexperience of some reporters, the pro-Arab sympathies of others, and the Israeli government's relative disregard for press relations—all contributed to a reduction in AIPAC's ability to develop a credible media-directed defense of Israel's activities during the summer of 1982 (Blitzer 1985, 166; Bookbinder Interview; Dine Interview; Kenen Interview; Rosenbaum Interview).

By the end of active hostilities in the early fall of 1982, the Reagan administration was virtually devoid of influential voices even moderately sensitive to Israel's position on the Lebanon conflict. Equally disturbing for AIPAC officials was the apparent fracturing of significant segments of Israel's previously consistent support from within Congress. Popular American disapproval of Israel's behavior in Lebanon led even some of its strongest friends in the House of Representatives and Senate to distance themselves from Jerusalem. At a meeting with influential American politicians, Israeli Prime Minister Begin became embroiled in a noisy dialogue with Senator Joseph Biden of Delaware, a proven friend of Israel who had worked hard in opposition to the AWACS sale (Bookbinder Interview; Dine Interview). Biden, reportedly, did not criticize Israel's intervention in Lebanon; indeed, he expressed general support of it. He nevertheless upset Begin by declaring his opposition to Israel's settlement policy in the West Bank. The ensuing discussion emboldened other participants, who then engaged Begin in vigorous debate over the conduct of the Lebanon War. The result was a well-publicized dispute between top Israeli officials and several members of the congressional pro-Israeli coalition (this dispute had the effect of strengthening the resolve of politicians more overtly critical of Israeli policy). Obviously, the incident did not assist AIPAC in its effort to contain public criticism of Israel's activities in Lebanon (Blitzer 1985, 111–13; Dine Interview).

The Lebanon War affected AIPAC's relations with several influential NGOs. The leadership of both organized labor and the Christian fundamentalist movement remained publicly supportive of Israel. In an official policy statement on August 5, 1982, the national leadership of the powerful AFL-CIO declared that "in destroying the PLO's military infrastructure, Israel has not only created the possibility of a free Lebanon; it has dealt a blow to international terrorism and set back Soviet influence in the Middle East—and this advanced the interests of the Western democracies" (Blitzer 1985, 182). The siege of Beirut and the Sabra and Shatila massacres decreased organized labor's level of support for Jerusalem's policies. Dissenting voices were heard throughout the movement's rank and file (Blitzer 1985, 184). The AFL-CIO leadership responded with a statement on September 24, 1982, that condemned the refugee camp deaths but suggested that the underlying cause of the tragedy was the absence of an independent and powerful Lebanese central government resulting from the continued presence there of foreign Arab armies (Blitzer 1985, 183).

American Jewish leaders were concerned about the significant domestic counterforce movement that arose in protest to the Israeli invasion of Lebanon. Gregory Orfalea, writing in *Before the Flames: A Quest for the History of Arab Americans*, suggested that the Lebanon War had an "extremely traumatic" effect upon Arab Americans, leading to an unprecedented level of communal unity for the purposes of political action (1988, x). During the war Palestinian solidarity and Lebanon solidarity movements proliferated throughout the United States (Goott and Rosen 1983; Kessler and Schwaber 1984). Although many of them were ad hoc issue-oriented interest groups (likely to dissolve as other issues and crises came to dominate the American Middle East foreign policy agenda), the Palestinian solidarity groups represented a short-term and long-term concern to AIPAC officials. In the short-term, such groups appeared to manifest growing popular discontent with Israel's specific policies in Lebanon. In the long term, although some of these groups would collapse, others might broaden their base of support and begin eroding the general pro-Israeli American popular consensus, leading ultimately to popular approval of a pro-PLO U.S. policy in the Middle East (Bookbinder Interview; Dine Interview; Rosenbaum Interview). The more established of the domestic Arab organizations, such as the National Association of Arab Americans (NAAA), the Arab-American Anti-Discrimination Committee (ADC), and the Association of Arab-American University Graduates (AAUG), took full advantage of Israel's controversial actions in Lebanon in order to significantly narrow the credibility gap that had heretofore existed between themselves and the American Zionist lobby (Blitzer 1985; Bookbinder Interview; Bookbinder and Abourezk 1987; Orfalea 1988).

AIPAC's attempt to sustain American popular support for Israel's activities in Lebanon was adversely affected by factors associated with the international political environment. The Israeli dimension, of course, was crucial. After the June 6, 1982, invasion of Lebanon, international criticism of Israel reached an unprecedented level. Israel was condemned by the United Nations Security Council, with the concurrence of the United States (Haig 1984, 345). The siege of Beirut and the Sabra and Shatila massacres prompted widespread criticism, as did the Likud government's blanket rejection of President Reagan's September 1, 1982, proposal for Middle East peace.

In the aftermath of the initial invasion, AIPAC undertook an intense public relations campaign. The campaign emphasized the tremendous restraint exhibited by the Israelis in the face of clear and obvious provocations from the PLO and the Syrians, and the transformation of Lebanon into a major base of international terrorism (*Near East Report*, June 11, 1982; July 2, 1982; July 16, 1982; August 6, 1982). Although claiming to have been somewhat successful in this crisis-management strategy, AIPAC officials acknowledge that Israel's continued activities in Lebanon did not make their task any easier (Dine Interview).

AIPAC adopted a posture on the Reagan Plan somewhat at variance with the Begin government's. Whereas Jerusalem rejected the plan as an overt appeasement of the Saudis, Jordanians, Egyptians, and Palestinians (*Jerusalem Post [International Edition]*, September 5–11, 1982, 1), AIPAC adopted a cautious wait-and-see approach, neither condemning nor praising the plan (*Near East Report*, September 10, 1982. See also *New York Times*, September 7, 1982, A3). AIPAC director Tom Dine acknowledged Israel's legitimate concern about the apparent divergence of the plan from the framework for Palestinian autonomy adopted at Camp David; however, he publicly asserted that the Reagan Plan might nonetheless serve as the framework for a workable settlement (*New York Times*, September 9, 1982, A1; *New York Times*, September 10, 1982, A10; *New York Times*, September 22, 1982, A16). He privately declared his concern about the possible political ramifications of the Begin government's swift repudiation of the plan (Dine Interview). Dine's cautious support for the Reagan initiative was echoed by other American Jewish leaders. Many of them shared Dine's concern about the rapid decline of Israel's standing in the United States resulting from the Lebanon misadventure (Bookbinder Interview; Rosenbaum Interview; Halperin 1982).

AIPAC officials acknowledge that their public divergence from Begin on the Reagan Plan was a tactical maneuver designed to demonstrate AIPAC's independence from the Begin government (Dine Interview; Rosenbaum Interview). A principal criterion of an ethnic interest group's influence is its perceived autonomy from a foreign government. The Lebanon War resulted in an inadvertent narrowing of the gap that exists normally between Jerusalem and AIPAC, a natural response of diaspora communities to crises confronting Israel. Realizing that the organization's carefully crafted political credibility was possibly jeopardized through "guilt by association," AIPAC sought to strike a policy stance somewhat at variance with Begin's and yet well within the mainstream of Israeli popular opinion (i.e., the more positive image of the Reagan Plan adopted by the Labor Party leader, Shimon Peres) (*Jerusalem Post [International Edition]*, September 5–11, 1982, 2).

AIPAC officials sought to present the Lebanon invasion as a standard and legitimate Israeli response to attacks upon Israel's northern settlements by Lebanese-based PLO forces (*Near East Report*, June 11, 1982). The goal was to de-emphasize the significance of the Lebanon War, to focus attention on other "more pressing" aspects of the U.S.-Israeli relationship. Even as the scope of the military operation broadened to include the encirclement of Beirut, AIPAC sought to present the Lebanon War as a noncrisis for Israel.

Although agreeing initially with AIPAC's conception of the invasion as an exercise in legitimate "hot pursuit" (Haig 1984, 335–42), the Reagan administration rapidly upgraded its level of concern with the Lebanon War. The administration's altered perception was based primarily on fears that Israel's actions would draw the Syrians (and hence, the Soviets) into an otherwise limited conflict. Equally important, Washington feared a possible weakening of America's credibility among the moderate Arab states (Haig 1984, 324–52). The decision of the Israeli government—or, perhaps more accurately, a handful of individuals surrounding Ariel Sharon—to dramatically escalate the scope and goals of the Lebanon operation caused the White House considerable alarm. A direct effect of this was AIPAC's reduced access to important loci of decisional authority (when AIPAC needed this access most) (Dine Interview; Blitzer 1985, 245–49; Rosenbaum Interview; Spiegel 1985, 415–18).

The Reagan administration adopted a policy response to the Lebanon War that was all but diametrically opposed to that preferred by AIPAC. The readiness of large segments of official Washington to openly criticize the Israeli government represents a situation of "minimal-nil" influence for AIPAC over the administration's policy on the Lebanon War. (The one saving grace of the affair was the White House's refusal to implement sanctions; hence a score of 2, rather than 1, on the index of influence.)

THE PALESTINIAN DISTURBANCES, DECEMBER 1987– DECEMBER 1988

Overview

Relations between the United States and Israel in the five year interval between the 1982 Lebanon War and the December 9, 1987, outbreak of the Palestinian disturbances in the occupied territories (commonly known as the *intifada*, or uprising) were typified by a series of peaks and valleys. By early 1983 much of the heated emotions produced by the Lebanon War had dissipated as the Reagan administration rapidly came to recognize the fundamental complexity of the Lebanese situation (and Israel's role in it). Congress approved additional foreign aid to Israel, despite the reported pleadings of some White House officials to use the opportunity to take a firm stand on relations with Jerusalem and its American Jewish supporters (Spiegel 1985, 422–23). The more positive mood in Washington concerning Israel was reinforced by the terrorist bombings of the U.S. embassy and Marine Corps headquarters in Beirut (in August and October 1983, respectively), and the signing of the U.S.-brokered de facto peace treaty between Israel and the Lebanese government of Amin Gemayal on May 17, 1983. Gemayal's abrogation of the agreement in early 1984 (under extreme pressure from President Hafez Assad of Syria) and allegations of Damascus's complicity in the two Beirut bombings drew Washington again toward Jerusalem: the Reagan administration recognized too late "that it was Syria, not Israel, that would not withdraw voluntarily from Lebanon" (Spiegel 1985, 425).

By mid-1983 the U.S.-Israeli relationship was seemingly back on course. The groundwork was laid for the greatest institutionalization yet of that relationship, including the signing of a Memorandum of Understanding on strategic cooperation; joint U.S.-Israeli cooperation against international terrorism; the creation of a U.S.-Israel free trade area; and the designation of Jerusalem as a principal non-NATO ally (with all of the attendant benefits) (*Near East Report*, December 21, 1987, 206; *Near East Report*, May 2, 1988, 71). In addition, throughout the 1982–87 period, financial and military aid to Israel reached unprecedented proportions. At both a substantive and symbolic level, the U.S.-Israeli relationship had returned to a state of normalcy following the strain of the Lebanon War.

There was, however, also a downside. A series of events undermined the more positive tone in relations between Washington and Jerusalem. Principal elements of strain included the Jonathan Pollard spying affair, allegations of Israel's direct involvement in the illegal transfer of American weapons to Iran (the infamous "Irangate" controversy), and the Reagan administration's continued pursuit of more stable relations with moderate Arab states. From the Israeli perspective, perhaps the most frustrating aspect of the Reagan administration's policy was that, in the aftermath of the Lebanon War and the Beirut bombings, the administration did not appear to have a policy on the Middle East. The net effect was to make highly complex the U.S.-Israeli relationship between 1982 and 1987.

Much of this complexity was manifested in Washington's attitude during the first year of the Palestinian disturbances. The Reagan administration responded with outward calm to the outbreak of the disturbances on December 9, 1987. Preoccupied with the stalemated Iran-Iraq War and the rapid renewal of détente with the Soviet Union, the White House adopted a wait-and-see attitude concerning the intifada. In late December Congress approved a $3 billion aid package to Jerusalem for fiscal 1988 (*Near East Report*, December 28, 1987, 209; *Near East Report*, July 18, 1988, 121). In the late winter and early spring of 1988, Secretary of State George Shultz initiated a series of visits to the Middle East for the purpose of convincing the regional actors of the merits of a peace proposal based loosely on an international peace conference. At the same time the White House fought vigorously to have the New York offices of the Palestine Liberation Organization closed (*Near East Report*, March 21, 1988, 47). In November 1988 Secretary Shultz, citing Yasser Arafat's record of support for international terrorism, refused to grant the PLO chairman a temporary visa to enter the United States to address the United Nations General Assembly's annual debate on Palestine (*Near East Report*, December 5, 1988, 201). Shultz's decision was reportedly made against the objections of most Middle East experts at the State Department and prompted widespread international condemnation of the United States, including charges that Shultz had violated many of the sacred tenets of the UN-host country arrangement.

And yet, even as Secretary Shultz maintained a firm hand against the PLO, there were strains appearing in Washington's relationship with Jerusalem. Even sympathetic American officials were beginning to grow impatient with the Israeli government. Prime Minister Yitzhak Shamir remained adamantly opposed to Shultz's plan for an international peace conference on the Middle East. To the American mind, Shamir offered little in the way of an alternative to the increasingly untenable status quo in the occupied territories. American patience with Jerusalem was further strained by daily televised images of Israeli soldiers implementing the Defense Minister Yitzhak Rabin's order to use an "iron fist" in putting down the disturbances. Arguably the lowest point in contemporary U.S.-Israeli relations occurred at the end of the period under consideration: on December 14, 1988—mere weeks after denying Arafat a visa and terming insufficient and ambiguous the November 15, 1988, declarations of the Palestine National Council (PNC) meeting at Algiers—Secretary Shultz announced that the United States would enter into a substantive dialogue with high-ranking representatives of the PLO. The PNC meeting of November 1988 produced a unilateral declaration of an independent Palestinian state in the West Bank and Gaza strip, renounced the use of violence and terrorism, and granted implicit recognition of Israel's right to exist by referring to United Nations Security Council resolutions 224 and 338. The turning point in U.S.-PLO relations, Shultz claimed, had come on December 14, at Geneva. Both in private consultations and in his formal address to the reconvened United Nations General Assembly, Arafat had seemingly met Washington's long-standing preconditions for diplomatic relations: the acceptance of Israel's right to exist, the embracing of UN Security Council Resolution 242 as the basis for peaceful settlement of the Arab-Israeli conflict, and the formal renunciation of terrorism. Despite Israeli and American Jewish pleadings, Washington accepted Arafat's words at face value and initiated its dialogue with the PLO (*Near East Report*, December 19, 1988, 209; *Near East Report*, December 26, 1988, 213). At the time of writing (Spring 1989), the true impact of the U.S.-PLO dialogue upon Washington's relationship with Jerusalem has yet to be determined. Nevertheless, it is clear that as the first year of the intifada came to an end, relations between the United States and

Israel had rarely been more tenuous. The situation presented the American Israel Public Affairs Committee with a challenge of unprecedented proportions.

Conceptual Analysis

AIPAC responded to the challenge of the intifada in the way anticipated of an institutionalized and effective ethnic interest group. However, as efficient as it was, there were limits to what AIPAC could reasonably hope to achieve. It could not control the course of developments in the occupied territories. And, by the end of December 1988, it could not control the dramatic shift in international and American popular opinion concerning Israel and the PLO. Increasingly, it found itself seeking merely to hold the line on U.S. policy toward the Middle East.

Throughout the first year of the Palestinian disturbances, AIPAC's level of lobbying was extremely high; it sought to explain Israel's actions in the occupied territories to as wide an American audience as possible. Its policy objectives were relatively constructive in tone: the goal was to maintain a business-as-usual approach to U.S.-Israeli relations; that is, to protect cherished aspects of those relations (especially foreign aid and strategic cooperation) by playing down the significance of the disturbances through presenting them as an unfortunate part of daily life in the "administered territories."

AIPAC's timing on the intifada was necessarily reactive. Nevertheless, by focusing on a business-as-usual approach to the broader U.S.-Israeli relationship, the committee sought to act in a formulative manner. AIPAC targeted a wide audience, including the White House, Congress, media, and general public. Increasingly, the focus was on the White House. The goal was to exploit President Reagan's and Secretary of State Shultz's demonstrated sensitivity toward Israel's concerns in order to (1) protect foreign aid allocations, (2) defend against possible calls for sanctions against Jerusalem, and (3) offset attempts by avowed Arabists at the State Department to use the disturbances as an opportunity to shift U.S. policy closer to the Palestinian Arabs and the PLO.

AIPAC attempted to counter popular allegations of widespread Israeli human rights violations in the occupied territories by disseminating the Israeli viewpoint and directing attention to other dimensions of the U.S.-Israeli relationship. There were widespread references to the images of Israel that had worked so successfully for AIPAC throughout the Reagan years: Israel as a "strategic asset" to the United States, and as a "beleaguered democracy" in a "sea of autocracies" (*Near East Report*, April 25, 1988, 67). The *Near East Report* gave extensive coverage to the State Department's 1987 *Country Reports on Human Rights*, which strongly criticized the human rights records of various Arab regimes (*Near East Report*, February 22, 1988, 30). AIPAC also focused attention on the Arab world's negative response to the Shultz peace initiative (*Near East Report*,

February 26, 1988, 34; *Near East Report*, April 4, 1988, 53; *Near East Report*, April 15, 1988, 61), and the imbalance prevailing in the Middle East arms race (*Near East Report*, September 5, 1988, 148).

An important intervening factor in AIPAC's targeting and strategy was that 1988 was an election year. This impacted both positively and negatively upon AIPAC's attempts to influence U.S. policy on the intifada. In pursuit of the much-valued "Jewish vote" many presidential and congressional candidates were likely to be somewhat restrained in their criticism of Israel (*Near East Report*, June 6, 1988, 96; *Near East Report*, July 4, 1988, 111; *Near East Report*, August 1, 1988, 125). By the same token, as a lame-duck president, Ronald Reagan was less able to dominate the policy process and was more susceptible to the influence of foreign policy professionals at the State Department and in the National Security Council (many of whom reportedly harbored sensitivities favoring the Palestinians).

The intifada presented AIPAC with severe (and perhaps unprecedented) threats to the cohesion of its American Jewish constituency. From all sides, American Jews—including several members of the American Zionist inner circle—publicly debated Israel's handling of the disturbances as well as the nature of their support for Israel generally (*Commentary*, February 1989; Fein 1989, 48–53; Shanks 1989, 4–6).

As they had voiced reservations during the 1982 Lebanon War, several prominent American Jewish performers, artists, and authors publicly voiced their reservations about Israel's handling of the intifada (*New York Times*, April 5, 1989, A28). American Zionist leaders were fairly successful in countering this criticism by questioning the Israel-related credentials of many members of this group. More problematical were strong criticisms of Israeli behavior raised from within the American Zionist mainstream. Dissent ranged from the extreme (including the group of American Jews who met privately with Arafat at Stockholm, Sweden, in November-December 1988) to the moderate (including those American Jewish leaders who chose not to attend Yitzhak Shamir's Prime Minister's Solidarity Conference in Israel in spring of 1989) (*Time*, April 3, 1989, 18–19). AIPAC officials sought to discredit the activities of the former group (*Near East Report*, December 12, 1988, 207; *Near East Report*, December 19, 1988, 209; *Near East Report*, December 26, 1988, 213) and to quietly cajole the latter group to tone down its criticism of the Shamir government (*Time*, April 3, 1989, 18–19). Zionist leaders sought to address the concerns of large segments of American Jewry about Israel's actions by referring to several of its timeworn strategies: denying that meaningful internal dissent existed; suggesting that "now, in Israel's time of crisis" was not the time for American Jews to question their faith in the Jewish state; and arguing that diaspora Jews could continue to support Israel even as they disapproved of the policies of a particular Israeli government. Community leaders cautioned their constituents not to weaken their faith in Zionism under the weight of sensationalized and biased media coverage.

These various strategies worked, to some extent, in calming American Jewry's collective anxiety. Nevertheless, latent frustration prevailed, threatening to crack the community's tenuous cohesion on support for Israel.[9]

The formal decision-making system was not entirely conducive to AIPAC's lobbying efforts during the first year of the intifada. President Ronald Reagan and Secretary of State George Shultz were demonstrably sensitive to Israel's security considerations. To the extent that they could dominate the foreign policy process, Reagan and Shultz effectively countered much of the anti-Israeli/pro-Palestinian sentiment reportedly prevailing throughout the executive branch. However, as the Palestinian disturbances progressed, Reagan and Shultz wavered in their support of Israel. Shultz returned from the Middle East frustrated by Israeli Prime Minister Shamir's seemingly intractable opposition to an international peace conference. Reagan appeared increasingly agitated by the unyielding position adopted by Jerusalem and allegations of Israeli human rights abuses in the occupied territories.

The intrusion of the 1988 elections impacted both positively and negatively upon AIPAC's lobbying efforts. The election broadened the decisional process to include candidates who, in the pursuit of Jewish electoral support, frequently went out of their way to avoid criticizing Israel. However, the fluidity in leadership associated with any preelection period effectively reduced the impact of the administration's interests over U.S. Middle East policy—primary responsibility for which then fell to the professionals at the State Department and the National Security Council (many of whom reportedly favored the Arabs over the Israelis).

The intifada resulted in a fairly significant change in attitude on the Middle East among elements of the domestic political environment. The Israeli political scientist Eytan Gilboa, having compiled a cross section of popular-opinion survey data, found some support for the proposition that Israel's response to the Palestinian disturbances had indeed been too harsh (table 3). However, the same data indicated that throughout the first six months of 1988 the American public remained significantly more sympathetic toward Israel than the Arabs (table 4).

Another survey, also conducted in the spring of 1988, indicated that 67 percent of Americans felt that there had been no change in their attitudes concerning Israel as a result of "recent events in the territories" (*Near East Report*, May 30, 1988, 90). These findings appear to reinforce an axiom that AIPAC spokesmen have always adhered to: average Americans may disapprove of the policies of a particular Israeli government; however, their support for the State of Israel remains strong and unyielding.

The intifada brought a renewal of the struggle between American Jewry and the media that had begun in earnest with the 1982 Lebanon invasion. AIPAC charged that many of the American print and electronic media were biased and unfair in coverage of the intifada. AIPAC said that by focusing exclusively— and in a sensationalist fashion—upon alleged Israeli excesses without reference to either the historical context within which the rioting was occurring or the way

Table 3
Has Israel's Response to the Uprising Been Too Harsh?

Date (1988)	Too Harsh	About Right	Too Lenient	Don't Know
Jan. 3-6	50%	23%	6%	21%
Jan. 20-24	36%	29%	12%	23%
Jan. 27-28	42%	17%	12%	29%
Feb. 3-4	43%	32%	17%	8%
Apr. 16-19	28%	26%	11%	34%
Apr. 19-May 1	32%	26%	11%	30%
May 9-12	34%	22%	10%	34%

Source: Gilboa 1989, 24.

Table 4
Do Americans Sympathize More with Israel or the Arabs?

Date (1988)	Israel	Arabs	Neither	Unsure	Both
January	47%	15%	13%	17%	8%
February	30%	12%	25%	23%	9%
March	49%	17%	26%	8%	--
April (avg)	49%	12%	22%	20%	11%
May	44%	13%	15%	22%	6%

Source: Gilboa 1989, 26.

in which the Arab states had responded to their own incidents of civil disorder, the media misrepresented the real picture in the occupied territories. AIPAC charged that media coverage incited further Palestinian violence: instead of simply reporting the news, journalists had effectively become newsmakers. Major newspapers were cited both for their slanted editorial bias and their willingness to serve as forums for "Israel bashing" (*Near East Report*, March 7, 1988, 40; *Near East Report*, April 4, 1988, 60).

To be sure, there were exceptions to such criticisms. Columnists George Will,

William Safire, and A. M. Rosenthal remained strongly supportive of Israel, as did conservative journals such as the *New Republic*. Several other journalists, including Joel Brinkley, David Shipler, and Thomas Friedman, were considered to be reasonably sensitive to—if not avowedly supportive of—Israel's perspective in their coverage of the disturbances and related developments. However, at least to the minds of many AIPAC officials, the balance in media coverage was skewed in favor of the pro-Palestinian perspective.

A particularly alarming aspect of the media's coverage of the intifada, mere inklings of which were detected in both the AWACS and Lebanon War cases, was a tendency of some of the American media to focus a critical eye not upon Israel's controversial military behavior but upon the lobbying activities of AIPAC. A case in point was a segment of CBS's "60 Minutes" that aired on October 23, 1988. The segment "promised a look at pro-Israel activities in the U.S., the American Israel Public Affairs Committee in particular. But judging by the story's content and conclusions, its purpose was to create doubt about Israel's value to the United States and to undermine support for U.S. aid" (*Near East Report*, October 31, 1988, 184). Jewish community leaders claimed that excessive media coverage of AIPAC "will only stimulate more activism on behalf of strong U.S.-Israel relations" (*Near East Report*, October 23, 1988, 184). Such coverage may, however, also have reflected broader popular discontent toward Israel and American Jewish political activism.

Throughout 1988 the U.S. Congress sent mixed signals to AIPAC and American Jewry. Congress granted overwhelming approval to unprecedentedly large aid allocations to Israel and obstructed various proposed weapons sales to the Arab world (*Near East Report*, July 11, 1988, 116; *Near East Report*, August 1, 1988, 123). While supporting the Shultz peace initiative in principle, members of Congress reminded the secretary of state of Washington's commitment to a Middle East peace built upon the provisions of UN Security Council Resolutions 242 and 338 and the Camp David Accords (*Near East Report*, March 7, 1988, 39). Nevertheless, there were significant rumblings of discontent within Congress, as even senators and congressmen with solid pro-Israeli credentials began to distance themselves from the Shamir government's policies in the occupied territories. The fact that 1988 was an election year impacted both positively and negatively upon Israel's and AIPAC's fortunes vis-à-vis Congress. Most candidates sought to avoid antagonizing Jewish voters; and yet, the presidential primaries and nominating conventions opened the two national parties, especially the Democrats, to the influence of anti-Israeli delegations (*Near East Report*, July 4, 1988, 111).

In the final analysis, Congress's support throughout 1988 for large aid allocations to Israel offset any anti-Israeli bias on the part of some politicians and in this sense represented a net advantage for AIPAC. However, this advantage was in turn countered by the nonlegislative quality of Shultz's diplomatic initiatives of late December 1988.

The intifada produced the most significant manifestation yet of a powerful

Arabist core within the American foreign service. This was most clearly shown in the considerable bureaucratic opposition to Secretary Shultz's attempt to close the PLO's UN office and Shultz's refusal to grant an entry visa to PLO chairman Arafat. (The latter decision was reportedly made by Shultz over the opposition of several key State Department Orientalists) (*Near East Report*, December 5, 1988, 201).

AIPAC was somewhat successful in retaining the support of the formal leadership of important NGOs, including Christian fundamentalists and organized labor. The following declaration was attributed to the leadership of the powerful AFL-CIO: "Israel, a thriving democracy with a strong tradition of respect for workers' rights is in the docket today alongside such heinous anti-worker states as Burma, Haiti, Malaysia and Syria" (*Near East Report*, November 28, 1988, 199). Although the support of the leaders of these movements was maintained, the attitudes of the rank and file and those of other important NGOs and groups (including other ethnic communities) tended to fragment on support for Israel in a fashion similar to the general American public (*Near East Report*, May 31, 1988, 90).

Domestic ethnic counterforce groups made significant strides toward enhanced political credibility during the intifada. Representatives of several of the more established Arab-American groups—including the National Association of Arab-Americans (NAAA), the American-Arab Anti-Discrimination Committee (ADC), and the Association of Arab-American University Graduates (AAUG)—were widely received by official Washington. In late March 1988 Secretary of State Shultz met formally for the first time with Professors Edward Said and Ibrahim Abu-Lughod and other Arab-Americans associated with the PLO and the Palestine National Council (*Near East Report*, April 4, 1988, 53). James Zogby, an Arab-American and cofounder (with former Democratic Senator James Abourezk) of the ADC, was alleged to have spearheaded an attempt to force anti-Israeli proclamations onto the policy platform of the Democratic party's 1988 national convention (*Near East Report*, July 4, 1988, 111).

The international political environment impacted both positively and negatively upon AIPAC's attempt to influence the U.S. response to the Palestinian disturbances. The protracted and extraordinarily violent Iran-Iraq War, the radicalization of the Persian Gulf, and the initiation of a new round of superpower détente (typified by the signing of the INF Treaty in late December 1987) diverted Washington's attention from events in the occupied territories, thus serving AIPAC's short-term lobbying interests. The negative response of most Arab regimes to Shultz's Middle East shuttle—and the refusal of West Bank and Gaza Palestinian leaders to meet with him—served to ameliorate some of the secretary's frustration concerning Shamir's rejection of the peace plan. The situation in Israel, including the seemingly paralyzed quality of the government and the confused military and political response to the Palestinian disturbances, worked against the lobbying interests of AIPAC. So did the stalemated results of the November 1, 1988, Israeli national election and the anxieties resulting from the attempt by various orthodox religious parties to force a showdown on the controversial "Who is a Jew?" question.

Equally problematic for AIPAC was the shift in international opinion concerning Israel and the Palestinian issue, which—while existing since at least the Lebanon War—reached a significantly higher level with the intifada and Yasser Arafat's "peace offensive" of November and December 1988.

AIPAC did not initially perceive the Palestinian disturbances as a crisis. It genuinely viewed the issue as "nothing out of the ordinary" in the daily life of the occupied territories and sought to present it as such to U.S. officials, the media, and the general public (*Near East Report*, December 21, 1987, 205). However, the intifada increasingly threatened several of AIPAC's cherished values. These included the relationship between Israel and the United States (especially in the areas of strategic cooperation and generous grants-in-aid) and the relationship between Israel and American Jewry. While these considerations surely heightened AIPAC's concern, AIPAC still appeared to view the situation as critical, but not impossible. This view changed, of course, with Shultz's December 14, 1988, decision to open a substantive dialogue with the PLO. Despite an outward appearance of calm, AIPAC clearly perceived the U.S.-PLO relationship as a fundamental threat to Israel and a crisis of the first order for American Zionism (*Near East Report*, December 19, 1988, 209; *Near East Report*, December 26, 1988, 213).

The Reagan administration's level of concern with the Palestinian disturbances also intensified over time, although never at a rate comparable to AIPAC's. The administration's initial response was one of restrained concern. It adopted a wait-and-see approach and cautioned moderation on Jerusalem. Essentially, there were two reasons for this: the White House had other, more pressing, items on its foreign policy agenda and the administration saw minimal room to maneuver. Washington had significantly downgraded its involvement in the Arab-Israeli peace process since the collapse of the May 1983 Israel-Lebanon accord; relations with Syria (a key actor in any peace settlement) were poor and Arafat and the PLO were perceived as still intractable.

As the Palestinian disturbances continued and spread, Washington's level of concern increased and culminated with the Shultz initiative in the spring of 1988. Although obviously sincere in his efforts, Secretary Shultz had limited time and resources to devote to Middle East peace; a breaking of the protracted Arab-Israeli stalemate would not come at the expense of enhanced relations with the Soviets.

Two other events influenced the administration's concern with the Palestinian disturbances: the outcome of the November 1, 1988, Israeli elections and some moderation in the PLO's posture. The administration's palpable frustration with the results of the Israeli elections and Arafat's moderate words at Geneva combined to alter Reagan's and Shultz's perception of the disturbances and to drive the United States in a policy direction not preferred by AIPAC.

This outcome appears to verify the hypothesis concerning the relationship between an ethnic interest group's level of influence and the government's perception of a particular issue. Until November-December 1988, the Reagan administration's relatively passive interest with the intifada permitted AIPAC to fairly effectively contain the damage to Israel's interests. However, once the administration chose to dramatically reactivate its involvement in the peace process, AIPAC's level of influence dropped appreciably.

In the final analysis, the first year of the intifada ended with AIPAC having low-moderate influence over U.S. policy (scored as 2). Obviously, AIPAC was dissatisfied with the U.S.-PLO initiative. Washington had adopted a policy that was *diametrically opposed* to the interests of Israel, AIPAC, and much of American Jewry. Paradoxically, although unable to significantly influence U.S. policy on relations with the PLO, AIPAC was able to maintain strong working relations with the U.S. government and to protect unprecedented levels of American financial and military aid to Israel, thereby affirming AIPAC's status as a fully institutionalized ethnic foreign policy interest group.

SUMMARY

Based on the criterion of domestic ethnic interest group influence used in this study, the following scores apply to the attempts by the American Israel Public Affairs Committee to influence U.S. Middle East policy between October 1973 and December 1988 (table 5).

Table 5
AIPAC and America's Middle East Policy, 1973–1988

Event	Degree of Influence				
	5	4	3	2	1
1973 War	X				
Kissinger's Diplomacy	X				
Boycott	X				
Carter's Diplomacy				X	
F-15s					X
AWACS					X
Lebanon				X	
Palestinian Disturbances				X	

NOTES

1. Steven Spiegel reports that some of the Pentagon officials perceived as being closest to the Israelis, especially at the Defense Intelligence Agency, were removed after the Yom Kippur War, possibly because it was felt that their judgment about the Middle East had been compromised by their Israeli contacts (1985, 222).

2. In practical terms, reassessment meant a suspension of all new U.S. arms sales to Israel. The sale of F-15 aircraft and Lance ground-to-ground missiles, approved after Prime Minister Yitzhak Rabin's November 1974 visit to Washington, was held in abeyance. Consideration of new economic assistance was also temporarily suspended. However, previously contracted purchases continued to arrive on time. The delay in fulfilling new commitments was designed to convey a clear message to Israel and its American supporters; in time, a delay in new aid and arms sales would erode Jerusalem's military budget and its military structure as well.

3. As cited in the *New York Times* of May 23, 1975, the Letter of 76 reads as follows: "We believe that preserving the peace requires that Israel obtain a level of military and economic support adequate to deter a renewal of war by Israel's neighbors. Withholding military equipment from Israel would be dangerous, and encouraging a resort to force. . . . Within the next several weeks, the Congress expects to receive your foreign aid requirements for fiscal year 1976. We trust that your recommendations will be responsive to Israel's urgent military and economic needs. We urge you to make it clear, as we do, that the United States, acting in its own national interests, stands firm with Israel in the search for peace in future negotiations, and that this premise is the basis of the current reassessment of U.S. policy in the Middle East" (8).

4. The Arab boycott of Jewish interests in Palestine dates informally from 1921. The boycott was formally instituted by the League of Arab States following the establishment of Israel in 1948. The boycott is essentially threefold in character. The "primary" boycott is a direct boycott of Israel and Israeli goods and services by Arab states, firms, and individuals. A "secondary" boycott is an attempt by Arabs to pressure firms or other countries to refrain from doing business with Israel or individuals sympathetic to Zionism as a precondition of trade with Arab states, firms, or individuals. The "tertiary" boycott of Israel entails pressure by Arab states to prevent firms of uninvolved third party states from dealing with firms of their own or other similarly uninvolved third party states because of the latter's relationship with Israel or its supporters as a condition for doing business with Arab states, firms, or individuals. A fourth type of boycott, known as a "voluntary" or "shadow" boycott or a "chilling effect," is the outgrowth of the secondary and tertiary boycotts; firms simply decline to deal with Israel or Jewish firms or individuals for fear of antagonizing present or prospective Arab clients (Chill 1976; Nelson and Prittie 1977; Stanislawski 1981b, 107–22; Stanislawski 1983, 205; Teslik 1982, 9–13; Turck 1977).

5. As finally implemented, the 1978 package provided for the sale of forty-two F-5E fighters to Egypt, sixty-two F-15s to Saudi Arabia, and thirty-five F-15s and seventy-five F-16s to Israel.

6. On October 14, 1981, the House of Representatives rejected the proposed sale by an almost three-to-one margin, 301 votes to 111. The following day the Senate Foreign Relations Committee voted nine to eight to recommend disapproval of the sale by the full Senate.

7. Included in the final approved package sale to Saudi Arabia were the following: 5 Boeing E–3A radar planes (AWACS), 1,177 Sidewinder air-to-air missiles for use by F-15 fighter aircraft, 101 pairs of fuel tanks for the F-15s, 6 KC707 tanker planes for in-flight refueling of the AWACS and the F-15s, and a complex of ground facilities including stations for receiving electronic and voice messages from the patrolling radar planes and ground radar stations (*New York Times*, October 29, 1981, A1).

8. Analysts charge that estimates of casualties and those made homeless by the Israeli invasion were calculated inaccurately on the basis of biased figures. Estimates provided by the Palestine Red Crescent, substantiated by a representative of the International Committee of the Red Cross, and reported subsequently—without verification—by the American media of 10,000 killed and 600,000 made homeless in the first four days of the invasion, did not correspond at all to official Israeli casualty figures (Chafets 1985, 300–302; *Near East Report*, June 18, 1982; July 9, 1982) or those reported primarily by David Shipler in the *New York Times* (July 14, 1982). A second frequently cited example of allegedly poor and biased media coverage relates to a widely distributed United Press International (UPI) wire service photograph of a Lebanese baby with a caption explaining that her arms had been blown off and her body severely burned as the result of Israeli bombardments of Beirut. Evidence revealed subsequently proved that both the photograph and the accompanying caption were inaccurate: the child's arms were bandaged as a result of burns suffered in a PLO attack against Christian-dominated East Beirut (Chafets 1985, 302–3. See also Bavly and Salpeter 1984, 139–59; Morris 1982; Muravchik 1983, 12; Peretz 1982; Simon 1983; Spiegel 1985, 417). Although an official retraction followed, the UPI picture further affected popular American moral sensibilities concerning the Israeli invasion and made even more difficult AIPAC's attempt to contain the domestic political fallout resulting from the Lebanon War (Dine Interview).

9. A survey of American Jewish attitudes concerning Israel, conducted by Queens College sociologist Steven M. Cohen (presented at the December 1988 Annual Meeting of the Association of Jewish Studies; cited in Shanks 1989, 5), found that in 1988 forty-five percent of respondents agreed with the following statement: "I am often troubled by the policies of the current Israeli government." (This compared to 40 percent of respondents in a 1986 survey). The 1988 survey also found that 82 percent of respondents agreed with the following statement (compared to 8 percent who disagreed and 10 percent uncertain/no opinion): "Even when I disagree with the action of Israel's government, that doesn't change how close I feel toward Israel." These two sets of findings suggest a continued strong general support for Israel among American Jews but significant concern about the 1987–88 policies of the government of Israel, presumably relating to the intifada (although possibly also resulting from the "Who is a Jew?" controversy that arose following the Israeli November 1988 national election).

5

The CIC and Canadian Middle East Policy: October 1973– December 1988

THE OCTOBER 1973 WAR

Overview

The official Canadian response to the October 1973 War was typical of Canada's traditional aloofness toward the Middle East and its conflicts. In marked contrast certainly to the Americans, but also to many of its Western European allies, the Canadian government responded to the outbreak of hostilities with a discernible indifference (Taras 1983). This indifference has been attributed to several factors. Canadians were preoccupied with a rapidly declining national economy, a minority Parliament, and all but imminent federal elections. Moreover, there was a widely held perception of Canada's limited capacity to influence events in the Middle East and an expressed desire on the part of Prime Minister Pierre Elliot Trudeau to move Canada away from traditional internationalism and toward enhanced bilateralism (Dewitt and Kirton 1983a, 68–75, 387–98; Kirton 1978). Also contributing to the Canadian government's limited response to the Arab-Israeli War was the fact that most decision makers were convinced that Israel "would win as quick and as decisive a victory as she had done in 1967" (Taras 1983, 306).

Parliament was not in session when the war began on October 6, 1973. No suggestion was made to cut short the prime minister's state visit to the Orient or to bring Parliament back into emergency session. When the House of Commons reconvened on October 15, the war was already into its second week. Regardless of large scale superpower intervention in the conflict, there was "no visible manifestation of crisis" among Canadian parliamentarians (Taras 1983, 311).

On October 16, in the first official statement of the government's position on the war, External Affairs Minister Mitchell Sharp condemned the use of force by all sides and reaffirmed Canada's continued support for a Middle East settlement based on the principles of United Nations Security Council Resolution 242. There was no formal condemnation of the joint Egyptian-Syrian attack of October 6 (Canada. Department of External Affairs 1973).

Other issues relating to the war received the same haphazard and noncommittal consideration by Canadian foreign policymakers. Even the superpower nuclear alert of October 24–25 failed to produce any forceful response from Ottawa. Many Canadian officials, including the prime minister himself, reportedly felt that President Nixon had used the alert as a pretext for diverting attention from the domestic political controversy over Watergate (Taras 1983, 33).

The issue of Canadian participation in Middle East peacekeeping provoked the most interest on the part of Canadian parliamentarians. The Trudeau cabinet responded with a marked lack of enthusiasm to a formal UN request for a Canadian peacekeeping contingent. Ottawa relented finally to American pressure to join the second United Nations Emergency Force (UNEF II) for the Sinai Desert, but the preconditions outlined by External Affairs Minister Sharp were so rigorous as to (he hoped) limit Canada's role in the force (Sharp Interview).

Conceptual Analysis

The organized Jewish community's lobbying activities during the October 1973 War fit only partly this study's assumptions about an influential ethnic interest group. The Canada-Israel Committee's level of activity was only medium-moderate. The community as a whole reacted vigorously to the unanticipated Arab attack upon Israel. But the CIC had to share leadership over communal lobbying with various other national groups and local federations, both permanent and ad hoc (Cotler 1974; Hayes 1974a).

The timing of the Jewish community's activities was necessarily reactive. The goal of achieving an official and explicit Canadian condemnation of the Arab attack upon Israel was sought through the lobbying of members of the cabinet and upper bureaucracy. External Affairs Minister Mitchell Sharp was a primary lobbying target, in part because of his proven sensitivity toward the Jewish perspective and because of the absence and relative disinterestedness of Prime Minister Trudeau (Bick Interview; Sharp Interview). Other members of the Liberal caucus and influential members of the opposition parties were approached regularly as well (Bick Interview; Sharp Interview; Stanfield Interview).

In selecting targets to lobby, the Jewish community demonstrated a fairly advanced comprehension of the way Canadian foreign policy is made. Because the cabinet and upper bureaucracy are the principal sources of decisional authority in the Canadian system, they received the lion's share of Canadian Jewry's attention. An attempt was also made to mobilize popular sympathy by lobbying the media and other influential segments of the general society.

The Canada-Israel Committee met only some of the organizational criteria usually attributed to an influential ethnic lobby. During the war the CIC's level of organizational sophistication was at best fledgling. The CIC was especially lacking in the areas of continuity and cohesion, stability and size of membership, and clear definition of priorities. At the outbreak of hostilities, the Canada-Israel Committee had been formally in existence for barely six years. It was not well known among its own constituents and was poorly funded and untested politically.

The CIC was the only Canadian organization mandated to lobby Ottawa on Israel's behalf. However, it lacked the authority to establish national direction or centralized leadership. During the war, the CIC's professionals found themselves bypassed by individual community power brokers reluctant to pass leadership over Israel-related matters to the upstart lobby group. Moreover, the CIC was frequently ignored by the leaders of its own constituent bodies, the Canadian Jewish Congress, B'nai B'rith, and the Canadian Zionist Federation (all of whom reverted to more traditional, semiautonomous methods of communal mobilization and representation) (Bick Interview; Dimant Interview; May Interview; Plaut Interview). Such parochialism had inhibited the organizational development of the Canada-Israel Committee prior to October 1973 and significantly restricted its lobbying effectiveness during the war.

Communal cohesion was strong, resulting from a widely shared sense of crisis. Solidarity in support of Israel was to some extent strong enough to compensate for the CIC's inability to coordinate the activities of its various constituent parts.

The structure of the Canadian foreign policy decision-making system in the fall of October 1973 was not entirely conducive to Canadian Jewry's lobbying efforts. Prime Minister Trudeau attempted to place the causes and likely consequences of the Arab-Israeli War within the context of Canada's domestic and international needs and concerns. The Jewish community's preference for Ottawa's formal condemnation of the Arab attack upon Israel did not mesh with Trudeau's conception of Canadian priorities in the Middle East (especially stronger bilateral economic relations with the Arab world's developing economies) (Dewitt and Kirton 1983, 167–93). While adequately received by the makers of foreign policy, Canadian Jewry was unable to influence the direction of Ottawa's official policy response to developments in the Middle East.

The Jewish community's standing in the domestic political environment also adversely affected its attempts to build support for an official condemnation of Egypt and Syria. Despite a general sympathy toward Israel, some Canadian politicians and elements of the attentive public were reportedly uncomfortable with the "ethnic" dimension of the Jewish community's response to the war (Sharp Interview; Stanfield Interview). Popular demonstrations of communal emotion are simply not the norm in Canada, where foreign policy is traditionally determined by a relatively isolated group of highly compatible politicians, bureaucrats, and selected nongovernmental opinion molders. Reinforcing official discomfort with the Jewish community's lobbying activities was the presence of an element of latent antisemitism in the Canadian political culture (which may have found its way into the locus of foreign policy decision-making) (Stanislawski 1981b; Taras 1983).

The Jewish community was unable to galvanize public opinion and the media during the war. A December 1973 Gallup Poll found that attentive Canadians were four times more supportive of Israel than of the Arab states (twenty-two to five percent). However, the most significant result was that a full seventy-three percent of the 1,044 respondents held a nonpartisan view of the Arab-Israeli conflict (forty-two percent claiming no sympathy for either side and thirty-one percent holding no strong opinion on the issue) (Canadian Institute of Public Opinion, December 22, 1973).

The Canadian media's coverage of the October War reflects popular ambivalence concerning the Middle East. Having analyzed the content of twelve major Canadian newspapers, David Taras found that most fell within a range of relative indifference (Taras 1983, 252). However, to the extent that differences could be detected in editorial bias, Taras suggested that many were moderately "pro-Arab" in orientation: "It can be argued that most of the major newspapers held an image of the conflict which lay closer to the Arab than to the Israeli viewpoint" (1983, 256).

Within Parliament, support for Israel during the war was at best moderate. To be sure, individual MPs, especially those of an older generation (with memories of the Holocaust or Israel's struggle for independence), remained generally sympathetic toward the Jewish state. However, such sympathies were not reflected in the policies of the three major federal political parties. Opposition leader Robert L. Stanfield claims to have felt no emotional commitment on the Middle East question (Stanfield Interview), and was "oriented almost totally to the rigors of the domestic political battle" (Taras 1983, 20). Demands within the Conservative party for a definitive Canadian condemnation of the Arab attack were heard—but not acted upon—by Stanfield (Stanfield Interview). The position of the New Democratic party (NDP) was complicated by a mixture of ideology and sentiment. The party's Jewish leader, David Lewis, had strong personal convictions about Israel and its social democratic roots. Such sentiment was shared by several other members of the party's old guard. There were, however, others within the party who criticized Israel on ideological grounds and argued that "support for Israel's cause might have to be tempered if the party was to play a constructive role" (Taras 1983, 21). Based on this divergence of opinion, the NDP did not seek to have the government of Canada explicitly condemn Arab actions but rather "to strongly affirm the rights and security of Israel" (1983, 21).

The October War and Canada's policy response to it were never formally addressed by the caucus of the ruling Liberal party, despite Canadian Jewry's long-standing alliance with it and the presence in caucus of one Jewish MP and several others with Jewish constituencies. Taras attributes this to the presence in the Liberal caucus of an even larger number of MPs from Quebec, whose

French-Catholic constituents held little affection toward Jews or Israel (Taras 1983, 22). Although enjoying fairly strong support from individual parliamentarians, Canadian Jewry was unable to garner the support of Parliament for the achievement of the desired official condemnation of the Arab attack upon Israel.

Canadian Jewry achieved strong support within the domestic political environment. Although seventy-three percent of Canadians considered themselves nonpartisan on the Middle East conflict, the attentive population supported Israel over the Arabs (by a ratio of four to one) in the fall of 1973.

Counterforce groups achieved only marginal success during the war. The Arab cause was represented primarily by the Arab embassies and the Arab League's Information Office in Ottawa. The domestic Arab-Canadian constituency was conspicuously passive throughout the war. This is largely explained by its relatively poor comprehension of the intricacies of Canadian political life, evidenced by a propensity toward loud, vigorous, confrontational, and generally "un-Canadian" encounters with politicians and foreign policy officials (Sharp Interview; Stanfield Interview; Former Assistant to the Secretary of State for External Affairs Interview; Official of the Middle East Division, Department of External Affairs Interview). The net effect of the Arab community's poor showing was to benefit Canadian Jewry's lobbying efforts.

The international political environment was not conducive to the Jewish community's attempt to influence Ottawa. A measure of independence from a foreign government is considered to be an important indicator of a domestic ethnic group's credibility. Its unprecedented solidarity with Israel during the war and its perceived lack of sources of information independent of the Israeli embassy were harmful to the Jewish community's lobbying of the Canadian government (Sharp Interview).

In the fall of 1973 relations between Ottawa and Jerusalem were relatively friendly. However, the basic ambivalence toward the Middle East exhibited by Prime Minister Trudeau and many of his key ministers significantly diminished the ability of Canadian Jewry's representatives to influence Ottawa's policy response to the Arab-Israeli War.

Finally, the Jewish community's and Ottawa's respective perceptions of the war did not contribute positively to the Jewish community's influence. Canadian Jews perceived the war with a sense of crisis unprecedented in the short history of Canadian Zionism. This perception was never shared by the Canadian government. Under the circumstances (and consistent with the hypothesized inverse relationship between the government's level of perceived crisis and the ethnic group's ability to influence policy), the Jewish community should have had influence over government policy. However, although its representatives enjoyed sufficient access to the decision makers, Canadian Jewry failed to move the Trudeau government to accept its preferred policy response (that is, a formal condemnation of the Egyptian-Syrian attack upon Israel).

The Jewish community's influence over Canadian policy on the October 1973 War is scored as moderate-high (4). Although the policy ultimately adopted by

Ottawa was far less pro-Israeli than that preferred by Canadian Jewish leaders, the almost complete indifference of the Canadian government to Arab Canadian groups and the acceptance of a limited Canadian role in UNEF II represented a policy that was basically satisfying to much of Canadian Jewry.

THE PLO IN CANADA

Overview

In 1970 the government of Pierre Trudeau, seeking to enhance the country's status as an important middle power, invited the United Nations to convene two major conferences in Canada: the UN Conference on Law Enforcement (the "Crime Conference") in Toronto in September 1975 and the "Habitat Conference" on housing and international settlement in Vancouver in May of 1976.

Controversy arose in early 1975 when the United Nations secretary general formally invited representatives of the Palestine Liberation Organization (PLO) to sit as participant-observers at both conferences. Many concerned Canadians, Jewish and non-Jewish, found the notion of PLO participation in international political forums, especially those relating to criminal activity, somewhat ludicrous if not hypocritical.

Ultimately, the issue proved too controversial even for the adroit Trudeau to handle. In July 1975 External Affairs Minister Allen MacEachen met with the UN secretary general to request a postponement of the Crime Conference (presumably to allow emotions to cool) (See MacEachen's statement in Stein 1976–77, 286). The secretary general rejected the Canadian request; the Crime Conference was transferred to Geneva. Significantly, Ottawa did not seek a postponement of the Habitat Conference. And, with only a modicum of public protest, that conference was convened on schedule in Vancouver with representatives of both the PLO and Israel in attendance.

Conceptual Analysis

Canadian Jewry responded to the PLO in Canada issue in a way generally anticipated of an influential ethnic interest group. However, the level of activity of the Canada-Israel Committee was at best moderate. As during the 1973 war, the CIC still had to share representation and leadership responsibilities with community notables and ad hoc groups.

The policy objectives articulated by Jewish and non-Jewish leaders—organized in groups such as Canadians Against PLO Terrorism (CAPLOT)—diverged somewhat from those anticipated of influential ethnic groups. The principal goal was antagonistic: to influence the Canadian government to bar the admission to Canada of representatives of the Palestine Liberation Organization. Although claiming to be sensitive to the potential costs to Canada's international political credibility resulting from a decision to not admit the PLO, Canadian Jewish leaders remained unyielding in their objective: if the PLO were not explicitly excluded from participating in the two conferences, then the government of Canada must declare its unwillingness to host them (Plaut, 1981, 263–64). The antagonistic quality of this objective suggests limited Canadian Jewish influence over government policy.

The community's timing on the issue was essentially reactive. It was responding to the UN secretary general's decision to include the PLO in the Crime and Habitat conferences. The efficacy of the community's timing was hindered by Ottawa's limited capacity to control the UN conferences. Canada was merely the host of the sessions; it had no formal capacity to dictate their agendas or scrutinize the list of participants and observers. Such actions are the exclusive prerogative of the UN secretariat. The Canadian government could conceivably restrict the admission of conference participants who fell short of the criteria for temporary entry visas to Canada, but the government was reportedly reluctant to use this administrative technicality in order to bar PLO representatives.

The leaders of the anti-PLO movement appeared to comprehend the decisional structure associated with the PLO in Canada question. The invitation to host the UN conferences was made by the prime minister and his cabinet; only they could withdraw the invitation. Similarly, the barring of delegates from entering Canada on administrative grounds was a discretionary power reserved to the minister of immigration (in consultation with his cabinet colleagues). Canadian Jewish leaders concentrated their lobbying efforts almost exclusively on members of the federal cabinet, especially those inclined toward Israel and Jewish concerns. Such behavior is consistent with that anticipated of an influential lobby.

The community's strategy was to exploit reported differences within the cabinet over the PLO admission question and to force the prime minister and external affairs minister to make a formal statement on the matter. Supplementing this strategy was a series of indirect strategies. These included the organizing of public demonstrations and the initiating of a media campaign to educate Canadians about the PLO's involvement in international terrorism. The CIC attempted to paint the PLO in the least favorable light and to emphasize the fundamental hypocrisy of permitting representatives of a "terrorist" organization to enter Canada to participate in conferences on international crime and housing. An important corollary to this emphasis was an attempt to domesticize the issue and to present it as one of concern to all right-minded Canadians, regardless of their ethnic background or their attitudes concerning the Arab-Israeli conflict (May Interview; Plaut Interview).

Canadian Jewry's response to the PLO admission issue exhibits some of the organizational attributes of an influential ethnic lobby. The Canada-Israel Committee was still lacking in cohesion, organizational membership, and active political experience. It was not the exclusive leader of opposition to PLO admission to Canada. Rather, the lead was taken by an ad hoc group of Jewish community notables, which was itself subsumed within the broader, nondenominational CAPLOT umbrella. To be sure, several Jewish community notables central to the Canada-Israel Committee were also actively involved in the organization and agenda-setting of CAPLOT. However, despite the obvious connection, the Canada-Israel Committee as an independent corporate entity did not play a lead role in the PLO in Canada debate.

Cohesion was also something of a problem for Canadian Jewry in seeking to influence the PLO in Canada debate. Most Canadian Jews objected to the PLO on principle. But only a handful of them were actively involved in opposing the admission of its representatives to Canada. Rabbi W. Gunther Plaut, then leader of the Canadian Jewish Congress, claims that for the Jewish community the PLO in Canada issue "was a time of unprecedented unity; we stood together, and it was the sense of common cause which communicated itself to the government. . . . We were to be reckoned with because we had a sense of oneness and purpose" (1981b, 268). This was undoubtedly the case for a few influential Jews living in the Toronto area. However, the sense of "oneness and purpose" that Rabbi Plaut wrote of was limited to these few.

The campaign to force Ottawa's hand on the PLO admission issue was elite-based, premised on personal lobbying of the executive branch of the federal government by key leaders of the Toronto Jewish community (buttressed by non-Jewish allies). The level of general communal concern with the issue dropped appreciably beyond this inner circle, and even more so beyond the geographic parameters of metropolitan Toronto. This was especially the case in Vancouver. There the small Jewish community presented only token opposition to PLO attendance at the Habitat Conference, and did so without the active support of the national leadership of Canadian Jewry living in central Canada.

The structure of the formal decisional process worked against the interests of the opponents to PLO admission. Prime Minister Trudeau and External Affairs Minister MacEachen saw the unimpeded convening of the UN conferences as politically imperative. They perceived four plausible policy options: Canada could request a transfer of the Crime Conference from Toronto to a less contentious locale, probably Montreal; it could bar representatives of the PLO from entering the country; it could proceed with the conferences, but prohibit the admission of known terrorists; or Canada could let the conferences take place as planned, with PLO attendance, but make an official statement against terrorism (Stein, 1976–77, 295). Each option implied its own set of problems for Canadian officials. The worst case scenario was a loss of political credibility if Canada were perceived as swimming upstream against the tide of moderating international opinion on the Palestinian issue.

Elements of the formal decision-making elite, including the prime minister himself, were reportedly quite uncomfortable with the extent to which the PLO had become an issue of popular debate in Canada (Plaut Interview; Sharp Interview). This popular debate was contrary to the statism typical of Canadian foreign policy-making. As a result, Jewish leaders found their attempt to change the Trudeau government's posture on the PLO admission question inhibited (Sharp Interview; Official of the Middle East Division, Department of External Affairs Interview).

Significant elements of the domestic political environment supported the anti-PLO campaign spearheaded by Canadian Jewry. Popular opinion was generally opposed to the PLO's record on terrorism (Stein 1976–77, 285–87). However, Jewish leaders acknowledged that they had failed to effectively secularize and domesticize the issue: "We [the organized Jewish leadership] did not succeed in 'Canadianizing' the issue sufficiently; important groups . . . supported us, but the image of the 'Elders of Zion' engineering the whole matter for Jewish purposes was never fully overcome" (Plaut 1981, 267–68).

The Canadian media, as was their traditional practice on matters relating to the Middle East, registered a basic ambivalence toward the PLO admission issue. Although there was some difference of editorial opinion on the issue, the majority of the Canadian media demonstrated basic indifference.[1] The one redeeming factor, perhaps, was that there was even less media support for the pro-PLO defense than the anti-PLO position. The net effect was to make the media uninfluential in the PLO in Canada debate.

Some analysts contend that an impending federal election campaign was a primary factor contributing to the federal government's decision to reconsider its position on the Crime Conference (Ismael 1976; Nossal 1985, 36). One analyst further argues that what permitted the federal cabinet to maintain its hard line on the Habitat Conference was the absence of a large Jewish population in Vancouver that might sanction the Liberal party in the forthcoming federal campaign (Nossal 1985, 36).

To explain the government's action as based on the election is inviting, but somewhat overstated. If the federal Liberals were so concerned with the sanctioning power of Canadian Jews (who made up but three percent of the national vote), why then did the cabinet consider transferring the Crime Conference from Toronto to Montreal, which also had two or three ridings in which the Jewish vote could be considered crucial? And why was the government willing to adopt a policy posture at the United Nations on the Palestinian issue and the PLO that was increasingly less responsive to the interests of a significant number of Jewish voters? The electoral dimension is undeniable. But it is an insufficient explanation for the federal government's decision-making on the PLO in Canada issue. Other factors, including the strong opposition of all three parties in the Ontario provincial government, the concern expressed by the city of Toronto, and the opposition of influential societal groups and individuals, may have combined with the federal government's concern with the electoral dimension to force the cabinet's hand on the issue.

Parliament was without influence on the PLO admission debate. Both major federal opposition parties declared their objection to granting entry visas to PLO members. However, Parliament as a whole was officially silent on the issue, owing to the nonlegislative nature of Trudeau's original invitation to have Canada host the UN conferences.

Far more important to the outcome of the debate was the intervention of several NGOs and provincial and municipal governments. By mid-July 1975, when the federal cabinet decided to seek a postponement of the Crime Conference, a broad array of nongovernmental organizations and local governments had declared formal opposition to the PLO's participation. These included the Law Society of Upper Canada, the International Association of Police Chiefs (and its Canadian affiliate), and a number of smaller permanent and ad hoc human rights groups, as well as the province of Ontario and the city of Toronto.

Foreign policy in Canada is constitutionally an exclusive prerogative of the federal government. The federal system, however, gives to the provinces (and, on occasion, also to the municipalities) a capacity to influence and affect foreign policy issues of concern to them. This influence played a part in the PLO in Canada controversy. The forceful anti-PLO posture adopted by all three parties in the Ontario provincial legislature and by the city of Toronto added significantly to the mounting pressure on the federal cabinet to reverse its position on the Crime Conference. By contrast, the province of British Columbia and the city of Vancouver offered only token opposition to the PLO's participation at the Habitat Conference, thus contributing greatly to the federal government's very different handling of that aspect of the controversy.

The principal counterforce to Canadian Jewry, the Arab ethnic community, was moderately active during the PLO admission debate (see Ismael 1976, 1984). The cabinet heard representations from groups such as the Canadian-Arab Federation and the Association Quebec-Palestine. However, the Arab Canadian community remained seriously divided along political, cultural, and religious lines (Abu-Laban 1980). Also contributing to the inefficacy of the Arab community's lobbying effort was its political behavior, which some government officials still considered to be less than purely Canadian (Sharp Interview; Stanfield Interview; Former Assistant to the SSEA Interview). For example, the leader of the Canadian-Arab Federation, George Hajjar, raised the spectre of possible Arab economic and diplomatic sanctions if Canada were to deny admission to the PLO. Although such concerns were also reportedly voiced by cabinet ministers and foreign policy officials (Sharp Interview; Former Assistant to the SSEA Interview), when voiced by members of the Arab community they appeared too much like the attempted OPEC economic blackmail of 1973–74 and provided an inadvertent advantage to their political opponents (*Montreal Star*, July 16, 1975, I; *Winnipeg Tribune*, July 18, 1975, 3).

Important aspects of the international political environment worked against Canadian Jewry's attempts to influence a prohibiting of PLO representatives in Canada. Leaders of the Jewish community acknowledge their failure to isolate the Israeli and Jewish components of the anti-PLO argument (Bick Interview; Plaut Interview). CAPLOT and other groups within the anti-PLO camp relied on information and logistical support from the Israeli embassy. This significantly limited the movement's range of political maneuverability and reduced its credibility in the eyes of Canadian foreign policymakers (Sharp Interview; Stanfield Interview; Official of the Middle East Division, Department of External Affairs Interview; Former Assistant to the SSEA Interview).

The quality of relations between Canada and Israel also restricted the influence of the anti-PLO forces. Primary among the issues of dispute between the two nations were discernible changes occurring in Canada's policy posture at the United Nations concerning the Palestinian issue. In the fall of 1974 Canada began to approve or abstain on measures favoring a broader diplomatic role for the Palestine Liberation Organization (Noble 1981, 1983). Canada's voting in international forums began to drift away from U.S. support of Israel and toward the European community's overt sympathy for the Palestinian cause (Dewitt and Kirton 1983a, 388; Stein 1976–77, 286–93; Stein 1983). The change in Canadian policy on the Palestinian issue, however subtle, caused strain in Canada-Israeli relations and served as a factor inhibiting Canadian Jewry's attempt to influence Ottawa on the PLO admission question.

Influential segments of Canadian Jewry perceived the PLO in Canada issue as a moderate-high crisis. The admission to Canada of representatives of the Palestine Liberation Organization was considered a threat to Israel's and Canadian Jewry's interests: it would represent a further deterioration in Canada's sensitivity toward the Israeli perspective to the Arab-Israeli conflict and it would provide further legitimacy to the "terrorist" PLO. However, Canadian Jewry also recognized that the consequence of the issue was more symbolic than real: Israel's security and existence would not be compromised by Ottawa's decision to permit representatives of the PLO to attend two United Nations conferences. The PLO in Canada issue, while important to many Canadian Jewish leaders, was not crucial (Bick Interview; May Interview; Plaut Interview). This perception contributed to a tempering of communal emotions, and permitted a compromise to be worked out with the federal government.

The Trudeau cabinet shared the Jewish community's general image of the situation, but for very different reasons. For the prime minister, the question of PLO admission to Canada was an irritant that unnecessarily politicized what would otherwise have been an uncontroversial assertion of Canada's role in international diplomacy (Official of the Middle East Division, DEA Interview; Sharp Interview). The more public the issue became, the greater the government's sense of crisis. The cabinet perceived itself to be in a no-win situation: If it allowed PLO representatives to attend the Crime and Habitat conferences, it risked the domestic political wrath of Canadian Jews and others offended by the PLO. However, if it refused to permit the PLO to attend, it risked facing both diplomatic embarrassment and economic sanctions from the Arab world. Nevertheless, although problematical, the PLO in Canada issue was never considered by the Trudeau cabinet to be as important as the domestic economic situation or the rapidly evolving constitutional debates. For the government, the issue constituted an unsolicited intrusion of the Middle East into the political affairs of Canada that had to be managed.

The symmetry of perceived views permitted the federal cabinet and leaders of the Jewish community to formulate a compromise over the Crime and Habitat conferences. While far from perfect, the arrangement was at least a satisfactory way for both parties to extricate themselves from a difficult situation.

The Canadian government's different responses to the two UN conferences might seem to indicate a greater amount of Jewish influence over the first conference than over the second. Through its alliances with the province of Ontario, the city of Toronto, and a variety of powerful nongovernmental actors, the Jewish community contributed considerably to the federal government's decision to adopt a position on the Crime Conference not very different from that which Canadian Jews preferred. By contrast, the Trudeau government's refusal to seek a similar postponement/cancellation of the Habitat Conference appears less satisfactory to Canadian Jewish interests. To be sure, Canadian Jewish leaders were unable to influence the federal cabinet to alter its position on the Habitat Conference. However, two considerations must be noted: first, the national Jewish leaders did not view the two UN conferences as equally threatening to its core concerns; and second, they did not see equal opportunities for success in both cases. They perceived PLO attendance at the Crime Conference to be more symbolically threatening than at the Habitat Conference. Similarly, their political advantage clearly lay in Toronto and the Crime Conference. National Jewish community leaders recognized both the unfavorable political conditions in Vancouver and the determination of the prime minister and cabinet to avoid total foreign policy embarrassment at the hands of societal forces (May Interview; Plaut Interview). They presented only token opposition to the PLO's attendance at the Habitat Conference; thus, they maximized their successes. They contributed to a symbolic political victory vis-à-vis the Crime Conference, and, by not resisting the federal cabinet on the Habitat Conference, the Jewish community built important political credit to be applied against subsequent issues on the Canadian-Israeli agenda.

THE ARAB ECONOMIC BOYCOTT IN CANADA

Overview

The Arab economic boycott of Israel had been a source of concern to Canadian Jewry since the boycott's inception in 1948 (See Stanislawski, 1981b). Canadian Jewish spokesmen had mounted occasional public campaigns of opposition. However, they had been largely unsuccessful in convincing the majority of Canadians that the boycott was an issue of concern beyond the narrow—and foreign—confines of the Arab-Israeli conflict. The first serious step toward Canadianizing the boycott resulted from the oil crisis of 1973–74 and Canada's subsequent drive toward enhanced bilateral commercial relations with the Arab states (Dewitt and Kirton, 1983a). Still, Canadian Jewry (now operating almost exclusively through the Canada-Israel Committee) failed to convey the relevance of the Arab boycott to the majority of Canadians and their elected representatives.

It was only when the boycott was introduced as a question in the House of Commons by a high profile Liberal member (a respected former member of the cabinet with an acknowledged commitment to Canadian economic nationalism) that the boycott became a prominent feature on the Canadian domestic political agenda. Herb Gray revealed in the House of Commons in April 1975 that the Export Development Corporation, an agency of the Canadian government, had been providing export insurance coverage for a number of Canadian firms undertaking contracts with Arab countries in full knowledge that those contracts included provisions demanding strict compliance to the secondary and tertiary boycotts of Israel and individuals doing business with Israel (Gray Interview; Stanislawski 1981b, 176–209). Once introduced in this way, the boycott issue developed a dynamic of its own and maintained its public importance well beyond the capacity of any one group to control or contain.

Throughout 1976 and 1977 the boycott attracted unprecedented attention. On October 21, 1976, the Trudeau cabinet responded to the growing clamor for action with a statement outlining a series of administrative guidelines concerning adherence to foreign boycott practices (Stanislawski 1981b, 310–13). But the administrative guidelines were in no way equivalent to a definitive parliamentary statement on the Arab boycott and its impact on Canadians and were only "haphazardly applied" by the Department of Industry, Trade and Commerce (Stanislawski 1981b, 208).

There were continued demands for tightening of the federal guidelines. Further pressure arose from the initiation of antiboycott legislation by the government of the province of Ontario (Stanislawski 1981b, 284–308).

Faced with charges of stonewalling on the issue, the Trudeau government announced in August 1978 a significant tightening of the administrative guidelines and pledged to enact legislation establishing a compulsory reporting mechanism for those Canadian firms or individuals receiving boycott requests from foreign governments (Stanislawski 1981b, 209). The proposed legislation, Bill C-32, was tabled in the House of Commons on December 15, 1978. Throughout the winter and spring of 1979, the bill was subjected to considerable debate and legislative maneuvering. Thursday March 22, 1979, has been described as the day "on which the drama, expectation, and activity on Bill C-32 reached its peak" (Stanislawski 1981b, 320). At the end of the daily question period, the opposition house leader announced his party's agreement to a special, one-day consideration and passage of Bill C-32. Representatives of the other opposition parties concurred. However, the suspension of normal parliamentary rules for special consideration of any bill requires the unanimous consent of the House of Commons; such consent was obstructed by two maverick MPs. Despite considerable behind the scenes politicking, the recalcitrant MPs would not be moved. Bill C-32 had to pass through the various time-consuming stages of the legislative process. It failed to pass through quickly enough and "died on the order paper on the eve of its expected passage" when Parliament was dissolved on March 26, 1979, in preparation for the May 22 national election (Stanislawski 1981b, 323).

The boycott issue received considerable attention during the subsequent election campaign. It was, however, eclipsed by Progressive Conservative party leader Joe Clark's pledge of April 25, 1979, to move the Canadian embassy in Israel from Tel Aviv to Jerusalem.

Conceptual Analysis

The Canada-Israel Committee's efforts throughout the boycott debate fit almost completely the criteria anticipated of a successful ethnic interest group. The only deviation from the anticipated criteria—and ultimately the only one that matters— was that for all of its efforts the CIC was unable to influence passage of federal antiboycott legislation.

The organization's level of activity was extremely high. Between 1975 and 1979 representatives of the Canada-Israel Committee and its constituent agencies met with the highest political, bureaucratic, and nongovernmental sources of decisional authority in the Canadian foreign policy-making process. The committee's principal objective was advocative; it sought to help formulate federal legislation that would address not only the parochial interests of Jewish Canadians about the Arab economic boycott of Israel but also the economic and civil rights of a wider spectrum of Canadians.

The CIC's timing on the boycott issue was purely formulative. Canadian Jews had long sought to increase popular awareness and debate of the effects on all Canadians of discriminatory Arab economic and religious practices. The CIC lobbied sympathetic politicians and bureaucrats, providing them with the information and expertise required to initiate the formal discussion of the issue in Parliament. Through its involvement, the CIC helped set both the policy agenda and the parameters of the debate. To the extent that the CIC's lobbying on the boycott question was directed at all phases of the legislative process, it should have had influence over the outcome of the legislative process.

The CIC lobbied cabinet members and key members of Parliament. It presented briefs before cabinet committees and interacted frequently with officials in the departments of External Affairs and Industry, Trade and Commerce. The highly technical and legal quality of the boycott debate lent itself more to a strategy of dialogue among experts than mass appeal (Plaut 1981b, 270).

The CIC's tendency toward elite interaction and quiet diplomacy throughout the boycott debate was appropriate for the traditions of Canadian politics. These methods should have resulted in increased CIC influence over the legislative process. So should have the relatively successful effort to deemphasize the Jewish and Israeli context of the boycott issue. In the words of one participant, the issue was "properly portrayed as a question of Canadian civil and human rights," enabling the CIC "to gain the sympathy and support of wide segments of the public" (Plaut 1981b, 270). The successful application of this strategy broadened the scope of the debate and directed further pressure upon the federal government to take action against the Arab boycott.

In its involvement in the boycott debate, the CIC met virtually all of the criteria associated with an institutionalized ethnic interest group: it demonstrated organizational continuity and cohesion, its membership was relatively stable and clearly defined, and its policy objectives were concrete and future oriented. In the aftermath of the Yom Kippur War and the PLO in Canada issues, the Canada-Israel Committee had evolved into "the unchallenged voice of Canadian Jews in matters concerning Israel" (Plaut 1981b, 269). By 1975 the CIC was *the* representative of Canadian Jewish concern in regard to the application of a forceful legislative response to the Arab economic boycott in Israel.

The increased organizational sophistication of the Canada-Israel Committee was indicated by the size of its budget and changes in its institutional structure. The antiboycott campaign contributed to a tightening of the CIC's internal forces (Bick Interview). Although membership remained role-based, the consultative base of the organization began to expand in several ways. The physical size of the committee increased, as an office was opened in Toronto and the committee's presence in Ottawa was greatly increased and made permanent. Other leaders in the community, such as McGill University law professor Irwin Cotler (the principal author of a public report highly critical of the Canadian government's response to the Arab boycott and other incidents of economic coercion), were made part of an informal network of consultation (Cotler 1974b).

The CIC also scored high with regard to community cohesion. The Arab boycott aroused considerable emotion among Canadian Jews. It was an issue about which most Jews, whatever their denominational or philosophical bent, could identify. Within the organized community there was some dissent over the CIC's leadership of the antiboycott campaign, relating mostly to the committee's intervention in what was essentially a domestic political issue (Bick Interview; May Interview). As W. Gunther Plaut writes, the boycott issue seemed more appropriately "to belong either to the [Canadian Jewish] Congress or to the Joint Community Relations Committee [operated conjointly by the congress and B'nai B'rith]" (Plaut 1981b, 269). Despite such concerns, most Canadian Jews realized that only the CIC had the personnel, the specialized knowledge, and the political experience in Ottawa required to effectively engage in a political campaign aimed at the achievement of meaningful federal antiboycott legislation (Bick Interview; May Interview; Plaut Interview).

The formal decision-making system was only partly conducive to the CIC's lobbying efforts. Prime Minister Pierre Trudeau sought to move cautiously on the boycott question. He publicly condemned discriminatory visa and trade practices as "alien to everything the government stands for and indeed to what in general Canadian ethics stand for" (Canada. House of Commons 1975). However, he then applied only a limited official response to the Arab boycott, in the form of a voluntary administrative guideline (which would supposedly make the point in principle without seriously compromising Canada's growing trade relations with the Arab world) (Gray Interview).

Trudeau's attempt to keep the official response to the boycott low-key was hindered by intense pressure for a more tangible legislative posture. Some of this pressure came from within the Liberal caucus and cabinet. Within these circles, concerns were raised about both the basic immorality of the boycott and the potential alienation of Jewish voters if the governing Liberals did not respond with forceful legislation (Gray Interview). Through persistent lobbying, the CIC contributed greatly to the setting of the government's general agenda on the boycott issue. Nevertheless, the Canadian foreign policy-making process remained fundamentally statist and isolated from nongovernmental pressures. Therefore, the CIC was unable to convert much of its relatively free access to the decisional process into actual influence over the outcome of that process.

On the boycott issue, CIC officials usually played by the "rules" inherent to Canadian foreign policy-making. The committee's emphasis on elite interaction and accommodation was consistent with the norms of Canadian politics. Nevertheless, some foreign policy officials perceived the Jewish community's motives and behavior as less than fully acceptable to Canadian customs and traditions (Bick Interview; Plaut 1981b, 270). Some officials were reportedly annoyed by what they considered to be the CIC's excessive stridency on the boycott question, as well as the committee's alleged attempt to orchestrate the parliamentary debate on Bill C–32 (Official of the Middle East Division, Department of External Affairs Interview; Former Assistant to the SSEA Interview). Such sentiments were harmful to the CIC's attempt to influence that debate's outcome.

Popular opinion favored the antiboycott cause. Such opinion may very well have been unrelated to sympathy toward Israel and associated instead with general popular concern about universal human rights and political and economic freedoms. Nevertheless, the very fact that popular opinion on the boycott question appeared to parallel the policy preferences of the Canada-Israel Committee should have enhanced the CIC's influence over the decision-making process.

The media were essential elements of the prolegislation campaign. Virtually all major newspapers in the country, regardless of their editorial postures toward the Arab-Israeli conflict, supported the call for government action against Arab boycott practices. In publishing a leaked confidential cabinet document on the Arab boycott and its implications for Canada, the *Globe and Mail* focused attention squarely on the issue (August 6, 1976, 3). This focus domesticized the issue and broadened popular interest about an essentially parochial foreign policy concern.

The CIC benefited in many ways from the strong media sympathy for its preferred policy option. Its professional staff made the CIC's unparalleled expertise on Arab boycott practices freely available to editors and commentators. The media—"ethnically neutral" and with an innate ability to focus popular attention on specific public figures and policy questions in ways that an ethnic interest group usually cannot—complemented the lobbying effort of the Canada-Israel Committee on the boycott question (Resnick Interview).

The media were invaluable allies to the CIC throughout the debate over antiboycott legislation. They "contributed to raising the issue, enhancing it in the public arena, constantly provoking controversy regarding it" (Stanislawski

1981b, 398). This is the private group-media relationship writ large, and it largely explains the level of success achieved by Canadian Jewry in increasing popular awareness of the Arab boycott of Israel.

Many of the benefits resulting from media concern with the boycott issue were countered by Canadian Jewry's rapidly deteriorating relations with members of the federal Liberal cabinet. There was reportedly a great deal of concern expressed within the Trudeau government and the Canadian foreign service about the possible impact of antiboycott legislation upon existing and anticipated commercial relations with the Arab world. The fear of significant costs to business (however unfounded, based on the experiences of antiboycott legislation in the United States and the province of Ontario) was pervasive. The federal minister of Industry, Trade and Commerce, Jack Horner, and his senior ministerial staff publicly expressed such fears. The prime minister was said to be of two minds on the matter of antiboycott legislation; despite his public view of boycott practices as repugnant to Canadians, the prime minister was "not keen to translate his disapproval into action" (Plaut 1981b, 270).

The impact of the electoral dimension must be considered. When the matter of the Arab boycott was first leaked to the media and then raised in the House of Commons in April 1975, the possibility of an election was distant for the governing Liberal party. Trudeau felt little pressure to move on the issue beyond announcing administrative guidelines. However, as time passed, the electoral imperative became increasingly relevant. By the time the draft of Bill C–32 was tabled in the House of Commons in December 1978, the likelihood of a federal election had become very real. The boycott issue had animated many Jews, especially those in the Toronto area, which was increasingly perceived as the linchpin of Liberal party electoral fortunes (Plaut 1981b, 270). The question on the minds of many Liberal strategists was a complex one: Was the anticipated loss of trade with the Arab states resulting from the application of antiboycott legislation more or less important than the possible loss of Jewish electoral support if the Liberal government did not move decidedly on the boycott?

Further complicating Liberal party strategy was the support given to antiboycott legislation by the two federal opposition parties. Trudeau, then, had to find some way to avoid alienating the Arab world and at the same time avoid losing potentially crucial Jewish votes to the Progressive Conservatives and New Democrats. One participant-observer suggests that Trudeau's advisers resolved that the government could achieve this careful balancing act by introducing Bill C-32 but then exploiting every possible delaying tactic available so as to ensure that the bill never became law or was so significantly watered down as to not offend the Arab states (Stanislawski 1981b, 402). Such conspiracy theories aside, clearly the Trudeau government was less than enamored with the prospect of implementing the type of meaningful antiboycott legislation preferred by the Canada-Israel Committee. This created an atmosphere of strained cordiality between representatives of the government and those of the Jewish community (Bick Interview). By the end of the boycott debate and with the closure of Parliament on March 26, 1979, government-Jewish community relations had degenerated into poorly disguised mutual contempt (Bick Interview; Plaut Interview).

Parliament's role in the boycott debate was far greater than its role in the two previous cases discussed in this chapter. A growing popular consensus found the administrative guidelines applied initially by the government to be an inadequate response to the Arab boycott of Israel. The focus of the debate shifted to a legislative response, which increased significantly Parliament's formal role in the policy-making process. Moreover, it was in Parliament that the boycott debate was initiated and given popular saliency. The fact that the Liberal MP Herb Gray chose to question his governing party's policies on the matter in the question period—rather than in the privacy of caucus—meant that the boycott issue was fair game for parliamentary debate. Finally, the boycott debate became intertwined with Parliament's preparation for national elections. Throughout the 1976–78 period, the Progressive Conservatives and New Democrats used the boycott issue as fodder against the Liberal government. The boycott increasingly became a partisan issue. This was especially the case for strategists of the Progressive Conservative party who, under new leader Joe Clark, saw the opportunity to break the Liberal party's hold over the Toronto Jewish vote by exploiting the boycott issue (Plaut 1981b, 270–71; Stanislawski 1981b, 324–31).

The Canada-Israel Committee and the antiboycott lobby had considerable support within Parliament. Even if the positions of the three parties on the issue wavered according to the political wind, the prolegislation sympathies of individual MPs were apparent. Insofar as a relatively large number of attentive Canadians were moved by the boycott issue, so too were their members of Parliament. This contributed to a significant narrowing of the policy parameters and the decisional latitude available to the government.

In the final analysis, the extent to which the boycott issue became a central focus of parliamentary debate was an essential factor in the CIC's relatively strong showing on the issue. The constant raising of questions in the House of Commons increased popular awareness of the Arab economic boycott of Israel and related discriminatory visa practices and forced the Trudeau government to acknowledge Canada's haphazard application of existing antiboycott regulations. The ultimate failure of Bill C–32 to pass safely through the legislative process is not a reflection of parliamentary indifference towards the issue, but rather of Parliament's limited capacity to stop a majority government from doing what it is intent on doing.

The strong support the CIC received from various nongovernmental organizations contributed positively to its lobbying efforts. Among the societal groups most active in supporting CIC was the Commission on Economic Coercion and Discrimination (the so-called Cotler Commission).[2] The intervention of human rights agencies (such as the Canadian Association of Statutory Human Rights

Agencies) was particularly significant in that it effectively secularized the issue and broadened the base of support for forceful antiboycott legislation. The Canadian Labour Congress (CLC), the principal umbrella group of Canadian labor, enthusiastically endorsed the call for federal antiboycott legislation. The CLC's largest provincial affiliate, the Ontario Federation of Labour (OFL), lobbied extensively on behalf of provincial antiboycott legislation.

The intervention of Canadian church groups on the boycott issue was somewhat restrained. In 1975 the influential Canadian Council of Churches formally condemned the Canadian government's policy of issuing certificates of religious affiliation to Canadians seeking entry into Arab countries maintaining anti-Jewish policies. This condemnation "helped erode any perception of legitimacy which the government was able to ascribe to its procedures" (Stanislawski 1981b, 393). However, the council's failure to explicitly advocate antiboycott legislation weakened the CIC's ability to list the church as a reliable political ally.

The province of Ontario was a principal extraneous player in the 1975–79 federal boycott debate. Ontario's own antiboycott legislation (Bill 112, implemented in November 1978) has been described as "the most important antiboycott legislative effort in Canada" (Stanislawski 1981b, 284). It served as a test case for the arguments for and against a federal statute. The Canada-Israel Committee honed its arguments and strategies for the federal debate in representations before committees of the Ontario legislature and in campaigns against the opponents of provincial antiboycott legislation. Ontario's Act to Prohibit Discrimination in Business Relationships set a clear and unambiguous precedent for federal legislation. It increased significantly the pressure upon the federal government to act more aggressively against the boycott. And the act increased the national public profile of the Canada-Israel Committee (Bick Interview; May Interview; Official of the Middle East Division, Department of External Affairs Interview).

It is difficult to calculate the impact of provincial actions on the federal government. However, it is reasonable to surmise that such actions caused decision makers in Ottawa to move more deliberately on federal antiboycott measures.[3] Such pressure was tremendously beneficial to the efforts of the Canada-Israel Committee and the prolegislation forces.

Domestic counterforce groups were somewhat active in their opposition to federal antiboycott legislation. Arab Canadian groups were largely ineffective throughout much of the boycott debate. Their interactions with government were infrequent and at times "unpleasant" (Stanislawski 1981b, 399–400). A far more credible opposition to federal legislation came through the interventions of leaders of the Canadian corporate sector. The captains of Canadian industry— many with strong personal, political, class, and corporate connections to the Progressive Conservative party of Canada—took quite seriously implied threats of dire Arab economic sanctions in retaliation for the passage of federal antiboycott restrictions (Clement 1975; Porter 1965; Presthus 1973, 1974a). Pressure from the corporate sector helped set the agenda and the parameters of debate concerning the Arab boycott and worked contrary to the interests of the CIC and other supporters of antiboycott legislation.

An effective ethnic group's assumed relationship with the fifth analytic variable, the international political environment, holds only moderately for the boycott case. The prolegislation lobby was strongly guided by both the Israeli embassy and the antiboycott experiences of Jewish groups in the United States. Rabbi W. Gunther Plaut recalls the visit to Canada by Israeli Prime Minister Menachem Begin in the fall of 1978 and the considerable pressure Begin placed upon Canadian Jewish leaders to push for federal antiboycott legislation (Plaut 1981b, 237–74). Regardless of the relatively successful efforts at secularizing the boycott debate, it clearly had a strong "Israeli" component, which hindered the CIC in presenting a credible "Canadian" defense of antiboycott legislation.

The CIC's leadership of the antiboycott campaign also worked against the perceived autonomy (and hence, independence) of the Canadian Jewish lobby. Some leaders within the Jewish community argued that in order to effectively domesticize the boycott question and to deemphasize its Israeli context, leadership of the campaign should be taken by either the Canadian Jewish Congress or the Joint Community Relations Committee (Plaut 1981b, 269). Despite such considerations, the CIC was in firm control of the campaign from the outset. The CIC was, by all accounts, the most talented and most able of the Jewish and Israeli lobbies in Canada. However, the goal of secularizing the issue was not enhanced by the CIC's lead role. The way in which the community distributed responsibility during the boycott debate restricted Canadian Jewry's ability to influence the debate's outcome.

At the initiation of the boycott debate, relations between Ottawa and Jerusalem were relatively amiable. However, there was also an element of tension, arising primarily from Canada's shifting voting pattern at the United Nations on resolutions relating to the Palestinian issue. There was also reportedly friction between Trudeau and Begin. This was exhibited in the fall of 1978, during Begin's first official visit to Canada. Trudeau refused to commit his government to Begin's request for a change in Canadian policy concerning either the Arab boycott or the location of the embassy in Israel (Plaut 1981b, 273–74). It is reasonable to speculate that the differences between Trudeau and Begin added to the difficulties already experienced by the CIC in seeking to influence the boycott debate.

Canadian Jewry wavered between interpreting the Arab boycott as either a moderate threat or as a serious threat to core values. Canada's unwillingness to submit to Arab "blackmail," and the opportunity for Canadian Jewry to influence a positive change in Canadian policy on the Middle East and to strike at the heart of the bureaucratic-corporate Arabist sentiment emerging in Ottawa represented, respectively, the perceived symbolic and tangible components to the issue (Resnick Interview). To a certain extent, much of the community's initial determination to pass boycott legislation dissipated over time. In part this was caused by Jerusalem's deliberate downgrading of the issue on its own agenda (in deference to the rapidly unfolding peace negotiations with Egypt). Moreover, as the boycott bill became mired in legislative procedure, some community leaders expressed fear that the issue might become a discernibly partisan one (Rose Interview). Although some leaders were apparently prepared to carry the boycott issue into a federal election campaign, others were concerned about the possible backlash of such a radical departure from Canadian Jewry's traditional nonpartisanship on Israel-related matters (Bick Interview; Rose Interview). Such differences of opinion presented the Canada-Israel Committee with a degree of strategic confusion and inhibited its prolegislation lobbying effort.

The Trudeau government, for its part, never perceived the Arab boycott issue as a high priority. Its first inclination was to bury the issue by dealing with it through the application of largely symbolic administrative guidelines. As the issue gained the attention of a wider segment of the population—and especially the influential media—and as the electoral imperative became more relevant, a more definitive legislative response was presented. Still, the federal cabinet was reluctant to put forth meaningful antiboycott legislation. This is most tellingly illustrated by the government's unwillingness to employ the various parliamentary procedures at its disposal to force Bill C-32 into law prior to the dissolution of the House of Commons in March 1979.

The Canada-Israel Committee's level of actual influence in its lobbying for passage of a forceful Canadian legislative response to the Arab economic boycott must be scored as marginal-low. Despite an intensive lobbying campaign, the CIC was unable to bring to fruition its goal of a federal antiboycott law comparable to the American prototype (Plaut 1981b, 272). The result of almost five years of political action—weak administrative guidelines and the unceremonious demise of antiboycott legislation on the parliamentary order paper—represents a situation of the government adopting a policy generally unsympathetic towards the interests of the ethnic foreign policy interest group (The one redeeming factor was that the end result of the boycott debate left the interests of Israel in no worse shape than they were prior to its initiation).

Some community leaders argue that the Canada-Israel Committee achieved a moral victory by forcing a public dialogue on the Canadian government's knowing acquiescence to discriminatory Arab boycott practices and by enhancing significantly the process of Canadian Jewish politicization (Bessin Interview; Bick Interview; May Interview; Resnick Interview). Rabbi W. Gunther Plaut carries this theme one step further. He suggests that the committee forced the federal cabinet into a compromise on the boycott, whereby the Canadian government, while denying the need for American-style antiboycott legislation, acknowledged that the Arab boycott was a problem that had to be officially addressed. Given the level of Canada's interests in the Middle East, Plaut asserts that this was the most Canadian Jewry could reasonably hope to achieve out of the boycott debate (Plaut 1981b, 272).

Such suggestions of a moral victory on the boycott issue are reasonable, at least in the abstract. However, the principal criterion of ethnic interest group influence remains the extent to which government policy parallels that preferred by the group. Under the circumstances, the Canada-Israel Committee's attempt to influence the passage of federal antiboycott legislation must be deemed a valiant, but ultimately unsuccessful, attempt at ethnic group intervention in the Canadian foreign policy-making process.

THE JERUSALEM EMBASSY: INITIATION

Overview

There are essentially three aspects to what has become known as the Jerusalem embassy affair: Progressive Conservative Party leader Joe Clark's initial promise to transfer the Canadian embassy in Israel from Tel Aviv to West Jerusalem (made during the 1979 federal election campaign); Clark's restatement of the pledge following the election; and the effective reversal of the pledge resulting from the appointment of a special one-man commission of inquiry into Canada's relations with the countries of the Middle East. This section examines the first two aspects of the Jerusalem embassy affair; the third is analyzed in the section following.

There is more wishful thinking than substance associated with the initiation of the embassy promise. Canada has never formally recognized Israel's claim to a united Jerusalem (Bercuson 1981; 1984; 1985). Prior to 1967 Canada gave de facto recognition to West Jerusalem as an integral part of Israel by conducting some diplomatic business there (although the embassy was based in Tel Aviv). Following the 1967 Arab-Israeli War, Israel extended its jurisdiction over the entire city of Jerusalem. Since then, Canada has maintained a policy of no unilateral alteration of the status quo. In November 1978 Israeli prime minister Menachem Begin made his first official visit to Canada. During that trip, Begin tried hard to convince Prime Minister Trudeau to move the Canadian embassy to Jerusalem, or at least to make a statement of principle regarding Canada's de jure recognition of Jerusalem as the "eternal" capital of the state of Israel. Trudeau declined.

During his visit to Canada, Begin also met with leading members of the Canadian Jewish community and impressed upon them the need to lobby their government for an embassy transfer (Plaut 1981b, 273–75). As Canadian Jewry considered Begin's call to political action, opposition leader Joe Clark was developing his own views on Jerusalem. Clark did not meet with Begin during the latter's state visit to Canada. Shortly thereafter, however, individual Jews associated with the Conservative party began to press for the formulation of a policy favoring an embassy transfer. They found a responsive constituency among Clark's key political advisers (Takach 1980; 1989).

Clark made his first visit to Israel in the early part of 1979. There he was exposed to at least three competing views on the Jerusalem question: Begin's view; the view of key Conservative party colleagues from the Toronto area (who saw the Jerusalem issue as a means through which to break the Liberal party's stranglehold over Jewish voters); and the view of Canada's ambassador to Israel, Edward Lee, who strongly advised against any decision by Clark concerning a proposed change to Canada's policy on Jerusalem (Adelman 1980, 9; Takach 1980, 28–32). Clark remained formally noncommittal. At a press conference in Amman, Jordan, he announced that any decision on the embassy in Israel would require both further review back in Canada and a successful realization of the Egyptian-Israeli peace process (Takach 1980, 30).

The next phase in the evolving drama occurred on April 25, 1979, three weeks into the federal election campaign. Prior to a meeting with leaders of the Canada-Israel Committee, Mr. Clark acknowledged that, with the achievement of the Egyptian-Israeli peace treaty, it was an opportune time for Canada to take "positive initiatives in the Middle East":

One such initiative would be the recognition of Jerusalem as the capital of Israel, with free access to its Holy Places provided to all faiths. As a symbol of this recognition, my government would be prepared to move the Canadian embassy from Tel Aviv to the western part of Jerusalem, which has been part of Israel since the creation of the country in 1948. . . . This foreign policy initiative is only a recognition of the political, administrative, demographic and legal realities of Jerusalem in 1979. . . . Jerusalem is and always has been the capital of the Jewish people and the Jewish spirit. 'Next Year in Jerusalem' is a Jewish prayer which we intend to make a Canadian reality. (*Toronto Star*, April 26, 1979, A1)

The election of May 26, 1979, resulted in a minority Progressive Conservative government headed by Joe Clark. The Conservative party had swept the Toronto area, taking all but one of the constituencies with large Jewish concentrations. On June 5 at his first formal press conference as prime minister of Canada, Joe Clark reaffirmed his government's intention to fulfill the pledge to relocate the Canadian embassy in Israel from Tel Aviv to West Jerusalem.

Conceptual Analysis

Canadian Jewry's involvement in the initiation of the Jerusalem embassy affair relates positively to many of the attributes usually associated with an influential ethnic interest group. This positive relationship is explained in part by the community's commitment to the unified status of Jerusalem. It is also a reflection of the evolving dominance of the Canada-Israel Committee on all issues relating to the Middle East and the CIC's ability to influence the Canadian foreign policy system to its best advantage.

The CIC's level of lobbying activity was high and its policy objectives were advocative. The CIC argued that the transfer of the Canadian embassy in Israel was a positive development, both with respect to the Arab-Israeli peace process and as an explicit acknowledgment of Canada's role in the Middle East.

A considerable amount of conjecture still remains as to the CIC's role in initiating Clark's embassy proposal. However, there is little doubt that, once the pledge was made, the CIC and Jews close to Clark's inner circle lobbied aggressively for its implementation.

The CIC's selection of targets on the embassy initiation indicates its advanced comprehension of the Canadian decisional process and the balance of political power. CIC officials recognized the personal quality of Joe Clark's commitment to an embassy relocation. They concentrated their lobbying upon Clark and his team of personal advisers instead of on the Progressive Conservative party establishment, which was concerned primarily with antiboycott legislation rather than with the embassy issue (Takach 1980, 25). CIC officials also did not expend great amounts of energy lobbying either the New Democratic party or the Liberals, whose leaders were either vague on the Middle East, as was the case for the NDP's Ed Broadbent, or adamantly opposed to any unilateral Canadian action on Jerusalem, as was the case for the Liberal prime minister, Pierre Trudeau (Takach 1980).

CIC representatives approached political decision makers and foreign policy officials directly. They also questioned electoral candidates on their position on the embassy issue. In addition, the CIC initiated a public education campaign addressing Canada's policy on Jerusalem and the likely implications of a transfer of the embassy from Tel Aviv to West Jerusalem (Canada-Israel Committee, n.d.).

The behavior of the Canada-Israel Committee met most of the criteria of an influential ethnic lobby. All other things being equal, this behavior should have resulted in a fair degree of influence over the outcome of the Jerusalem embassy debate.

But all other things were not equal. Canadian Jewry met only moderately the organizational criteria of an influential ethnic interest group. The CIC's level of organizational development wavered between mature and institutionalized. Some criteria of institutionalization were met; others were not. Organizationally, the CIC had benefited from the cancellation of the Crime Conference and from fighting "the good fight" on antiboycott legislation. The CIC was now more well recognized and well respected in Ottawa, and its budget was more consistent with that expected of an efficient foreign policy lobby group (Bessin Interview; Bick Interview; Resnick Interview).

Detracting from this enhanced organizational sophistication, however, were deficiencies with regard to group cohesion and unity of purpose. The Jerusalem embassy initiative caused serious divisions to emerge within the ranks of Canadian Jewish leadership that threatened to make impossible the lobbying efforts of the Canada-Israel Committee. Intraorganizational differences arose first in response to Prime Minister Begin's urgings that Canadian Jews lobby their government more aggressively on the Jerusalem embassy issue. Virtually all Jewish Canadians were sympathetic to such a request, for all considered a unified Jerusalem to be the legitimate eternal capital of the state of Israel. However, there was dissent concerning the timing of Begin's request and the appropriate strategy to be adopted with a federal election pending (May Interview; Plaut Interview, 1981b, 274–75).

The cautious approach taken by some members of the CIC's inner circle was rejected by others. There were some members, the so-called Jerusalem activists, willing to make a proposed embassy transfer a partisan cause and an issue of debate in the upcoming federal election (Bick Interview). The activist perspective, adopted primarily by representatives of the Canadian Zionist Federation and especially the B'nai B'rith, clashed constantly with the political caution counseled by the Canadian Jewish Congress (Dimant Interview; May Interview; Plaut Interview, 1981b, 274–75; Rose Interview, 1980). The tactical disputes were reportedly significant enough not only to stalemate the lobbying effectiveness of the Canada-Israel Committee but also to threaten CIC's very dissolution.

Joe Clark's April 25, 1979, pledge to move the embassy increased disputes within the CIC. All CIC members welcomed the Clark initiative as morally correct and long overdue; differences were based on the intrusion of the issue into the federal election campaign and the fear of alienating a portion of the Jewish community from its traditional locus of political support within the Liberal party (Plaut 1981b, 275). A compromise of sorts was eventually reached. The CIC would engage in a low-key information campaign on the Jerusalem embassy question directed both at the Canadian public, Jewish and otherwise, and at electoral candidates of all three federal political parties. The campaign would not, however, require candidates to declare themselves formally on Clark's proposed embassy transfer (Plaut 1981b, 275; Takach 1980, 22–27).

The compromise did little to smother the fires of intracommunal dispute over the proper handling of the Clark initiative. As one participant writes, "The underlying result of the controversy was that the Jewish community was deeply split" (Plaut 1981b, 276). Moreover, the dispute was not kept in house. Despite the attempt by its leaders to contain the debate, it soon became clear to many people—including makers of Canadian foreign policy and opponents of the embassy transfer—that the CIC was in the midst of serious internal disruption over the Jerusalem embassy question (Official of the Middle East Division, DEA Interview; Former Assistant to the SSEA Interview). Community leaders acknowledge that to the extent that debates internal to the Canada-Israel Committee on the Jerusalem embassy issue became public knowledge, the group's influence over the policy issue was reduced (May Interview; Plaut Interview; Rose Interview).

The structure of the decision-making system was fairly conducive to the CIC's attempts to influence the embassy issue. The decision to move the embassy was based primarily on the personal considerations of Clark and a few of his key personal political advisers, no doubt in consultation with specific Jewish political activists in the metropolitan Toronto area. During the transition of power following the May 1979 election—but prior to Clark's June 5 press conference—a briefing paper, drafted jointly by the Department of External Affairs and the Privy Council Office, warned the prime minister-elect not to proceed with his election promise regarding the embassy (Takach 1980, 45). This advice went unheeded by Clark in part because Clark did not trust much of the existing bureaucracy in Ottawa (which he considered to be loyal to the previous Liberal regime) (Cox 1982; Simpson 1980; Takach 1980) and in part because of Clark's "highly personal, populist approach to foreign policy . . . [and] instinct toward the privatization of Canadian foreign policy" (that is, the willingness to formally involve communities and nongovernmental groups in the consideration of foreign policy of interest to them) (Kirton and Dimock 1983–84, 77–79). Clark's views worked to the advantage of the Canada-Israel Committee's lobbying effort.

The domestic political environment contributed only moderately to the CIC's influence over the embassy issue. Fifteen percent of respondents to a July 1979 Gallup Poll favored a transfer of the Canadian embassy in Israel, fifteen percent were not sure or offered no opinion, and seventy percent opposed the transfer (*Toronto Star*, August 18, 1979, 1). Put simply, seventy percent of Canadians opposed the policy preference articulated by the Canadian Jewish community and the Canada-Israel Committee.

The Canadian media appeared to take their lead on the Jerusalem embassy issue from popular opinion. Many of the media were critical of Clark's initial pledge of April 25, 1979, but in an undemonstrative way, perceiving it as only a campaign promise likely to be forgotten once the federal election had passed. Clark's June 5 reaffirmation of the pledge caused a discernible shift in the tone of media comment. The majority of editorial pages came out fully against Clark's initiative, most citing Arab economic sanctions as a negative repercussion likely to result from an embassy transfer.[4]

As the threats of Arab economic sanctions continued to mount, there was a slight change in stance of some of the Canadian media; while still highly critical of Clark's initiative, some editorialists urged the Canadian government against "knuckling under" to Arab economic blackmail. For example, the *Toronto Star* suggested that, whatever the failings of Clark's embassy pledge, the Canadian government and people could not tolerate "the brazen efforts mounted by the Arab Lobby and its allies to intimidate the new government. It [the new government] should tell the Arab ambassadors to observe the norms of diplomatic behavior and to end their campaign of threats" (*Toronto Star*, June 23, 1979, B2). While increasingly in evidence, such editorial sentiment remained in the minority; the Canadian media were predominantly critical of the proposed embassy transfer. Some Jewish community leaders suggested that media comment extended beyond criticism of the Clark pledge. They charged that by emphasizing the alleged role of Jews in the embassy pledge, the media manifested a latent antisemitism rooted deeply in Canadian culture and politics (Plaut 1981b, 276). Such charges are, of course, impossible to verify empirically. Nevertheless, it is quite plausible that the Canada-Israel Committee's attempt to influence the implementation of the embassy transfer was adversely affected by the amount of media attention focused upon its activities concerning the initiative of the original pledge.

Prime Minister–elect Joe Clark and the team of political advisors surrounding him clearly supported the embassy pledge. Whether motivated by moral or political considerations, Clark initiated the issue by making the embassy pledge and then reaffirming it. Obviously, the early support of Clark and his inner circle for the embassy move was a major boost to the fortunes of the Canada-Israel Committee.

The intrusion of the issue into the federal election campaign contributed both positively and negatively to the CIC's influence. The timing of the pledge gave the CIC maximum media coverage and public attention. The Jerusalem embassy question became one of the election campaign's hot items, and the CIC was in the forefront throughout the proceedings, interacting with representatives of all three federal political parties and key media commentators. The timing, moreover, allowed the CIC to force other Canadian-Israeli agenda items, including antiboycott legislation, temporarily back onto the political front burner (Bessin Interview).

The timing of the issue, however, also negatively affected the CIC's influence over the policy outcome. By politicizing the Jerusalem embassy question and making it an indisputably partisan one, large segments of Canadian Jewry were effectively alienated from the federal Liberal party. The extent to which the fate of the embassy question was tied to the electoral fortunes of the Progressive Conservative party was a major departure from the nonpartisanship traditionally practiced by the Canada-Israel Committee and its institutional precursors (Hayes 1979; May Interview; Plaut 1981). The politicization of the issue also caused a major rift to develop between the CIC staff (and other Jewish community professionals) and their counterparts in the Canadian foreign service. The latter had come to respect CIC representatives for their expertise, professionalism, and relative objectivity (Official of the Middle East Division, DEA Interview). Many foreign service officials regarded the Jewish community's role in politicizing the Jerusalem embassy issue as inappropriate and a demonstration of excessive stridency and unprofessionalism (Official of the Middle East Division, Department of External Affairs Interview; Former Assistant to the Secretary of State for External Affairs Interview).

Parliament had absolutely no role to play in Clark's decisions to announce and then reaffirm the embassy pledge. The House of Commons had been dissolved on March 26, 1979, and did not reconvene until late in the summer. The embassy issue received much attention during the election campaign from both the Liberals and the New Democrats. The Liberal party's reaction was predictable; Prime Minister Trudeau immediately seized upon it as an "irresponsible" policy proposal and an indication of Joe Clark's "flip-flop" on substantive issues (Stanislawski 1981b, 328–31; Takach 1980, 73–74).

Various individuals and NGOs joined with the Liberals and foreign policy officials in opposing Clark's embassy initiative. Several respected academics had reportedly sought to informally persuade Clark not to make his proposal and viewed with considerable cynicism the Conservative leader's policy announcement of April 25, 1979 (Lyon 1982b, 1984). Few apparently expected Clark to fulfill his pledge, assuming that the embassy proposal would be lost in the hoopla of electioneering. It was only with the June 5 reaffirmation that most groups opposing the embassy move began to participate actively in the debate.

This pattern of reacting also typified the business community's response. Elements of the Canadian corporate sector had been sensitized to Middle East questions by the boycott debate. Business leaders had reportedly met with the leaders of all three federal political parties urging them to stay away from the Middle East and to not use the federal election campaign as a forum for initiating changes in Canadian policy on either the Arab boycott or the status of Canada's embassy in Israel (Stanislawski 1981b, 324–31). Clark's original embassy pledge produced a surprisingly restrained response from the business community, primarily because few businessmen thought that Clark was foolish enough to try to actually implement the controversial campaign promise (Takach 1980, 78–79). Business responded by employing its many ties to the Conservative party establishment to indicate its displeasure with any intrusion by the Canadian government into the Middle Eastern morass. Tentative moves were made to revitalize the corporate-bureaucratic alliance forged in the late 1970s in opposition to antiboycott legislation. As was the case with other NGOs, however, the business lobby apparently failed to take seriously enough Clark's commitment to fulfill his promise to transfer the embassy. This was reflected in the corporate community's shocked response to Clark's reaffirmation of the pledge on June 5.

The haphazard response of many domestic political actors to the original Clark initiative strengthened the lobbying position of the Canada-Israel Committee. In the absence of vigorous and unified opposition to its policy preferences, the CIC was able to achieve a fairly high degree of influence over Clark's decision to announce and then reaffirm his government's intention to move the embassy.

The reaction of Arab Canadian groups and the Arab states to Clark's first and second decisions on the embassy issue was expectedly swift and declaratory. Following the April 25, 1979, pledge, the Arab Palestine Association—an organization comprised of some five thousand Canadians of Arab descent—sent a strongly worded telegram to the Conservative leader, warning him that his promise on Jerusalem, if fulfilled, would be detrimental to Canadian economic interests in the Middle East (Takach 1980, 50). Such sentiments were expressed by other Arab Canadian groups and Arab Canadian newspapers in Montreal and Toronto. Statements of protest were also forthcoming from the Arab embassies and the Arab League Information Office in Ottawa (*Toronto Star*, June 7, 1979, 3). A theme running consistently throughout much of the Arab community's response to Clark's April statement was an emphasis on Canada-Arab economic relations, an issue of legitimate concern to Canadian politicians and foreign policy bureaucrats. Idle and amorphous retaliatory threats were rarely heard; the Arab-Canadian community was steadily evolving into a corporate entity capable of providing effective opposition to the influence of the Canada-Israel Committee.

The various assumptions associated with the international political environment hold only partly for the CIC's attempt to influence the Jerusalem embassy issue. The Canada-Israel Committee was perceived as only partly independent of Jerusalem. It is of course conceivable that Conservative party leader Joe Clark would have presented his embassy pledge, and the CIC would have aggressively responded to it, regardless of the activities of the government of Israel. However, it is also true that the tone and quality of the CIC's campaign on the embassy issue were largely a consequence of the CIC's close working relationship with the Israeli government. The CIC's reliance on the Israeli embassy for information, guidance, and advice moreover contributed to a perceived melding of the CIC's and Israel's position on the Jerusalem embassy question, regardless of the actual direction of Israel's guidance on the issue (Former Assistant to the Secretary of State for External Affairs Interview; Official of the Middle East Division, DEA Interview). CIC activists acknowledge that such perceptions were detrimental to their lobbying efforts (Bick Interview; Rose Interview).

The perceived influence of Israel on the CIC also affected the CIC's performance of its role as a bridge linking the Canadian and Israeli governments. Although the committee enjoyed effective access to the decision makers in both Ottawa and Jerusalem, its influence was severely constrained by the fact that a large number of Canadian foreign policy professionals viewed it as little more than a handmaiden to the Israeli government on the embassy question. Community leaders acknowledge that the CIC's inability (and perceived unwillingness) to adopt a position on the Jerusalem embassy issue somehow different from Israel's harmed the organization's credibility and reduced its potential influence over the embassy debate (Bessin Interview; May Interview; Plaut Interview; Resnick Interview).

Despite tactical differences, there was agreement among Canadian Jewish leaders that the Clark embassy pledge represented both a symbolic and a tangible goal of the highest order. The Clark team came to share the CIC's perception of the Jerusalem embassy issue, but for reasons quite different from the Jewish community's reasons. For Clark there was both an electoral imperative (that is, drawing Jewish voters away from the Liberal party) and a political imperative (that is, Clark's desire to prove his skill as an international statesman and establish effective control over the Canadian foreign service).

Joe Clark determined the transfer of the Canadian embassy to be an issue of medium-high intensity. According to the inverse relationship theory of influence, the CIC should not have enjoyed great influence over either the April 25, 1979, initial pledge or (especially) the June 5, 1979, reaffirmation. Nevertheless, it did.

The Jerusalem embassy affair is given a score of 5 on the index of influence; a situation of greatest ethnic interest group influence over foreign policy decision-making. The drawing of a direct causal relationship between the activities of the Canada-Israel Committee and the Clark embassy initiative is inhibited by both the high degree of conjecture concerning the origin of the plan and the introduction of a complicating extraneous factor (the federal election campaign). Nevertheless, in the definition of influence used in this study, the emphasis is on parallelism of policy preferences rather than absolute and unambiguous causation. To the extent that Clark's first two (of three) decisions on the Jerusalem question paralleled almost completely the policy preferred by the vast majority of Canadian Jews, significant influence must be attributed to the Canada-Israel Committee.

THE JERUSALEM EMBASSY: REVERSAL

Overview

On June 5, 1979, at his first press conference as Canada's prime minister, Joe Clark restated his government's intention to move the Canadian embassy in Israel from Tel Aviv to Jerusalem. This action prompted weeks of intense domestic political controversy unprecedented in the recent history of Canadian foreign policy-making. The controversy reached a turning point on June 23, 1979. On that day, Prime Minister Clark announced that the respected former leader of the federal Progressive Conservative party, Robert L. Stanfield, had been appointed special representative of Canada and ambassador-at-large. Mr. Stanfield was asked to undertake a detailed investigation into the implementation of the policy on Jerusalem, so that the Canadian government could decide how and under what circumstance to proceed.[5]

Stanfield was appointed to relieve pressure on Clark and the new Conservative government and to effectively put the Jerusalem embassy question on the political backburner. Nevertheless, in the days and weeks following Stanfield's appointment, significant corporate, diplomatic, and bureaucratic pressure was placed on Clark, External Affairs Minister Flora MacDonald, and International Trade Minister Michael Wilson.

The controversy culminated on October 29, 1979, when the beleaguered prime minister received and accepted Robert Stanfield's interim report on Canada's relations with the Middle East and North Africa. Clark read the two and one-half page letter to the House of Commons. Ambassador Stanfield recommended that the Conservative government immediately rescind its offer to transfer the Canadian embassy to Jerusalem, on the grounds that "a change in the location of the Canadian embassy . . . would be seen as prejudging negotiations concerning parties in the Middle East, and might in fact work against progress toward a just and lasting peace settlement" (Canada. House of Commons, 1979). Clark made the following declaration:

The purpose of this government is to encourage that peace. Consequently, the government accepts the recommendation that no action be taken on the location of the Canadian embassy until the status of Jerusalem is clarified within a comprehensive agreement between Israel and its neighbors. . . . Until there is such a clarification within the context of a just and lasting settlement, the Canadian embassy will stay in Tel Aviv. (Canada. House of Commons, 1979, 697)

In late December 1979 Joe Clark's minority government was defeated on a parliamentary motion of nonconfidence. The Liberal party, under the leadership of Pierre Trudeau, was returned to power in the February 1980 elections, with a significant majority of the vote. Shortly thereafter, on February 20, 1980, Ambassador Stanfield submitted to Parliament his final report on Canada's relations with the Middle East and North Africa. The report was perfunctorily received, thus bringing the Jerusalem embassy affair to an anticlimatic end.

Conceptual Analysis

Coming in the immediate aftermath of its successful intervention in the Jerusalem embassy initiation, the Canadian government's decision to reverse that initiative represented a major defeat for the Canada-Israel Committee. This is indicated by the committee's rather poor showing on many of the key criteria associated with an influential ethnic interest group.

The CIC's level of activity throughout the embassy reversal was extremely high. Canadian Jewry's representatives interacted frequently and forcefully with politicians and foreign service officers and submitted formal briefs to the Stanfield Commission of Inquiry. The benefits theoretically derived from this activism, however, were offset by other aspects of the CIC's behavior. The committee's policy objectives on the reversal were essentially antagonistic. In the opinion of several Canadian officials, the CIC's argument against a reversal of the controversial embassy pledge contained little of substance other than its urgings for Canada not to submit to Arab and domestic corporate pressures (Former Assistant to the Secretary of State for External Affairs Interview; Official in the Middle East Division, DEA Interview). The CIC was viewed as only seeking to deny a political victory to the Arabs and their domestic supporters; it was seen as adding little constructive to the policy debate. In this sense, the CIC's objectives failed to meet the criteria usually associated with an influential ethnic interest group.

The CIC's timing on the reversal was exclusively reactive. Most Jewish leaders were ill-prepared for the policy reversal because it did not fit their preconceived images of the preferred situation and because they had faith in Clark's commitment to implement his pledge (May Interview; Plaut Interview). The CIC was then forced into a purely reactive position, trying to halt the rapid deterioration of its capacity to influence Canada's posture on the Jerusalem embassy question. The CIC's targeting on the embassy reversal was complicated by confusion as to who was making policy in the Clark government (Cox 1982; Kirton and Dimock 1983–84, 77–79; Official of the Middle East Division, DEA Interview; Takach 1980, 100–101).

The CIC's strategy of direct and formal lobbying of government was supplemented by appeals to the media and other NGOs. Two factors complicated the CIC's strategic response to the reversal. The CIC had to fight a rearguard action to counter the popular perception of the embassy pledge as an electoral stratagem foisted upon Clark by an excessively strident Canadian Jewish community (Rose 1980, 8–9). Moreover, the organization's strategic response was complicated by a severe cracking of internal cohesion over the entire embassy issue (Bick Interview; May Interview; Rose 1980; Plaut 1981b, 276).

In its response to the embassy reversal, the CIC met only some of the criteria of institutional sophistication. Its organizational base had expanded to incorporate representatives of other national groups and local Jewish federations. However, the potential benefits of an enhanced participatory base were countered by the debilitating effect of reduced cohesion resulting from strategic disputes among leaders of the CIC. Although many of the more pressing disputes resulting from the embassy pledge had been resolved or made less imperative by the course of developments, the reversal of Clark's pledge also produced a high degree of intraorganizational dissent. Some of the CIC's volunteer and professional leadership felt that the Jewish community must maintain an active and aggressive posture and take all steps possible to force Clark to return to his original commitment. Other CIC activists—possibly a majority—reasoned that "Clark should be let off the hook as quickly and painlessly as possible" (Plaut 1981b, 276). They felt this way not because the embassy transfer had suddenly become less important, but because continued stridency on the controversial matter would exacerbate the negative images of Canadian Jews resulting from the embassy affair (Bessin Interview; May Interview; Plaut 1981b, 276; Rose Interview, 1980).

Disputes within the CIC over the embassy reversal weakened the credibility of the Jewish lobby in the eyes of some Canadian officials (Gray Interview; Former Assistant to the SSEA Interview; Official of the Middle East Division, DEA Interview; Stanfield Interview). This view, in turn, had the effect of strengthening the resolve of domestic counterforce groups (Abdallah Interview).

The structure of the formal decision-making system worked against Canadian Jewry's antireversal lobbying efforts. The embassy pledge resulted, in part, from a temporary widening of the foreign policy decision-making process. Its reversal saw the return to a more typical, concentrated, and statist policy-making structure (Kirton and Dimock 1983–84, 77; Nossal, 1983–84, 1–22; Nossal 1985, 101–7).

Key aspects of the domestic political environment provide further explanation of the CIC's limited influence over the Jerusalem embassy reversal. A Gallup Poll taken during the summer of 1979 found that only fifteen percent of respondents favored a move of the embassy whereas an overwhelming seventy percent either opposed the proposed transfer or held no opinion (*Toronto Star*, August 18, 1979, 1). Jewish community leaders acknowledge that public opinion was clearly against their efforts to convince Clark to maintain his policy line on the Jerusalem embassy issue (Rose 1980, 8–9).

The Canadian media's coverage of the embassy reversal also did not enhance the CIC's influence. Following Clark's June 5, 1979, policy reaffirmation—but prior to the June 23 appointment of the Stanfield Commission—the Canadian press gave considerable attention to the embassy question. Many newspapers were overtly critical of Clark's policy and the alleged Jewish influence in its formulation (*Ottawa Journal*, June 6, 1979, 7; *Peterborough Examiner*, June 8, 1979, 5; *Windsor Star*, June 8, 1979, 4; *Toronto Star*, June 8, 1979, A1; *Winnipeg Tribune*, June 8, 1979, 6). Other papers focused on reports and rumors of imminent economic and diplomatic peril if the Canadian embassy were transferred to West Jerusalem (*Globe and Mail*, June 7, 1979, 1; *Montreal Gazette*, June 7, 1979, 1; *Toronto Star*, June 7, 1979, A1; *Toronto Sun*, June 7, 1979, 1).

Threatened and implied Arab economic sanctions against Canada prompted an interesting division within the media. Some newspapers sensationalized the damages likely to occur to Canada in the event of the embassy move (*Ottawa Citizen*, June 19, 1979, 1; *Globe and Mail*, June 20, 1979, 1; June 21, 1979, 1). The growing threats of Arab economic sanctions led other papers to urge Clark to hang tough against attempted Arab economic blackmail (regardless of the wisdom of his policy) (*Toronto Star*, June 20, 1979, A1; June 21, 1979, A1; June 23, 1979, A1; *Toronto Sun*, June 21, 1979, 1; June 26, 1979, 1).[6]

Although designed as a dignified way out of the embassy imbroglio, the June 23, 1979, appointment of the Stanfield Commission was declared by much of the press to be a sellout to Arab blackmail and domestic corporate pressure (*Globe and Mail*, June 26, 1979, 1). The press also reported that Stanfield's appointment did little to quell Arab threats of economic sanctions (*Toronto Star*, September 15, 1979, A1). Although perhaps benefiting indirectly from the generally sensationalized reporting, the CIC's influence was clearly only marginally enhanced by media coverage of the embassy reversal affair.

The CIC's influence over the reversal was harmed by its declining base of support within the executive branch of the Canadian government. Prime Minister Joe Clark's personal support for the embassy transfer—so instrumental in its initiation—dissipated rapidly. By the summer and early fall of 1979, Clark's determination to fulfill the Jerusalem policy had been tempered by a strong dose of political realism, in the form of the obviously unanticipated domestic political fallout associated with his pledge (Cox 1982; Simpson 1980; Stanislawski 1981b; Takach 1980). Clark had been embarrassed personally and harmed politically by the embassy affair. There were also suggestions that the prime minister was frustrated by what he considered to be the CIC's abuse of the opportunity to have its interests considered in a populist foreign policy-making environment (Official of the Middle East Division, Department of External Affairs Interview). Such allegations were, of course, denied by most Jewish community activists, who in turn charged that Clark used the CIC as a convenient scapegoat to deflect the legitimate charge that he had fumbled the ball on the embassy question (Bick Interview; May Interview; Plaut Interview, 1981b, 276–77; Resnick Interview).

The Canadian foreign service remained consistently opposed to any embassy transfer. The foreign service's support of the reversal of Clark's initiative was based on a number of considerations. These included the following: a fear of Arab economic retaliation; a concern that the fulfillment of the embassy transfer would reinforce the pro-Israeli tilt that had allegedly prevailed in official Ottawa since the late 1940s (Lyon 1982b; Kirton and Lyon 1989); and the feeling on the part of some career foreign service officers that a unilateral Canadian move on the question of Jerusalem was simply "not a just and fair-minded thing to do" (Former Assistant to the SSEA Interview; Official of the Middle East Division, DEA Interview; Stanfield Interview).

The influence of bureaucratic opponents to the embassy transfer was initially countered by Joe Clark's determination to use the issue as a means to establish his government's control over the Canadian foreign service. However, as Clark's resolve on the issue weakened, the concerns of opponents to the embassy transfer came to dominate the debate (Bessin Interview; Bick Interview; May Interview; Plaut Interview, 1981b; Resnick Interview; Stanislawski 1981b; Takach 1980).

Parliament was an important actor in the process leading to the reversal of the Clark government's stand on the embassy question (Takach 1980, 74–78). The thirty-first Parliament served as "a potent forum" for the Liberals and the New Democrats to pursue and embarrass Clark and the Conservative party (Takach 1980, 78). Throughout the fall of 1979 "question after question hit the Conservative front benches with devastating effect" (Takach 1980, 78). It was largely through government responses to opposition questions in Parliament that substance was given to the sensationalist rumors in the newspapers of impending economic peril if the embassy pledge were fulfilled. And it was in the House of Commons that Clark announced his decisions of June 23, 1979, to establish the Stanfield Commission, and of October 29, 1979, to reverse the embassy pledge.

During the reversal phase of the embassy affair, a number of societal groups dedicated to denying Canadian Jewry influence over policy on the Middle East became fully mobilized. Most conspicuous of these were the business community, the Church, and significant elements of the academic community. The corporate sector reacted with great concern to the threatened or imagined Arab response to Clark's June 5, 1979, reaffirmation of the embassy pledge. Three sectors of Canadian business were primarily involved in the campaign to have Clark reverse the pledge: oil importing companies (mostly American-owned multinationals with Canadian affiliates or subsidiaries), banks and other financial institutions, and manufacturers and engineering firms with significant contracts or contracts pending with Arab countries. In addition, several trade associations also were active throughout the summer of 1979 in making the business community's opposition to the embassy transfer clear to Clark and the government of Canada (Adelman 1980; Stanislawski 1981b, 331–53; Takach 1980, 78–83).

In its lobbying effort, the Canadian business community employed virtually every available political strategy. There was "a corporate storming" of official

Ottawa following Clark's June 5 press conference (Takach 1980, 79). A steady stream of letters, telephone calls, telexes, and telegrams—supplemented by "a massive effort of personal representations by literally scores of businessmen"— was targeted at the offices of the three ministers responsible for international trade. So substantial was the flow of comment and information that the foreign service was instructed to bypass the standard departmental filtering process and direct all material received on the Jerusalem embassy issue immediately to the office of the secretary of state for international trade, Michael Wilson (Takach 1980, 79).

Canadian corporate leaders enjoyed free and frequent access to the prime minister throughout the reversal phase of the embassy affair. Arguably the most important meeting of the entire affair occurred on June 22, 1979, when Prime Minister Clark received thirteen of the country's most powerful corporate leaders in his parliamentary offices (Takach 1980, 79–80). Although there is evidence that the decision to reverse the Jerusalem embassy policy was already in the works, it is significant that one day after this meeting Clark announced the appointment of the Stanfield Commission, setting in motion the process by which the government could "withdraw with honor" from its Jerusalem embassy misadventure.

Whether attributed to inordinate influence peddling on the part of the export and oil industry or the traditionally close affinity between big business and the federal Progressive Conservative party, "the business community's concerns found ample expression. The corporate lobby enjoyed a degree of entrée to politicians and bureaucrats throughout the Embassy Affair that no other group came close to equalling" (Takach 1980, 82–83). To the extent that it can be considered a monolith, the Canadian business community acted as an independent constraint upon the CIC's attempt to influence the Clark government not to reverse itself on the Jerusalem embassy question.

Demands for reversal of the embassy pledge also came from noncommercial segments of the domestic political environment. The Canadian Council of Churches reminded the prime minister of Canada's traditional opposition to any unilateral change in the status of Jerusalem and reiterated its call for a unified city under international jurisdiction (Adelman 1980, 17; Bessin and Willmot 1984, 48–52; Takach 1980, 68). The United Nations Association of Canada, at its June 1979 annual meeting, passed a resolution urging the government to reverse its Jerusalem embassy policy on the grounds that a transfer of the embassy would constitute an undermining of both the UN's nonrecognition of Israeli jurisdiction over territories occupied since the June 1967 War and Canada's neutrality on the Arab-Israeli conflict (Takach 1980, 68–69).

· Several prominent academics went on record in opposition to the Conservative government's policy (Takach 1980, 68–70; *Montreal Gazette*, June 19, 1979, A3; *Toronto Star*, June 7, 1979, A6; June 19, 1979, B3). Some analysts have suggested that many academics opposed the embassy transfer because of the broadly held perception that such constituted a departure from "responsible international citizenship'' in Canada's Middle East diplomacy (Takach 1980, 70–72).

There is limited evidence to suggest that either the clergy or the academic community had a direct effect upon the Clark government's decision-making on the embassy question. However, their opposition to the transfer no doubt contributed to the increasingly inhospitable domestic political environment within which the CIC had to function in attempting to influence the government to fulfill its transfer pledge.

Domestic ethnic counterforce groups performed competently though unspectacularly in their attempt to move the Canadian government toward a policy position on Jerusalem antithetical to the interests of Canadian Jewry. To be sure, the argument could be made that Arab Canadians simply rode on the coattails of the protesting Arab ambassadors (working in tacit association with the corporate-bureaucratic lobby) (Stanislawski 1981a). Such an analysis, while essentially correct, is incomplete; it ignores the enhanced politicization of the Arab Canadian community. Throughout the second half of the 1970s, Arab Canadians became increasingly politically active (Abu-Laban 1988). Moreover, the growing respectability in Ottawa of the Arabist perspective, and the concomitant effect of this upon the political fortunes of domestic Arab ethnic interest groups, should be recognized (Abdallah Interview; Resnick Interview; Sharp Interview). As the credibility of the Canada-Israel Committee dipped temporarily under the combined weight of the domestic controversy resulting from the embassy affair and the collapsing confidence and popularity of the Clark government, an increase in the political fortunes of the principal counterforce group, the Arab-Canadian lobby, could be expected. Although they sought to play down its significance, Jewish leaders acknowledged this occurrence (May Interview; Plaut 1981b, 275; Resnick Interview; Rose Interview, 1980).

By the fall of 1979, then, several important elements of the domestic political environment supported a reversal of the Clark government's commitment to transfer of the embassy to Jerusalem. The net effect of these elements was to severely constrain the Canada-Israel Committee's attempt to influence the government to implement the embassy transfer.

In the reversal phase of the embassy affair, the Canada-Israel Committee was at best semiautonomous of the Israeli government. The guidance of the Israelis was evident in at least two ways: by the fact that the Canadian Jewish leadership was seemingly prepared to sacrifice a revitalization of antiboycott legislation in pursuit of the embassy transfer, and in that the CIC continued to pursue the Jerusalem embassy issue long after the fulfillment of Clark's commitment ceased to be a likely outcome of the debate. There is ample evidence of a two-way flow of guidance on the reversal; that is, some leading Canadian Jews attempted to persuade the Israelis to maintain the pressure on Clark even after the policy reversal had been implied through the appointment of the Stanfield Commission (Bick Interview; Dimant Interview; May Interview; Plaut Interview). The failure of the Canada-Israel Committee to adopt a policy line distinguishable from that of Israel's appeared to confirm the suspicions of some Canadian officials that the CIC was merely the handmaiden of Begin and Israeli policies on the Jerusalem question (Former Assistant to the SSEA Interview; Official of the Middle East Division, DEA Interview; Sharp Interview; Stanfield Interview).

Influential members of the decision-making core on the Jerusalem embassy issue contend that the converging of Israeli and Canadian Jewish preferences on the embassy reversal reduced the CIC's capacity to properly perform its function as a bridge between Canadian and Israeli officials (Official of the Middle East Division, DEA Interview; Stanfield Interview). Canadian Jewish leaders concur with this perception (Bessin Interview; Resnick Interview). Some analysts contend that the CIC's influence over the reversal should have benefited from the strengthening of relations between Ottawa and Jerusalem resulting from the embassy initiation (Lyon 1982b). Others argue that the warm Canadian-Israeli friendship resulting from Clark's initiative was an atypical diversion from the pattern prevalent throughout much of the post-October 1973 period (Bick Interview; Stanislawski 1981b). In other words, the cooler interstate relations resulting from the embassy pledge reversal represented a return to normalcy following the brief anomaly of warmer relations associated with Clark's original pledge.

The final variable, level of crisis that the policy issue represents to the interest group and the government, reinforces the image of the CIC's limited influence over the embassy reversal. The committee saw a reversal of the embassy pledge as both a symbolic and tangible threat to several of its cherished values. The threat was tangible to the extent that a reversal would constitute a lost opportunity to achieve a major item on the Canadian Jewish political agenda and symbolic in the sense that community leaders realized that a defeat on the embassy question would both weaken the credibility of the CIC and strengthen the resolve and political influence of domestic counterforce groups (May Interview; Plaut Interview; Resnick Interview). In a word, the CIC viewed the embassy reversal as crucial, and it sought to salvage something positive from a rapidly deteriorating situation.

Canadian foreign policymakers shared the CIC's sense of crisis over the Jerusalem embassy issue, though for different reasons. The Clark cabinet and the Conservative party had been badly hurt by the Jerusalem embassy affair. The image of incompetence resulting from the incident had embarrassed the government and cut deeply into its already diminished stockpile of credibility. Clark needed to find a quick way out of the controversy without completely destroying his personal credibility and mandate to govern. The professional foreign service saw the embassy reversal as imperative in order to extricate Canada from the Middle East morass with the least amount of economic and diplomatic cost. They also saw the reversal as a means to reestablish the "appropriate" relationship between the Prime Minister's Office (PMO) and the Department of External Affairs, and between political and national interests (both of which were seemingly upset by Clark's refusal to accept the department's professional advice concerning the plan to transfer the embassy to Jerusalem) (Official of the

Middle East Division, DEA Interview; Former Assistant to the SSEA Interview). The Canada-Israel Committee's failure to influence Clark not to reverse the embassy pledge is then consistent with the relationship assumed between the level of an ethnic interest group's influence and the extent of the government's perceived stake in a policy issue.

The Clark government's reversal of policy on the Jerusalem embassy issue represents a situation of "least influence" for the Canada-Israel Committee (scored as 1 on the index of influence). While arguing that they were put in a no-win situation—having been handed an unsolicited offer on the status of Jerusalem that they could not reject—Canadian Jewish leaders acknowledge that the Jerusalem embassy affair rapidly turned into a disaster for the Canada-Israel Committee and its ethnic constituency (Dimant Interview; May Interview; Plaut Interview, 1981b; Resnick Interview). As put succinctly by one participant, "The battle for Jerusalem in 1948 was won by the Jews. The battle in 1979 was lost by us in Canada" (Plaut 1981a, 276; Plaut 1981b, 276).

THE LEBANON WAR OF 1982

Overview

The enhanced anxiety felt by the Jewish community about Canadian-Israeli relations resulting from the Jerusalem embassy affair seemingly climaxed with the Israeli invasion of southern Lebanon in the summer of 1982. Since his return to power in 1980, Prime Minister Pierre Trudeau had exhibited a certain shift in his personal perspective toward the Middle East. He appeared more inclined toward a sympathetic view of the right of the Palestinian Arabs to a definable homeland, and he had become increasingly more critical of various aspects of Israel's foreign policy—especially those relating to the occupied territories and the broader Arab-Israeli peace process (Former Assistant to the SSEA Interview; Official of the Middle East Division Interview; Resnick, Interview). This contributed to what a former CIC national executive director describes as an "incremental deterioration" throughout the late 1970s and early 1980s in Canada's policy toward Israel and a fair and just settlement of the Arab-Israeli dispute (Resnick Interview).

Increasingly, Trudeau's criticism of Jerusalem focused on Israel's alleged contribution to the collapse of central authority in Lebanon. On June 5, 1982, Trudeau sent a letter to Israeli Prime Minister Menachem Begin counseling restraint in the face of accelerating PLO attacks upon Israeli settlements in the northern Galilee region, and suggesting that certain Israeli policies over the past months had given "Israel's friends certain cause for concern, to say nothing of its enemies" (*Canadian Middle-East Digest*, September-October 1982, 1). Trudeau reacted strenuously to Israel's military incursion into southern Lebanon on the following day. On June 9 he sent a second letter to Begin, informing the Israeli leader that Canada was "dismayed by the subsequent escalation of the conflict represented by the massive movement of Israeli forces into Lebanon." Although his government understood Israel's "natural concern" for security and "condemned heinous acts of terrorism," Trudeau also informed Begin that he could not "accept the proposition that the present military activities are justified or that they would provide the long-term security that you seek for the Israeli people." The Canadian leader appealed to Begin to withdraw Israel's forces "immediately and unconditionally" from Lebanon, as demanded by United Nations Security Council Resolution 508 (*Canadian Middle-East Digest*, September-October 1982, 1).

By expressing his concern in such unconditional terms, Trudeau seemed to be suggesting that it was the Israeli invasion that was principally responsible for the death and destruction in Lebanon and that only a unilateral Israeli withdrawal would grant to the Lebanese the possibility of "ever returning to normalcy" (*Canadian Middle-East Digest* September-October 1982, 1).

The course of the Lebanon War prompted further change in Canada's position toward Israel and the Palestinian issue. In late July 1982 External Affairs Minister Mark MacGuigan announced that preliminary contacts were being sought with PLO officials in Beirut. Hints were dropped of the possibility of Canada establishing more permanent political relations with that organization at an unspecified future date (*Canadian Middle-East Digest*, September-October 1982, 1–3; *Montreal Gazette*, October 23, 1982, A1). The siege of Beirut, widespread allegations of Israeli complicity in the Sabra and Shatilla refugee camp massacres, and Begin's unequivocal rejection of Reagan's September 1, 1982, plan for Middle East peace, produced a popular sense of frustration with Israel in Ottawa similar to that found in most Western capitals. This frustration widened the gulf between Ottawa and Jerusalem and resulted in a greater willingness on the part of members of the Trudeau cabinet to publicly criticize the Israelis (Former Assistant to the SSEA Interview; Gray Interview; Official of the Middle East Division, DEA Interview; Sharp Interview; Stanfield Interview).

Canada eventually adopted a less strident policy response to Israel's activities in Lebanon. Taking its lead essentially from the American's, Ottawa demanded the withdrawal of all foreign forces from Lebanon and supported the return to sovereignty of the Lebanese central government.

Conceptual Analysis

The Canada-Israel Committee's attempt to influence the official Canadian response to the Lebanon War meets only some of the criteria associated with an influential ethnic interest group. During the Lebanon War, the CIC's level of activity was high, although its activity was constrained somewhat by the atmosphere of animosity prevailing between much of the Jewish community's leadership and senior ministers of the Trudeau cabinet (resulting from Trudeau's rather blunt public criticism of Israel's intervention in southern Lebanon) (Former

Assistant to the SSEA Interview; Official of the Middle East Division, DEA
Interview; Resnick Interview).

The CIC's influence was also constrained by the antagonistic nature of its
policy objectives. Its principal goal was to stop the perceived incremental deterioration in Canada's Middle East policy (Resnick Interview). Although an
attempt was made to place the Lebanese invasion into its "proper" historical
perspective, Canadian Jewish leaders acknowledge that they were generally perceived as defending essentially indefensible Israeli military activities (Bessin
Interview; May Interview; Resnick Interview).[7]

The CIC's concentration on the cabinet and the top echelon of the foreign
service was appropriate, given the statism of Canadian foreign policy-making.
This strategy paid some dividends. Throughout much of the Lebanon War, CIC
officials had fairly regular access to the Department of External Affairs and some
members of the cabinet. The transformation of access into influence was constrained by Trudeau's disaffection for Israel's policies and by a determination
on the part of influential Ottawa insiders to use the Lebanon War as an opportunity
for moving Canadian policy toward a more explicitly pro-Arab perspective (Official for the Middle East Division, DEA Interview). Nevertheless, the CIC's
targets were appropriate, and this fact indicates fairly complete comprehension
of the Canadian foreign policy process on the part of the Canadian Jewish leaders.

The CIC scores well with regard to several aspects relating to the organization
of an influential ethnic interest group. By June of 1982 the CIC had achieved
the status of an institutionalized domestic ethnic lobby. The committee had grown
tremendously during the latter half of the 1970s (despite its failure to achieve
clear political victories in the antiboycott and Jerusalem embassy debates). The
CIC was universally acknowledged as the principal spokesman for Canadian
Jewry on Israel-related questions and had acquired a budget appropriate to its
vastly expanded responsibilities (Bessin Interview; Resnick Interview). Organizationally, the CIC remained federated, role-based, and elitist, although its
consultative and decisional base was being expanded laterally to include more
ex officio members and representatives of other national organizations and local
federations.

Many of the advantages offered by its enhanced organizational sophistication
were effectively offset by a significant weakening during the Lebanon War of
the CIC's ability to maintain communal cohesion. Compared to the severe disputes that they had over the Jerusalem embassy question, CIC leaders were
virtually all of one mind on the Lebanon invasion. This was not the case for
Canadian Jewry as a whole, which at several points during the Lebanese situation
exhibited significant strain and fragmentation. Much of the community supported
Israel's original incursion into southern Lebanon. The goal of eradicating the
threat of PLO terrorism was supported by the majority of Canadian Jews. The
relative ease with which the Israel Defense Forces accomplished this task was
a source of pride to many. The movement of Israeli forces into a military siege

of Beirut and the seemingly indiscriminate bombing of the Lebanese capital were far less well received. News of some type of Israeli complicity in the Sabra and Shatilla tragedies stimulated a wave of soul searching on the part of many Canadian Jews. While the majority suffered in silence, some elements of the Jewish community publicly opposed the policies of Prime Minister Begin and Defense Minister Ariel Sharon (*Montreal Gazette*, July 10, 1982, A3; *Montreal Gazette*, September 29, 1982, B3; *Toronto Star*, September 24, 1982, A21; *Toronto Star*, September 27, 1982, A3).

The Canada-Israel Committee had to undertake a rearguard action: managing intracommunal dissension concerning the Lebanon War while at the same time attempting to confront the anti-Israeli/pro-Palestinian sentiment reportedly prevalent in the federal cabinet, the Department of External Affairs, and Parliament, as well as the media and increasingly large segments of the general public. CIC officials sought to stem the tide of intracommunal dissent by insisting that Canadian Jewry's continued support for Israel did not necessarily mean support for the specific policies and actions of a particular Israeli government. They further argued that intracommunal debate, if reasoned and well timed, is inherent to Zionism and the Jewish political tradition (Canada-Israel Committee 1982; *Canadian Middle-East Digest*, September-October 1982, 1; *Toronto Star*, September 27, 1982, A3). However, the authority of the Canada-Israel Committee to even speak for Canadian Jewry on issues relating to Israel and Canada-Israel relations was questioned by groups such as the Ad Hoc Committee of Concerned Jews, whose representatives claimed that the Canadian Jewish establishment, led primarily by the CIC, "had given the false impression that all Jews support the invasion" (*Montreal Gazette*, June 30, 1982, B1; *Montreal Gazette*, July 20, 1982, A3). Such groups represented but a fraction of Canadian Jewry.[8] Arguments supporting the activities of the CIC far outweighed those critical of it (*Montreal Gazette*, July 10, 1982, A3; *Montreal Gazette*, July 23, 1982, B2; Weinfeld 1982). However, the very fact that the Canada-Israel Committee had to expend valuable political energy defending itself against critics from within the Jewish community, while at the same time defending Israel from attacks from the general Canadian political environment, demonstrates the extent to which Canadian Jewry's traditional consensus on Israel was weakened by the Lebanon War. This intracommunal dissension also reduced, at least temporarily, the CIC's credibility in the eyes of Canadian foreign policymakers (Former Assistant to the SSEA Interview; Gray Interview; Official of the Middle East Division, DEA Interview; Sharp Interview; Stanfield Interview).

By the summer of 1982 Prime Minister Pierre Elliot Trudeau had little desire to foster participatory democracy in the making of foreign policy decisions. Trudeau's brief flirtation with the concept during the late 1960s and 1970s (Kirton 1978) and Joe Clark's fumbling of a populist foreign policy-making process helped to convince Trudeau that the fewer number of nongovernmental actors involved in the consideration of foreign policy, the better (Kirton and Dimock

1983–84). Affected most severely by the return to a tightly confined, statist foreign policy process was the Canada-Israel Committee, which (as already indicated) had several near confrontations with Trudeau during the second half of the 1970s. The existence of an exclusivist Canadian decision-making system (combined with an apparent shift in Trudeau's mind-set on the Palestinian issue generally) inhibited the CIC's effort to ameliorate the deteriorating quality of Canada-Israel relations resulting from the Lebanon War (Bessin Interview; May Interview; Plaut Interview; Resnick Interview).

Important aspects of the domestic political environment contributed to the CIC's inability to influence Ottawa's policy response to the Lebanon War. Israel's incursion into southern Lebanon and the siege of Beirut were not supported by the Canadian public. A November 1982 Gallup Poll asked the following question: "Do you find yourself more in sympathy with the Arabs or the Israelis?" In 1982, thirteen percent of Canadians supported the Arabs (compared to seven percent in 1978 and five percent in 1973); seventeen percent sympathized with the Israelis (twenty-three percent in 1978 and twenty-two percent in 1973); and seventy percent supported neither side or had no opinion on the issue (seventy percent in 1978 and seventy-three percent in 1973) (Canadian Institute of Public Opinion—Gallup Poll, November 27, 1982). CIC officials acknowledge that the near doubling of support for the Arabs between 1978 and 1982 and the six percent decrease in support for the Israelis during the same period were trends that, if maintained over an extended period of time, might significantly affect the way in which Ottawa views the Arab-Israeli conflict (Bessin Interview; Resnick Interview).[9]

The Canadian media's posture on the Lebanon War (and their impact on Ottawa's policy response to the war) remains a matter of considerable conjecture. Some analysts contend that the Canadian print and electronic media presented an unbiased, objective, and factual view of events in Lebanon (consistent with the Canadian tradition of nonpartisanship and detachment from the Arab-Israeli conflict) (Keenleyside, Soderlund, and Burton 1985). Other analysts argue, as did the CIC itself, that the Canadian media's coverage of the Lebanon War was sensationalist, selective, and, moreover, indicative of a growing general bias in media sentiment in the favor of the Arab and Palestinian Arab causes (Abella 1982; Dewitt and Kirton 1989; Kirton, Barei, and Smokum 1985). An interesting aside on this debate is represented by yet another school of thought, which not only acknowledged the Canadian media's bias toward the Arabs during the Lebanon War but claimed that such bias was appropriate in light of Canada's alleged traditional tilt toward Zionism and the state of Israel (Ismael 1984; Lyon 1982a, 1982b; 1984).

The debate continues. The one perspective missing from most analyses of the Canadian media's coverage of the Lebanon War was that of any explicit sympathy toward Israel, suggesting that few within the Canadian media picked up on the CIC's contention that the Lebanon invasion was a reasonable act of self-defense.[10] The failure of the Canadian media to integrate this defense into its coverage of the Lebanon War (in the way that some influential segments of the American media did) added to the CIC's already burdensome lobbying agenda during the summer and fall of 1982.

The federal cabinet was highly critical of Israel's military incursion into southern Lebanon. Guided largely by Prime Minister Trudeau's strong public criticism of Jerusalem, members of the Liberal party's influential Quebec caucus led a major push for an immediate upgrading of Canada's official relations with the Palestine Liberation Organization as an appropriate response to Israel's military actions in southern Lebanon (Dewitt and Kirton 1989). This push was reportedly stalled only by the intervention of influential Liberal senators and party officials (Dewitt and Kirton 1989). Elements of the Canadian foreign service took considerable latitude during the Lebanon War in calling for the adoption of a more discernibly pro-Arab Canadian policy on the Middle East (Dewitt and Kirton 1989; Kirton and Lyon 1989). Typical of the changing mood in Ottawa precipitated by the Lebanon War was the Canadian government's unwillingness to censure the increasingly anti-Israeli comments attributed to Canada's ambassador to Lebanon, Theodore Arcand (Abella 1982; *Montreal Gazette*, July 29, 1982, A1; *Montreal Gazette*, August 7, 1982, B1; *Montreal Gazette*, August 18, 1982, B3). CIC activists acknowledge that the net result of the anti-Israeli mood prevalent within both the federal cabinet and the foreign service was to severely restrict the CIC's attempts to soften Ottawa's official response to the Lebanon War (Bessin Interview; May Interview; Resnick Interview).

In the summer and fall of 1982 Parliament became still another venue for criticism of Israel. All three federal caucuses publicly condemned Israel's military action in Lebanon; moreover, there was a concurrence by all parties on a parliamentary resolution demanding that Israel accede to the United Nations Security Council's call for immediate, unconditional withdrawal from Lebanon (*Canadian Middle-East Digest*, September-October 1982, 3). Some members of Parliament exhibited empathy for Israel (or at least counseled the government of Canada to maintain an even-handed approach toward the Arab-Israeli conflict). However, such voices of moderation were lost amidst the rumble of the anti-Israeli/pro-Palestinian popular and official mood resulting from the Lebanon War. Jewish leaders acknowledge the debilitating impact of such parliamentary sentiment upon the CIC's ability to have Canada hold the line on the Lebanon War.

The sentiments of some influential nongovernmental organizations also shifted significantly as a result of the Lebanon War. The Ontario Federation of Labor (OFL) called for Canadian recognition of the PLO and for the creation of an independent, PLO-dominated Palestinian state in the West Bank and Gaza. Although the declaration was suppressed by the OFL's umbrella group, the Canadian Labour Congress, the OFL's willingness to adopt such a radical policy posture on an issue well beyond its traditional domain of primary concern is typical of the anti-Israeli/pro-Palestinian mood that arose primarily during the Lebanon War and pervaded any number of religious, cultural, and social groups.

The discernible shift in Canadian governmental and popular sympathies resulting from the Lebanon War encouraged Arab Canadians and their supporters to dramatically increase their level of political activity. Throughout the summer and fall of 1982 Palestinian solidarity groups proliferated in virtually every Canadian city and on every Canadian university campus. Although usually controlled from the Arab League and the Palestine Information Offices in Ottawa, such groups also represented the climax of a generation of growth in Arab Canadian political consciousness and an activist Arab Canadian response to the groundswell of sensitivity toward the cause of the Palestinian Arabs (Abdallah Interview; Abu-Laban 1989). Moreover, Arab Canadians were emboldened by the apparent disunity of Canadian Jewry caused by Israel's controversial military activities in Lebanon (Abdallah Interview). The net effect of official criticism of Israel and the new aggressiveness of Arab Canadians was that the Canada-Israel Committee was forced to operate in a much more "crowded" domestic political environment relating to Canada's Middle East foreign policy (an environment that Canadian Jewry had traditionally dominated by default) (Bessin Interview; Bick Interview; Resnick Interview).

Throughout the Lebanon War, the Canada-Israel Committee was perceived by much of official Ottawa as strongly related to the Israeli government. The CIC attempted to present a credible explanation for Israel's invasion of Lebanon and siege of Beirut; however, this was widely perceived by Canadian officials as an exercise in defending the indefensible (Former Assistant to the SSEA Interview; Official of the Middle East Division, DEA Interview; Sharp Interview; Stanfield Interview). CIC activists acknowledge the existence, if not the accuracy, of such perceptions. One went so far as to privately suggest that the popular image of the CIC's inseparability from Israel was reinforced by the lobby group's rather ambiguous response to the Reagan Plan (Resnick Interview).

Although Canada was still among Israel's strongest supporters in the international community, relations between the two countries had become somewhat strained by the early 1980s, further compromising the CIC's ability to influence Canadian policy on the Lebanon War. The rift between Ottawa and Jerusalem widened during the summer of 1982, a consequence largely of Trudeau's public condemnation of Israel's political and military policies toward southern Lebanon. This estrangement inhibited the CIC's performance of its function as a bridge linking Ottawa to Jerusalem. Prominent Canadian Jews experienced relatively good access to the loci of foreign policy decision-making throughout much of the Lebanon War; however, this did not translate into the CIC having influence over Canada's official response to Israel's part in the war (Resnick Interview).

The leadership of the Canada-Israel Committee perceived Ottawa's policy response to the Lebanon War as a threat to many of Canadian Jewry's core values. It feared that unrestrained official Canadian criticism of Israel might contribute to Ottawa's supporting the imposition of threatened international sanctions against Jerusalem and an acceleration in the incremental deterioration in Canada's position vis-à-vis the Palestinian issue (Bessin Interview; May Interview; Plaut Interview; Resnick Interview). The CIC's sense of crisis was heightened by the fact that both during and after the Lebanon War Prime Minister Trudeau and External Affairs Ministers Mark MacGuigan and Allan MacEachen made overt references to Canada's endorsement of the possibility of an independent Palestinian state in the occupied territories (*Canadian Middle-East Digest*, September-October 1982, 1–3; Noble 1983).

The government of Canada, for its part, perceived the Lebanon War as being a crisis of moderate-high intensity. Prime Minister Trudeau reportedly viewed Israel's invasion of Lebanon as problematic for several reasons: it was unlikely to eliminate the threat of PLO terrorism; the war in Lebanon threatened to escalate into a superpower confrontation; and, depending on how the government responded to events in Lebanon, Canada might stand to lose profitable commercial investments in the Arab world (Official in the Middle East Division, DEA Interview; Stanfield Interview).

The Canada-Israel Committee's attempt to influence Ottawa's official response to the Israeli invasion of Lebanon is scored as 2, representing a situation of moderate-least influence. The Trudeau cabinet, through its outright condemnation of Israel's actions, adopted a policy line diametrically opposed to that preferred by the Canada-Israel Committee (which sought to have Canada demand the withdrawal of all foreign armies, Arab and Israeli, from Lebanon). The one redeeming aspect of the affair was that—while implying to do so—the Trudeau government did not use the Lebanon War as an opportunity to dramatically upgrade Canada's diplomatic relations with the PLO (that did not occur until March 1989).

THE PALESTINIAN DISTURBANCES, DECEMBER 1987– DECEMBER 1988[11]

Overview

Between the end of the Lebanon War and the initiation of the intifada, relations between Canada and Israel could best be described as cordial yet cool. Although Prime Minister Trudeau backed away from his implied threat to upgrade relations with the PLO as an appropriate Canadian response to Israel's conduct of the Lebanon invasion, an element of strain was still vividly apparent. This was tellingly manifested by the report of the Standing Senate Committee on Foreign Affairs, published in June 1985, concerning Canada's relations with the countries of the Middle East and North Africa. Although wide ranging in its scope, the Standing Committee's report gave considerable attention to the Arab-Israeli conflict and the Palestinian issue. It was critical of Israel's policy on Jewish settlements in the occupied territories. It affirmed the Canadian government's respect for the legitimate political rights of the Palestinian Arabs and criticized Israel's alleged intransigence concerning implementation of the autonomy plan formulated at Camp David. And, while not prepared to recognize the Palestine Liberation Organization as the sole representative of the Palestinian people, the committee's report nevertheless recommended a widening of official contacts with the PLO (Canada. Standing Senate Committee on Foreign Affairs 1985, 7–68). The controversial report was effectively shelved by the new prime minister, Brian Mulroney, who chose to move cautiously on the delicate matters of Canada-Israel and Canada-PLO relations (Kirton and Lyon 1989).

Strains were nevertheless emerging. Canada refused to accredit Israel's proposed military attaché to Ottawa, General Amos Yaron, privately citing Yaron's part in the Lebanon invasion (Kirton and Lyon 1989, 199). And Canada's delegation at the United Nations and other international forums reverted to an earlier practice of abstaining on resolutions critical of Israel's policies in the occupied territories, rather than voting against them (Stein 1983). However, Canada continued to reject resolutions supporting self-determination for the Palestinians, explaining that self-determination is frequently assumed to be synonymous with independence; Canada's favoring of Palestinian self-determination would then effectively prejudge the outcome of negotiations (*Globe and Mail*, September 3, 1987, 2).[12]

The thin tightrope Mulroney sought to walk between support for Israel and defense of Palestinian political rights and struggles between the Prime Minister's Office and the professional foreign service officers at the Department of External Affairs for control over Canada's Middle East policy characterized Canada's response to the first year of the intifada.

The Palestinian disturbances produced the type of foreign policy-related controversy seldom experienced in Canada (beyond the narrow confines of the Canada-United States relationship). From the outset, there was widespread criticism of Israel's allegedly excessive management of the disturbances. However, such criticism was significantly moderated by the initial response of the prime minister. In his annual year-end television interview with the Canadian Broadcasting Corporation (CBC), Brian Mulroney declared that Israel had shown considerable "restraint" in its handling of the disturbances. He also declared "false and odious" any attempt to compare the situation in the occupied territories with that in South Africa (CBC transcript, December 21, 1987).

The first indication of serious divergence of Canadian opinion on the intifada emerged two days after the prime minister's television interview. On December 24, 1987, it was announced that an assistant deputy minister in the Department of External Affairs, Marc Brault, had written to the Saudi Arabian ambassador, expressing Canada's "profound concern" over Israel's actions in the occupied territories (*Globe and Mail*, December 24, 1987, A9).

In mid-January 1988 External Affairs Minister Joe Clark called in Israel's ambassador, Israel Gur-Arieh, for what has been described as a tough "dressing down." While Clark did not lodge a formal complaint at the time (concerning Israeli Defense Minister Yitzhak Rabin's promulgation of an "iron fist" policy and CBC allegations that Israeli forces were deliberately withholding food supplies from Palestinian refugee camps), the secretary of state reportedly had been stern in saying things "that sometimes need to be said between friends" (*Toronto Star*, January 22, 1988, A5). Later in January 1988 Prime Minister Mulroney seemingly relented from his adamant support of Israel: "There have been changes on an ongoing basis. The profile is changing. Secretary of State Joe Clark has stated our concern about developments in that area. He said food ought not to be used as a weapon" (*Toronto Star*, January 23, 1988, A1, A4).

Throughout January and February 1988 the popular criticism of Israel's actions reached unprecedented proportions. It spread throughout many of the media and to all sides of the House of Commons (Canada, House of Commons, *Debates*, January 17, 1988; *Montreal Gazette*, January 30, 1988, B6; *Calgary Herald*, February 18, 1988).

Canada's criticism of Israel climaxed with Secretary of State Clark's address to the annual policy conference of the Canada-Israel Committee on March 10, 1988. Over one thousand parliamentarians, civil servants, and Canadian Jews attended the CIC's parliamentary dinner on March 9. Prime Minister Mulroney took the unprecedented step of making a brief appearance at the predinner reception. The following day the conference participants heard from the leader of the federal New Democratic party, Ed Broadbent, and from the leader of the Liberal party, John Turner. The conference's last scheduled speaker was External Affairs Minister Clark. He stepped into a highly charged atmosphere and appeared tense, perhaps anticipating the type of reaction his comments were likely to elicit from the partisan audience.

Clark's address was mainly a stinging attack on Israel's alleged violation of the human rights of West Bank and Gaza Palestinians. According to Clark, Israeli soldiers were using human rights abuses as "deliberate instruments of the so-called 'iron fist' policy, designed to re-establish control by force and fear." The daily violence inflicted upon Palestinian civilians, he said, "tears at our consciences and our hearts as it tests our convictions." Clark's charges against Israel continued: "The use of live ammunition to restore civilian order, the withholding of food supplies to control and collectively penalize civilian populations, the use of tear gas to intimidate families in their homes, of beatings to maim so as to neutralize youngsters and pre-empt further demonstrations, have all been witnessed these past months" (Canada. Department of External Affairs, 1988, 2–3). When members of the audience charged that his facts were unfounded or deliberately misleading, Clark responded boldly: "I learned long ago that disputing reality won't change reality" (Author's personal transcript).

Clark's address was soon disrupted by the audience's response to the minister's claim concerning the peaceful intentions of moderate Arab states: "My discussions with the leaders of Jordan, Saudi Arabia, and Egypt leave me in no doubt that they seriously want a just and lasting peace, and to that end are willing to lend their assistance in negotiations" (Canada, Department of External Affairs 1988, 4). His intimation that Israel was the stumbling block to peace caused many in the audience to perceive a complete about-face in Canada's Middle East policy; a noisy exit by perhaps 50 members of the audience of approximately 400 began.

Lost in the commotion was Clark's declaration of Canada's support for the Shultz peace initiative and his call to the Palestinians to accept Israel's right to exist alongside a Palestinian homeland in the West Bank and Gaza. Also lost was Clark's suggestion that the Canadian government sponsor a dialogue between Arab and Jewish Canadians (Canada. Department of External Affairs 1988, 7).

After the minister concluded his remarks, the CIC chairman, Winnipeg lawyer Sidney Spivak, admonished Clark for his criticisms of Israel, suggesting that many of his accusations—especially concerning the withholding of food—were "myths that became facts." Spivak also hinted at electoral retaliation: "Israel will have an election . . . as will we soon" (Author's personal transcript). Emerging from a postconference emergency meeting of its executive committee, the CIC demanded, "a definitive clarification of [Canada's] policy immediately" (*Canadian Jewish News*, March 17, 1988, 1). The president of the Canadian Jewish Congress termed Clark's intimation that Israel was primarily responsible for the failure of peace efforts in the Middle East "grotesque": "It is the refusal of the Arab states to recognize Israel that is the root cause of the conflict. . . . Mr. Clark's inability to perceive the Arab-Israeli conflict within the context of history, rather than relating to isolated incidents, is a serious failure on his part" (*Canadian Jewish News*, March 17, 1988, 1).

In the immediate aftermath of Clark's speech considerable efforts were made to calm the waters between the Conservative government and the Jewish community. A delegation from the CIC met with Clark, and although Clark refused to retract any of his allegations the mood was reportedly cordial and somewhat relaxed—there was an implied "agreement to disagree" (Willmot Interview). The prime minister sent a personal letter to the CIC chairman Spivak. While expressing concern with the violence in the occupied territories, Mulroney also declared unambiguously Canada's continued support for Israel: "Canadian policy toward Israel is clear, consistent and unchanged: Israel is our friend. Israel has a right to exist in peace, to be recognized by its neighbors and to be secure. This is an unshakable commitment" (*Toronto Star*, March 25, 1988, A22). Such sentiment was underscored by Clark. In an address before the Jewish community of Edmonton, Alberta, Clark declared that Canada is "a firm and unyielding friend of Israel. . . . Canada will protect, defend and endorse the State of Israel forever" (*Globe and Mail*, April 20, 1988, A11). Although obviously displeased with Clark's refusal to back down from his various allegations concerning Israel's alleged human rights violations, CIC spokesmen declared general satisfaction with the different tone and emphasis of Mulroney's letter and Clark's Edmonton speech: "It's pretty clear the government has made a serious effort to address concerns and has gone a long way towards meeting them" (*Globe and Mail*, April 20, 1988, A11).

A modus vivendi of sorts had seemingly been reached between the Mulroney government and Canadian Jewry. The same could not be said of Canadian Jewry and the media. From the outset the media had been critical of Israel's handling of the intifada. In the immediate aftermath of Clark's CIC speech, this media criticism of Israel's actions was coupled with widespread comment on the alleged dual loyalty of Canadian Jews: "Que les membres en regle du comite Canada-Israel penseront a Israel quand ils voterant au Canada? Est-ce qu'on peut avoir deux parties et une *double loyalte*? Il est vria que les cardinaux de la sainte Eglise sont citoyens du Vatican. Mais cette qualite ne les entraine pas a trahir leur patrie charnelle" ("Do the members of the Canada-Israel Committee think about Israel when they vote in Canada? Do they have dual-loyalty? It is true that Cardinals of the Roman Catholic Church are citizens of the Vatican. But this does not affect their patriotism to their native land.") (*La Presse*, March 12, 1988, 7. Translation by author. Emphasis added). Similar comments were articulated in the English-language press, including the *Toronto Star* and the *Ottawa Citizen* (Aikenhead 1988, 13–14; Hayes 1988, 31–35, 56, 60, 62).

Clark's speech to the CIC and its aftershock represented the climax to Canada's response to the first year of the intifada. However, less dramatic domestic controversies also occurred. The convening of a symposium involving a select group of 30 Arab Canadians and Canadian Jews in late April 1988 went virtually unnoticed. The meeting, held at the luxury resort of Montebello, Quebec, was organized by the Canadian Institute for International Peace and Security on behalf of the Department of External Affairs. It resulted from the proposal raised at the end of External Affairs Minister Clark's March 10, 1988, speech to the Canada-Israel Committee to have the federal government sponsor an ongoing dialogue between Canadian Arabs and Jews about the Arab-Israeli conflict and Canada's role in it (Canada, Department of External Affairs 1988, 7). The proposal was all but forgotten amidst the furor of the Jewish community's response to other aspects of Clark's speech.

The convention, nonetheless, attracted the attention of articulate conservative elements within the Canadian Jewish community, many of whom claimed after the fact that they had been denied invitations to participate in the conference because of the organizers' predisposition to stack the deck with moderates from both sides (Waller 1988). Critics also charged that those Jews who did attend the Montebello meeting—many of whom were associated with Peace Now—were unrepresentative of the mainstream of Canadian Jewish opinion on Israel and the Arab-Israeli conflict (Waller 1988). They charged additionally that the tremendous secrecy with which Montebello was organized was an inappropriate way for a democratic state to go about making its foreign policy on controversial matters: or more to the point, that it was not the place of Canadian Jews, or of Canadian Arabs for that matter, to decide how Israel and the Arab states should go about making peace (Waller 1988). These accusations were strenuously denied by several of the Canadian Jews who participated in the Montebello discussions (Confidential interviews by author). Nevertheless, the dispute caused further fragmentation to a Canadian Jewish community already under tremendous strain. (Willmot Interview).

In early May 1988, Geoffrey Pearson, outgoing director of the Canadian Institute for International Peace and Security, announced that a planned second meeting at Montebello had been postponed indefinitely. This represented the denouement of Canada's 1988 posturing on the Middle East.

National events overshadowed the Middle East. The House of Commons was dissolved for national elections and the election campaign was dominated by the debate over the proposed free-trade agreement with the United States. Canada's official response to Arafat's November-December 1988 peace offensive was decidedly low key. Much to the chagrin of Arabists in Ottawa, Prime Minister Brian Mulroney—returned to power with an overwhelming majority of the vote—declared that Canada "was not in a race" to follow the U.S. lead concerning relations with the PLO (*Toronto Star*, January 7, 1989, A3). The first year of the intifada ended relatively quietly in Ottawa. It was not until the spring of 1989 that changes occurred in Canadian policy.

Conceptual Analysis

In seeking to influence Canada's policy response to the Palestinian disturbances, the Canada-Israel Committee met some, but not all, of the criteria generally associated with an influential ethnic foreign policy interest group.

The committee's level of activity was high. It lobbied aggressively, convened its annual parliamentary dinner and policy conference, and published and distributed two handbooks (one on responding to criticism of Israel's handling of the disturbances, the other a briefing book on lobbying effectively during the impending federal election campaign).

The CIC's policy objectives were largely reactive and nonconstructive. Its goal was to hold the line against attempts by Arabists to use the intifada as an opportunity to press Ottawa toward a shift in Canadian policy, involving, at a minimum, an upgrading of relations with the PLO (Dewitt 1988). The CIC's timing was purely reactive; there were few other substantive issues on the Canadian-Israeli political agenda (and, hence, little opportunity for the CIC to divert attention away from the intifada).

From the outset of the disturbances, the primary targets of the CIC's lobbying were avowed friends within the federal cabinet, including the prime minister. The goal was to exploit Brian Mulroney's proven sensitivity toward Israel and Jewish community concerns in order to counterbalance the Arabist mood prevailing at the Department of External Affairs (Kirton and Lyon 1989). The CIC also sought to lobby friends of Israel within Parliament and the media to counter the rising tide of anti-Israel popular sentiment resulting from daily doses of sensationalist media coverage of events in the occupied territories.

Strategically, the CIC sought to downplay the significance of the disturbances. It criticized the media for biased and sensationalized reporting and denied (and, when possible, tried to prove fallacious) alleged Israeli human rights excesses. The Canadian Jewish lobby tried to focus attention upon (1) the "real cause" of the Arab-Israeli conflict (that is, the refusal of all Arab states, except Egypt, to recognize and negotiate peace treaties with Israel) and (2) the dubious human rights records of the Arab states and the PLO (Canada-Israel Committee 1988a, 1988b).

In terms of timing and strategy, the CIC benefited somewhat from the intervention of the federal election campaign. The committee was able to imply the application of electoral sanctions against politicians deemed excessive in their criticism of Israel. However, this strategy was only partially successful, primarily because of the extent to which the free-trade issue dominated the election campaign. (Paradoxically, this was beneficial to the CIC's lobbying interests, in the sense of temporarily getting Israel out of the headlines of daily media coverage).

The CIC demonstrated itself to be a well-organized and fairly institutionalized ethnic lobby. It had, in the aftermath of the Jerusalem embassy and Lebanon cases, broadened its participatory domain extremely to include a wider spectrum of Canadian Jews (although membership in the national organization was still formally role-based). Regardless of these organizational advances, the CIC suffered from a significant fragmentation of intracommunal cohesion. Throughout the intifada the CIC was attacked from all quarters within the Jewish community: the left accused it of being too quick to launch a strident defense of Prime Minister Shamir's policies in the occupied territories and the right attacked the CIC for not being strident enough (Aikenhead 1988, 13–14). One CIC activist suggests that one of the primary factors contributing to the stridency with which External Affairs Minister Clark addressed the Canada-Israel Committee was the (ultimately inaccurate) belief that the majority of Canadian Jews had significantly modified their attitudes concerning Shamir and Israel's policies in the territories (confidential interview with CIC official). It was further suggested that this belief was fostered by a few Canadian Jews associated with the Department of External Affairs and prominent within the camp of Peace Now. The CIC's inner core remained fairly cohesive throughout the Palestinian disturbances.

Initially, important dimensions of the formal decision-making system impacted positively upon the CIC's lobbying efforts. The committee was able to exploit the prime minister's December 1987 public defense of Israel's actions, as well as the long-standing struggles between Mulroney and Clark for dominance over the Progressive Conservative party, and between the Prime Minister's Office and the Department of External Affairs for control over Canada's Middle East policy (Kirton and Lyon 1989). However, as media reports continued unabated, and as pressure from within the cabinet and the Conservative party's caucus reportedly mounted, Mulroney's support of Israel weakened, as did his willingness to battle Clark and Arabists at External Affairs. To be sure, contentious debates continued to rage within the federal cabinet; however, they were now less over *whether* to publicly distance Canada from Israel and shift Ottawa's official position toward the Palestinians and the PLO, but *when* and *how* to do so at the least political cost to the Conservative party.

Much of the foreign service had consistently opposed the alleged pro-Israel tilt to Canada's Middle East policy and advocated, at a minimum, an upgrading of relations with the PLO as an appropriate response to the intifada (Kirton and

Lyon 1989). Initially, the foreign service was constrained by Mulroney's decidedly pro-Israeli stance. The prime minister's wavering represented an opportunity for the Arabists to win the day. Even so, they were constrained by Mulroney's inclination to proceed slowly on the Middle East, especially in an election year. The real opportunity for policy adjustment did not present itself until the change in U.S. policy in mid-December 1988: the Mulroney government, on March 30, 1989, announced the upgrading of relations with the PLO to the ambassadorial and ministerial level.

The CIC's lobbying effort was adversely affected by the response to the Palestinian disturbances of several influential segments of the domestic political environment. A majority, fifty-three percent of respondents to a national popular opinion survey, disapproved of Israel's handling of the rioting. Twenty-three percent characterized themselves as pro-Israeli while fourteen percent described themselves as pro-Arab. A majority of respondents claimed no preference for either side (*Globe and Mail*, March 30, 1988, A1). Another poll found that twenty percent of Canadians blamed Israel alone for the violence in the occupied territories; twenty percent put the onus solely on the Palestinians, while twenty-four percent blamed both sides equally. A majority of those expressing an opinion believed that the media's coverage of the intifada had been fair, as had been Joe Clark's criticism of Israel at the CIC's national conference (*Calgary Herald*, April 2, 1988, A1).

The media played a central role in constraining the CIC's attempt to hold the line on Ottawa's response to the intifada. The media's coverage brought a sharp reaction from the organized Jewish community. The media were condemned for one-sided and superficial reporting, for having been manipulated by the PLO, and for having an obsession with Israel's every move (*Canadian Jewish News*, January 21, 1988, 11; *Canadian Jewish News*, January 28, 1988, 20; *Canadian Jewish News*, February 25, 1988, 27; *Canadian Jewish News*, March 10, 1988, 19; *Canadian Jewish News*, May 26, 1988, 12; Hayes 1988; *Globe and Mail*, February 19, 1988, A7; *Toronto Star*, January 19, 1988, A15). Although many Jews were troubled by the Canadian media's reporting of events in the occupied territories, they were more deeply offended by the dual loyalty charges that arose in the immediate aftermath of Clark's CIC speech: "Canadian ethnic groups remain particularly vulnerable to the disloyalty charge. Can one imagine those lobbying against free trade being smeared as disloyal? Would the [Toronto] *Star* feel it necessary to remind pro-life or pro-choice groups that they are Canadian? Obviously not. Why then is it necessary for ethnic communities to be subject to this form of abuse when exercising their rights as Canadians?" (Troper 1988, 3).

During the first year of the intifada, Parliament was a forum for strong, bipartisan criticism of Israel. Typical of the sometimes impassioned criticisms were remarks by the New Democratic party's parliamentary critic on human rights: "When thousands of people are imprisoned in camps, when even children protesting their oppression as they must fall before lethal ammunition, and when the nations of the world condemn the excesses of the occupying army of Israel, our Prime Minister commends the restraint of the oppressive conqueror'' (Canada. House of Commons 1988, 2401).

Parliamentary criticism of Israel crossed party lines. A rump group within the Conservative caucus associated with the Canada-Arab World Parliamentary Association pressed the cabinet for formal condemnation of Israel's actions. Similar groups were active within the Liberal and New Democratic caucuses. The mood of their rank and file was reflected in the words of the leaders of the two federal opposition parties. In his address to the Canada-Israel Committee conference, New Democratic leader Ed Broadbent declared unyielding support for Israel; however, he also expressed his personal outrage at Israel's actions in putting down the disturbances and affirmed his party's recognition of the PLO as a suitable negotiating party for Israel. Liberal party leader John Tucker rejected the PLO's status, but reaffirmed his party's position that the Palestinians have the right to a homeland in the West Bank and Gaza Strip (Author's personal transcript). And Prime Minister Mulroney, while rejecting demands from within the Conservative caucus for a dramatic change in Canadian-Israeli relations, made clear his displeasure with Israel's actions. This was achieved by his backing away from his initial defense of Israel and his office's reported approval of the text of External Affairs Minister Clark's speech to the Canada-Israel Committee (*Toronto Star*, March 25,1988, A22; Confidential interviews by author with CIC officials).

Several influential NGOs were overt in their criticism of Israel's handling of the intifada. The Canadian Labour Congress passed a resolution in May 1988 strongly condemning Israel for "senseless and brutal violence," and called for an independent PLO standing at an international peace conference on the Middle East (*Canadian Jewish News*, May 19, 1988, 12). The Canadian Council of Churches issued a resolution calling for PLO participation in all negotiations, the withdrawal of Israel from all territory occupied in the 1967 War (including East Jerusalem), and the establishment of a sovereign Palestinian state in the occupied territories (*Canadian Jewish News*, May 19, 1988, 12). In January 1989 the council presented a brief, prepared by its Middle East Working Group, before a meeting of various NGOs with the Department of External Affairs in preparation for the 45th session of the United Nations Commission on Human Rights. The brief, highly critical of Israel's alleged human rights abuses in the territories, prompted a formal response from the Canada-Israel Committee and various other national Jewish agencies (Confidential interviews by author with CIC officials; Confidential B'nai B'rith memorandum). In June 1989 the Council of Canadian Catholic Bishops and the United Church of Canada added their voices to forceful criticism of Israel's Palestinian policies (*Canadian Jewish News*, June 8, 1989, 3). CIC officials acknowledge that the anti-Israel postures adopted by so many influential NGOs were detrimental to organized Canadian Jewry's attempt to contain official Canadian criticism of Jerusalem's actions (Willmot Interview).

A final segment of the domestic political environment significantly upgraded its level of activism in Ottawa during the intifada—Arab Canadian counterforce groups. In early January 1988 the National Council on Canada-Arab Relations, directed by a former Liberal MP from Quebec, Ian Watson, released a letter critical of Prime Minister Mulroney's claim about Israeli "restraint." The letter was signed by twenty-seven individuals, including members of Parliament, several members of the Ottawa-based Middle East Study Circle, former diplomats, and academics (Abu-Laban 1988). The Canadian Arab Federation and other Arab community groups organized public demonstrations in Toronto, Montreal, and Ottawa, and provided a steady stream of letters to the editors of major national newspapers. The Palestine Information Office (the designated representative of the PLO in Canada), and its director, Abdallah Abdallah, provided logistical support and literature to the domestic ethnic constituency. The Arab ambassadors to Ottawa met several times with the External Affairs minister, lobbying for a more forceful Canadian condemnation of Israel. As it had in the Lebanon War, the counterforce Arab ethnic lobby made significant political advances in Ottawa during the intifada at the expense of the Canada-Israel Committee (which was perceived by many Ottawa insiders as attempting to defend Israel's indefensible behavior).

The international political environment worked against the interests of the Canada-Israel Committee. Canadian officials were exposed to daily film footage of events in the occupied territories. Whether accurate or biased, such coverage affected the moral sensibilities of Canadian foreign policymakers. This news coverage prompted an increased concern in Ottawa for the human and political rights of the Palestinian Arabs, which upset Ottawa's attempt to balance friendship and support toward Israel with respect for the legitimate rights of the Arabs (Bercuson forthcoming; Dewitt 1988). The resulting decisional confusion was reflected in Canada's voting behavior at international forums: a greater willingness to criticize Israel's human rights record but—as at the Quebec francophone summit—a hesitance to approve the call for Palestinian self-determination.

Many professional foreign service officers found such policy confusion embarrassing and contrary to Canada's international interests. For them, Canada's primary international priorities included the maintenance of Canada's image as an honest broker in the Middle East and the distinguishing of Canadian policy from the decidedly pro-Israeli stand of the Reagan administration in the United States (Kirton and Lyon 1989; Lyon 1988). Also pressing Canadian officials was the need to maintain credibility with the nonaligned bloc of nations, so as to secure Canada's nomination in the fall of 1988 as a nonpermanent member of the United Nations Security Council. It was generally conceded that one of the best ways to secure the nomination was for Ottawa to establish a harder line toward Israel (Goldberg and Taras 1989, 213–14; Kirton and Lyon 1989; Lyon 1988). Finally, several foreign service officers were reported to have quietly voiced their concern about the extent to which the political interests of the Prime Minister's Office were inhibiting the achievement of Canada's core international priorities (Dewitt 1988, 12).

Under the circumstances, the CIC's relations with the prime minister and his immediate staff did remain fairly strong. However, the anti-Israel/pro-Palestinian mood prevailing throughout much of Ottawa adversely affected the CIC's ability to contain criticism of Israel or serve as an effective bridge between Ottawa and Jerusalem.

The Canada-Israel Committee viewed the intifada as a threat to its most basic values, both in a symbolic and actual sense. Symbolically, official Canadian criticism of Israel's actions was tantamount to desertion by one of Israel's closest international friends and further isolation of the Jewish state. In addition, there was the very real possibility that Arabists in Ottawa would use Israel's controversial handling of the Palestinian disturbances as an opportunity to reinforce the incremental deterioration in Canadian-Israeli relations over the Palestinian issue ongoing since the mid-to-late 1970s. This deterioration, it was feared, might take various forms: Ottawa's sanctioning of commercial relations with Jerusalem, a shift in Canada's voting at the UN in support of overtly anti-Israeli resolutions, or a dramatic upgrading of relations with the PLO (Willmot Interview). There was, finally, a palpable concern expressed by Jewish officials that the Canadian response to the intifada might cause further—and perhaps permanent—fracturing of Canadian Jewish attitudes on Israel (Willmot Interview).

The government of Canada, for its part, perceived the issue as being of moderate-high crisis intensity. For Prime Minister Brian Mulroney and his immediate advisers, there was an electoral imperative; that is, the political costs to be paid by the Progressive Conservative party for the anti-Israel tone adopted by Canadian officials, including External Affairs Minister Joe Clark. Mulroney was also reportedly concerned about having Canada move too quickly on the Middle East issues because they threatened to direct attention away from the greater goal of achieving the free-trade agreement with the United States and because Mulroney personally found the PLO untrustworthy (Kirton and Lyon 1989). The Prime Minister's Office was also concerned about keeping control of foreign policy beyond the grasp of the apolitical technocrats at the Department of External Affairs (Dewitt 1988; Kirton and Lyon 1989).

Secretary of State Clark and the professionals at External Affairs saw the Palestinian disturbances as an opportunity to move Canadian policy on the Middle East in a direction closer to the mainstream of international opinion. Not to take advantage of the situation would mean resigning Canada to a position of diplomatic isolation (along with the United States and Israel), with attendant losses to Canada's credibility and its likely election to the UN Security Council. By the end of December 1988 the Clark/External Affairs perspective came to prevail in official Ottawa—resulting in the upgrading of relations with the PLO the following March. This supports the theory of an inverse relationship between the level of an ethnic lobby's influence and the government's level of concern with a particular foreign policy issue.

The Canada-Israel Committee was clearly unhappy with the explicit criticism of Israel voiced by the highest authorities in the Canadian government (including the Secretary of State for External Affairs), as well as the concomitant deterioration in Israel's—and its own—credibility among key political and societal elements. Particularly disturbing was the perceived attempt, unprecedented in Canadian foreign policy, by the government to domesticize the Arab-Israeli conflict and to drive a wedge between various segments of Canadian Jewry (Confidential interviews with CIC officials). Although significantly troubled by these developments (and their possible long-term ramifications for Canadian-Israeli relations), CIC spokesmen were moderately satisfied at the end of December 1988 by the fact that Canada's official policy on the Middle East and the Arab-Israeli conflict remained unchanged. Joe Clark and others may have publicly criticized Israel's actions but no sanctions had been applied. Canadian delegations continued to reject (or abstain from voting on) resolutions overtly critical of Israel or supportive of Palestinian self-determination. And, most important, Canada had not upgraded its relations with the Palestine Liberation Organization (Willmot Interview). This unchanged Canadian policy had the effect of ameliorating somewhat a difficult situation for the Canada-Israel Committee. The situation was obviously less than satisfactory, but not yet desperate. (The CIC's sense of dissatisfaction, of course, increased with the upgrading of Canada-PLO relations in March 1989.)

SUMMARY

Based on the criterion of ethnic interest group influence used in this study, the following results are discerned concerning the influence of the Canada-Israel Committee over Canada's Middle East policy between October 1973 and December 1988 (table 6).

Table 6
The CIC and Canada's Middle East Policy, 1973–1988

	Degree of Influence				
Event	5	4	3	2	1
1973 War		X			
PLO in Canada		X			
Boycott				X	
Embassy Initiation	X				
Embassy Reversal					X
Lebanon				X	
Palestinian Disturbances				X	

NOTES

1. See, for example, the *Globe and Mail*, July 16, 1975, A7; *Montreal Gazette*, July 14, 1975, A5; *Montreal Star*, July 16, 1975, A6; *Winnipeg Tribune*, July 18, 1975, 3; and *Time*, July 18, 1975, 23, and August 4, 1975, 19.

2. The Commission on Economic Coercion and Discrimination was headed by McGill University law professor Irwin Cotler and was composed of a number of highly respected individuals from the political and academic domain, including a former Liberal cabinet minister and the former leader of the federal New Democratic party. It was mandated to examine the political, economic, and social ramifications for Canadians of the Arab boycott of Israel as well as other forms of economic, political, and religious discrimination. Its final report, published in January 1977, was highly critical of the Canadian government's handling of evidence about the knowing acquiescence by Canadian private companies and public agencies to discriminatory practices demanded by Arab governments (See Canada. Commission on Economic Coercion and Discrimination 1977).

3. The Province of Manitoba also considered the application of antiboycott legislation. Although never enacted, such consideration "illustrated the widespread support which anti-boycott efforts could achieve" (Stanislawski 1981b, 284).

4. For example, a headline in the June 8, 1979, *Ottawa Journal* declared that "Arabs Threaten Economic 'War' Against Canada" (A1). The *Montreal Star* of the same day reported that "The Arab's Reply Could Cost 55,700 Jobs" (A1). The *Toronto Star*, in a June 8 editorial entitled "A Bad Foreign Policy Move," implored Ottawa to "give up the [embassy] promise as contrary to Canada's peacekeeping interest and its economic ties with the Arab world" (A1).

5. The mandate of the Stanfield Commission of Inquiry was actually much broader. The commission was asked to place the Jerusalem embassy question within the context of Canada's overall relations with the Middle East and to provide "recommendations on ways of developing our relations with all the countries of the Middle East and North Africa to take full advantage of the many interests we share, and on the implementation of our policy on Jerusalem in a way that will be compatible with the efforts that are being made to achieve a comprehensive peace settlement in the Middle East" (Canada. Department of External Affairs 1979; *Final Report of the Special Representative of the Government of Canada Respecting the Middle East and North Africa* 1980).

6. In an editorial entitled "Tell the Arabs Where to Go," the *Toronto Star*, on June 23, 1979, called the lobbying campaign for policy reversal "unconscionable propaganda coupled with frequently undiplomatic moves by Moslem diplomats in Ottawa." The *Toronto Sun* recommended that Canada make it known that its foreign policy "is made in Ottawa, not in Baghdad, Riyadh, Teheran—or Jerusalem" (*Toronto Sun*, June 21, 1979, 7). And the *Ottawa Citizen* decried "the Arab arrogance" on the embassy issue and recommended that "Canada should simply ignore that rudeness and blackmail and refuse to be intimidated" (*Ottawa Citizen*, July 25, 1979, 10).

7. As indicated by the Canada-Israel Committee, the proper historical context concerning the Israeli invasion of Lebanon included the following: the destruction that the so-called Syrian peacekeepers had inflicted upon the authority of the Lebanese central government, and especially upon Lebanon's Christian population, since the civil war of 1975–1976; the way in which the PLO, with the support and concurrence of the governments of Syria, Libya, and the Soviet Union, had transformed the southern half of Lebanon into a veritable headquarters of international terrorism; and the way in which

the PLO had used the July 1981 cease-fire with Israel as an opportunity both to rearm itself and to strike violently at Israeli and Jewish targets throughout the world (*Canadian Middle-East Digest*, September-October 1982; Canada-Israel Committee, 1982).

8. The Ad Hoc Committee, for example, claimed a total membership of fifty persons and was confined to the Montreal area (*Montreal Gazette*, July 10, 1982, A3; *Montreal Gazette*, July 23, 1982, B2). Similar groups located elsewhere in the country drew equally small numbers.

9. A survey commissioned by the Canada-Israel Committee found that by a proportion of about two-to-one (fifty-eight percent to thirty-three percent), Canadians approved rather than opposed Israel's 1982 incursion into Lebanon (Bessin and Willmot 1984, 43–46). The editors of the report nevertheless acknowledged that "Canadians were unsure whether Israel's rooting out of the PLO would accomplish Israel's primary objective—the removal of the PLO threat to Israel" (Bessin and Willmot 1984, 46).

10. See, for example, *Calgary Herald*, June 29, 1982, 1; July 27, 1982, 3; *Globe and Mail*, June 30, 1982, A1; July 6, 1982, A3; July 9, 1982, A7; July 21, 1982, A13; *Montreal Gazette*, July 10, 1982, A1; *Toronto Star*, July 17, 1982, A1; September 27, 1982, A1; October 19, 1982, A14; November 11, 1982, A7; *Vancouver Sun*, July 10, 1982, A3; September 29, 1982, A3; October 2, 1982, A13; October 12, 1982, A10; November 30, 1982, A13; *Winnipeg Free Press*, July 15, 1982, 7; July 19, 1982, 13; July 29, 1982, 11; October 11, 1982, 16.

11. A version of this section is to be found in two articles contributed by the author to *The Domestic Battleground: Canada and the Arab-Israeli Conflict*, edited by David Taras and David H. Goldberg (Montreal: McGill-Queen's University Press, 1989).

12. Such explanations drew critical fire from the Arab states and reportedly also from within the Canadian foreign service. The foreign service perceived losses in terms of Canada's international credibility and standing as an honest broker in the Arab-Israeli conflict if Canada continued to lag behind much of the rest of the world in recognizing self-determination for the Palestinian Arabs (Lyon 1988, 17–18; Lyon and Kirton 1989, 191).

6

Findings and Conclusions

This study has, to this point, examined separately the relationship between the various criteria of analysis and American and Canadian Jewry's respective levels of influence over their government's policies toward the Middle East and the Arab-Israeli conflict between 1973 and 1988. However, in order to produce generalizable conclusions about the relationship between the variables and the level of influence of an ethnic foreign policy interest group, it is necessary that the two pro-Israel lobbies be systematically compared. It is to this task that much of this concluding chapter is directed.

FINDINGS: LEVEL OF INFLUENCE

Based on the criterion of ethnic interest group influence employed in this book (that is, the extent to which a government's response to a particular policy issue parallels the preferences articulated by the group), the findings in tables 7 and 8 are discovered concerning American and Canadian Jewry's respective influence over policy for the Middle East from October 1973 to the end of December 1988.

BEHAVIORAL ATTRIBUTES

Activity

The level of activity of both AIPAC and the Canada-Israel Committee were high throughout much of the 1973–88 period. The only variance for AIPAC occurred during the antiboycott campaign, when Jewish community leadership was taken formally by a triumvirate of national Jewish defense organizations.

Table 7
AIPAC's Scoring on the Index of Influence

	Degree of Influence				
Event	5	4	3	2	1
1973 War	X				
Kissinger's Diplomacy	X				
Boycott	X				
Carter's Diplomacy				X	
F-15s					X
AWACS					X
Lebanon				X	
Palestinian Disturbances				X	

Table 8
CIC's Scoring on the Index of Influence

Event	5	4	3	2	1
1973 War		X			
PLO in Canada		X			
Boycott				X	
Embassy Initiation	X				
Embassy Reversal					X
Lebanon				X	
Palestinian disturbances				X	

The CIC's level of activity was moderate during both the 1973 war and the PLO in Canada issue, primarily because it had to share political leadership with various ad hoc groups and assorted influential individuals and other semiautonomous groups. Nevertheless, Canadian Jewry was actively involved in the lobbying process. Level of activity, then, does not explain considerable variance between AIPAC and the CIC.

Policy Objectives

A positive relationship is anticipated between a group's level of influence and its articulation of constructive policy objectives. During the 1973–88 period, AIPAC and the CIC each adopted policy objectives that were both antagonistic and constructive in character. While this may help explain the less-than-complete level of influence experienced by each group in particular cases, the pattern, as such, does not provide much comparative insight.

Targets and Strategies

Similarly, the targeting and strategies of each group suggest a limited basis for comparison. Each ethnic lobby exhibited considerable comprehension of its respective government's policy-making process and an ability to play by the rules of that process. The only significant variation from this understanding was the Canada-Israel Committee's targeting during the Jerusalem embassy reversal. At that time, there was considerable confusion as to who was making decisions resulting from the transfer of power to the Progressive Conservatives and Prime Minister Joe Clark's struggle to establish control over the Canadian foreign service.

Timing

Somewhat more significant comparative findings are revealed with regard to the timing of each group's lobbying activities. AIPAC's inclination toward relations with both the executive and congressional/legislative branches of American government and the CIC's concentration on the prime minister, cabinet, and senior civil service suggest differing perceptions of likely lobbying success, which may, in turn, reflect broader structural differences in the distribution of effective foreign policy decision-making authority within the presidential-congressional system and the parliamentary form of government.

In summarizing the behavioral attributes category, it appears that the most important difference between AIPAC's and the CIC's experience relates to the timing of each's lobbying activities, suggesting a greater distinction relating to the structure of the governmental system in which an ethnic interest group must operate.

ORGANIZATIONAL CHARACTERISTICS

Level of Institutionalization

Throughout the 1973–88 period AIPAC exhibited many of the traits usually associated with an institutionalized ethnic interest group. The same cannot be said for the Canada-Israel Committee. In both the 1973 War and the PLO in Canada case, the CIC was at best fledgling in an organizational sense; it was lacking in several of the more basic characteristics of institutionalization. And, although it had achieved far greater organizational sophistication by the late 1970s, the Canadian Jewish lobby wavered between mature and institutionalized status on the Jerusalem embassy pledge. This was primarily due to the severe intraorganizational disputes concerning the organization's appropriate strategic response to Joe Clark's election campaign pledge to transfer the embassy to West Jerusalem.

Structure and Cohesion

An examination of the two groups with regard to the structure and cohesion dimension of the organizational variable offers further comparative insight. AIPAC is formally autonomous of all other American Jewish organizations; many of its members and executive officers also may be affiliated with other national agencies and local Jewish federations, but membership in AIPAC is open rather than role-based. And because it is a registered lobby, AIPAC's financing must be based on private, taxable contributions. In contrast, the Canada-Israel Committee is a fully federated organ of the national Canadian Jewish community. Formal membership is role-based, being confined to representatives of B'nai B'rith, the Canadian Jewish Congress, and the Canadian Zionist Federation (and, since the late 1970s, also to delegated representatives of other national organizations and local federations). The CIC's budget is established in concurrence with a community agency—the National Budgeting Conference— and is therefore dependent on the allocations provided by its constituent organizations and the budgetary demands of other community-supported agencies.

Intraorganizational cohesion is another area of significant difference between AIPAC and the CIC. AIPAC exhibits a slightly greater tendency toward intraorganizational uniformity, although significant strains began to emerge within the American Zionist lobby during the Lebanon War and (especially) the Palestinian disturbances. By contrast, the Canada-Israel Committee demonstrates a tendency toward only moderate levels of cohesion. The Yom Kippur War witnessed a tremendous level of community solidarity. But the mounting of a united national lobbying campaign was constrained by the tendency of various groups to operate independently of each other. The PLO in Canada issue failed to catalyze the entire Canadian Jewish population. The Jerusalem embassy affair—both its initiation and reversal—caused significant fragmentation at the CIC's inner core;

community leaders failed in their attempts to keep internal dissent over the issue in-house. And although internal cohesion was maintained, the Lebanon War and the intifada resulted in a marked weakening of the Canada-Israel Committee's credibility among influential elements of its principal constituency, the Canadian Jewish community. The comparative findings for this index suggest that the organization of the ethnic interest group, and its level of internal cohesion, have a large bearing on its level of influence over government policy.

STRUCTURE OF THE DECISION-MAKING SYSTEM

The data for the two test groups provide some important comparative insight concerning the assumed relationship between the level of an ethnic interest group's influence over foreign policy decision-making and the structure of the formal decision-making process. A particularly important part of this structure is the extent to which the system and political culture generally are open and receptive to interventions in the policy process by nongovernmental groups and organizations.

Although there are some important exceptions, the evidence suggests that throughout the 1973–88 period AIPAC was working in an American political culture that was (both constitutionally and attitudinally) receptive to nongovernmental group intercession in the making of foreign policy. By contrast, during much of the same time period the Canada-Israel Committee was confronted by a decisional environment characterized by its closedness and exclusivity. A direct consequence of this environment was a severe delimiting of the influence of domestic groups operating in the Canadian system, especially those—like the CIC—concerned with controversial foreign policy questions. The only significant variation from this was Prime Minister Joe Clark's brief flirtation in 1979–80 with a populist policy process (involving the formal inclusion of NGOs and communities with vested interests in the outcome of the foreign policy issue under consideration). The complete failure of that experiment, manifested in the unprecedented domestic controversy resulting from the Jerusalem embassy affair, forced Clark to quickly return to a more traditional, isolated style of foreign policy-making. The net effect was adverse consequences for the CIC's attempt to influence the outcome of the Jerusalem debate and all subsequent Israel-related issues confronting the Canadian government during the 1980s.

The openness of the American process relative to its Canadian counterpart allowed AIPAC to exploit fairly effectively intragovernmental rivalries endemic to the U.S. system of government in order to protect Israel's interests. The CIC sought to behave in a similar fashion as its American counterpart, especially by exploiting the pro-Israel sensitivities of Prime Minister Brian Mulroney and the power struggles between his office and the Department of External Affairs. However, the CIC frequently came up against the realities of a tightly centralized and insular foreign policy-making process (increasingly controlled, CIC activists believed, by individuals holding images of the Middle East antithetical to Israel's concerns). Although, by the end of December 1988, AIPAC also was confronted by a more decidedly Arabist foreign policy bureaucracy in Washington, its activists were able to counter much of this sentiment by targeting other loci of decisional authority in the American system.

The comparative examination of each group's relationship with the formal decision-making system represents an important independent indicator of different levels of influence experienced by AIPAC and the CIC during the period of October 1973-December 1988. This analysis, in turn, suggests that the structure of the decision-making system within which it must function will have a significant impact upon the level of political influence experienced by an ethnic foreign policy lobby group.

DOMESTIC POLITICAL ENVIRONMENT

Various aspects of the domestic political environment also help to explain differences between AIPAC and the CIC.

Public Opinion

Israel received considerably greater popular support in the United States than in Canada. To be sure, there was variation (mostly slippage) in popular support in response to specific policies of particular Israeli governments. This was most pronounced in the latter part of the period under consideration, especially relating to the Lebanon War and the Palestinian disturbances. Nevertheless, general support for the state of Israel remained strong, significantly greater than that for the Arabs. By contrast, Canadian popular opinion has traditionally been less overtly supportive of Israel. While attentive Canadians have generally favored Israel over the Arabs by a fairly wide margin (between three to one and four to one), the most relevant finding of public opinion surveys over the past forty years has been the significant proportion of Canadians that had no opinion about or felt no sympathy toward either side of the Arab-Israeli conflict. Such widespread ambivalence represented an important constraint upon the influence of the Canada-Israel Committee in the 1973–88 period.

It is hypothesized that the greater the popular support for an ethnic interest group and its core concerns, the greater its influence over policy relevant to its interests. Based on the evidence discovered in this study, it must be concluded that AIPAC had a distinct advantage over the Canada-Israel Committee in this regard.

Media

Similar conclusions are achieved concerning relations between the North American Zionist lobbies and their respective national media. The American media demonstrated a measure of support for Israel throughout a good segment of the 1973–88 period. Significant variation from this theme was found only in the latter portion of the period, when specific issues of concern to AIPAC activists became entangled in U.S.-Israeli controversies over Jerusalem's political policies and military behavior in Lebanon and the occupied territories. Although this media criticism was intense, it never reached what might be considered crisis proportion. Even at the height of the controversial Lebanon War and the intifada, elements of the American media remained generally supportive of Israel or at least attempted to place Israel's actions into their proper historical and political context. This support appeared to have a moderating effect upon governmental and popular criticism of Israel and American Jewry.

The Canadian media, on the other hand, tended to reflect the public's ambivalence toward the Middle East and the Arab-Israeli conflict. To be sure, in specific cases the CIC received moderate-high support from segments of the elite media or indeed established working coalitions with them (the role of the *Globe and Mail* in breaking and pursuing the Arab boycott issue is a case in point). However, such cooperation was more the exception than the rule in CIC-media relations. The Jerusalem embassy affair, Lebanon, and the intifada all resulted in strong media criticism of Israel and, increasingly, of Canadian Jewry's alleged dual loyalty in support of Israel. Such allegations created an air of tension between much of the organized Jewish community—represented by the Canada-Israel Committee and its constituent agencies—and the influential Canadian media.

Alliances

The findings with respect to alliances and alliance formation provide further evidence of AIPAC's greater potential influence relative to the CIC's. In the early part of the 1973–88 period, AIPAC maintained moderate-high relations with the White House and the foreign policy establishment. Although these relations dropped to a moderate level in the latter part of the period (especially concerning Carter's diplomatic strategy and the F-15s), even at the worst of times AIPAC was able to keep open the lines of communication. By contrast, the CIC maintained poor-moderate relations with the federal cabinet throughout much of the 1973–88 period, with the possible exception of during the Jerusalem embassy initiation and the earliest days of the intifada (when Prime Minister Brian Mulroney defended Israel's actions as restrained). This is not to suggest that the CIC was not without a degree of access to the Canadian government on specific issues of concern. However, if influence is measured by the extent to which governmental policy resembles that preferred by an ethnic interest group, then the CIC's access to government infrequently resulted in influence.

Legislative Process

Throughout much of the 1973–88 period, AIPAC maintained important ties with influential segments of the U.S. Congress, primarily in the Senate. The only deviation occurred (temporarily) during the Lebanon War and over the intifada. To be sure, such alliances were not always helpful. A case in point is Congress's inability to confront Carter's nonlegislative diplomatic strategy and the defeat of congressional measures disapproving the sale of F-15s and AWACS to Saudi Arabia. However, in those legislative defeats, AIPAC and the pro-Israel congressional coalition were able to defend Israel's broader concerns and to achieve passage of important aid concessions for Jerusalem. And the Lebanon War and the Palestinian disturbances, while certainly resulting in temporarily reduced congressional patience with the government of Israel, did not constrain Congress from either appropriating substantial military and financial assistance to Israel or opposing the Reagan administration's proposed sale of weapons to Saudi Arabia and Jordan.

Canadian Jewry has always enjoyed friendly relations with individual members of Parliament. However, such support has rarely resulted in definitive pro-Israeli government policy. Various factors explain this incongruence: parliamentary indifference toward the Middle East and a preoccupation with domestic political matters (as in October 1973); a lack of policy consensus within Parliament (as in the boycott issue); and the cabinet's general indifference toward the foreign policy concerns articulated by governmental backbenchers or members of the opposition parties. On most issues during the 1973–88 period, at least one federal political party offered general support to Israel; however, unless it was the governing party that held such a posture, there was no assurance that parliamentary sympathies would be translated into government policy.

Nongovernmental Organizations

Further differences between the CIC and AIPAC are suggested by their alliances with other nongovernmental organizations. Although both AIPAC and the CIC had relations with NGOs in their respective political systems, AIPAC appeared to have had greater success in maintaining such ties during much of the 1973–88 period (and in turning them to Israel's favor). Even at the height of the Lebanon War and the Palestinian disturbances, Israel received the formal support of the leadership of the AFL-CIO labor movement and the Christian fundamentalists, as well as influential segments of the Black congressional caucus and other ethnocultural communities. The CIC, by contrast, appeared to have less success in achieving and maintaining societal alliances. The climax of several years of acrimony with a powerful traditional ally, the United Church of Canada, occurred as a result of the Yom Kippur War. The Jerusalem embassy affair, both its initiation and reversal phases, caused a number of traditionally friendly or indifferent societal groups to openly criticize Israel and Canadian Jewry. This was also the case with the Lebanon War. The Palestinian disturbances precipitated even more significant shifting in the positions of many NGOs on the Arab-Israeli conflict, including the Canadian Labour Congress, the Canadian Council of

Churches, the United Church of Canada, and the Council of Canadian Catholic Bishops.

Counterforce Groups

There is very little difference between AIPAC and the CIC on the matter of domestic Arab counterforce groups. In both the United States and Canada, the level of activity and the perceived respectability of Arab ethnic and pro-Arab groups increased as the 1973–88 period progressed. In both countries, an enhanced political consciousness on the part of North American Arabs and the closing of the gap that had traditionally prevailed between the Zionists and their ethnic political adversaries occurred. Since AIPAC and the CIC confronted the same types of development by counterforce groups, this factor does not explain different levels of influence experienced by the American and Canadian Zionist lobbies.

The comparative findings for this category suggest that AIPAC should have been moderately more influential than the Canada-Israel Committee, based upon its relations with important dimensions of the domestic political environment. These results generally suggest that an ethnic interest group's success is very much dependent upon the domestic political environment in which it must operate.

INTERNATIONAL POLITICAL ENVIRONMENT

Theorists anticipate a correlation between an ethnic lobby's freedom of maneuverability vis-à-vis a foreign government and its level of influence over its own government's foreign policy process. The two subject groups vary slightly on this point. AIPAC demonstrated a fairly strong inclination toward semiautonomous relations with the state of Israel. AIPAC officials most certainly interacted on a regular basis with their Israeli counterparts, but they also had independent sources of funding and information. The one significant exception to this was AIPAC's reliance upon the overly optimistic reports of battlefield conditions coming from the Israeli embassy in the early days of the Yom Kippur War. However, the potential damage to its credibility resulting from the conduct of Israel's military campaign in the 1982 Lebanon War contributed to AIPAC's taking a posture on the Reagan peace plan at variance to that of the Begin government's. Some AIPAC officials also publicly criticized Israel's policies in handling the Palestinian disturbances between December 1987 and December 1988.

The Canada-Israel Committee is formally independent of Jerusalem and the Israeli embassy in Ottawa. However, on occasion the committee was perceived as too ready to accept Jerusalem's guidance or at least reticent to diverge from support of Israel's policies, good or bad. An example of this is offered by the CIC's lackluster response to the Reagan plan; little attempt was reportedly made to follow AIPAC's lead in finding something positive to say about Reagan's initiative. And, in the Palestinian disturbances, elements within the Jewish community associated with the Peace Now movement criticized the CIC for its being too quick to articulate a strident defense of Israel's hard-line policies. Several current and former Canadian foreign policy officials voiced the opinion that the Canada-Israel Committee's perceived lack of freedom from the Israelis reduced its credibility and influence over the policy process.

The comparative findings discerned in regard to the international political environment variable suggest that AIPAC has been moderately more influential than the Canada-Israel Committee. More generally, the findings suggest the importance of relations between a home government and an ethnic interest group's foreign policy concern in determining the influence of the group: the ethnic foreign policy lobby exists primarily because of its relationship with the foreign concern; it is, in turn, affected by the foreign government's policies and behavior.

THE POLICY ISSUE

Theorists suggest an inverse relationship between an ethnic foreign policy interest group's level of influence over a policy issue and the intensity with which its government feels concerned about that issue. The relationship holds in most cases for both AIPAC and the CIC. In those cases in which the level of government concern was high (for example, the Yom Kippur War, the F-15 and AWACS sales, and Lebanon for AIPAC, and the boycott, embassy reversal, and Lebanon for the CIC), the influence of the two Zionist lobbies tended to wane. The only significant variation from the anticipated relationship occurred, for AIPAC, with regard to Kissinger's diplomatic strategy, and for the CIC, in the Jerusalem embassy initiation. In those two cases, the Zionist lobbies had a considerable degree of influence *despite* their respective government's high degree of concern with the policy issues at stake. Therefore, this index does not appear to represent a powerful—or reliable—explanation of an ethnic interest group's level of influence over government policy.

CONCLUSIONS

Several conclusions are derived from the data presented in this book. The most basic, perhaps, is that neither AIPAC nor the Canada-Israel Committee were as influential in dealing with a series of crisis issues confronting them and their ethnic constituencies during the October 1973-December 1988 period as they themselves or their detractors considered them to be. Neither the American nor the Canadian Zionist movements demonstrated any extended capacity to directly affect the quality or substance of policy toward the Arab-Israeli conflict adopted by their respective governments during the period between October 1973 and December 1988, the end of the first year of the intifada.

Beyond this general assertion, however, it does appear that AIPAC was moderately more influential than its Canadian counterpart. This conclusion has little to do with the different levels of interest in the Middle East expressed by Washington and Ottawa. Rather, as the comparative data indicate, it relates to differences between the two groups based on organizational, structural, and environmental factors. Organizationally, AIPAC was better suited to represent the Israel-related concerns of American Jewry. Its formal independence from all other organizations and its level of organizational sophistication were in marked contrast to the CIC's federated structure and the often severe limits imposed upon its agenda-setting and priority-setting by its dependence on others within the community for funding. The CIC also frequently needed to spend valuable political resources resolving disputes internal to the organization before even beginning the process of lobbying the government on issues relevant to Canadian-Israeli relations. And the structure of the American decision-making system, moreover, provided AIPAC with opportunities for influence beyond compare with those experienced by the Canada-Israel Committee. The American system is correctly characterized as a weak state and a strong society in the sense that the officially designated decision makers have only limited capacity to disregard the demands of societal groups. The American brand of liberal pluralism, warts and all, is generally more receptive than its Canadian counterpart to intervention in the public policy process by well-organized and motivated NGOs (Dahl 1967, 1976; Lowi 1967, 1979).

Ultimately, it is the organization of the two ethnic lobbies and the different ways in which the American presidential/congressional and the Canadian parliamentary structures of government relate to NGOs generally (and ethnic interest groups in particular) that most distinguish AIPAC from the Canada-Israel Committee. The most important comparative finding of this book is the following: for an ethnic interest group to increase its likely influence over its government's foreign policy, it must organize itself to fit the parameters and structural constraints of the political system in which it must function.

Bibliography

BOOKS, MONOGRAPHS, AND THESES

Abella, Irving, and Troper, Harold. *None Is Too Many: Canada and the Jews of Europe, 1933–1948*. Toronto: Lester and Orpen Dennys, 1982.

Abraham, Sameer Y., and Abraham, Nabeel, eds. *The Arab World and Arab-Americans: Understanding a Neglected Minority*. Detroit: Wayne State University, 1981.

————, eds. *Arabs in the New World: Studies on American Arab Communities*. Detroit: Wayne State University, 1983.

Abu-Laban, Baha. *An Olive Branch on the Family Tree: The Arabs in Canada*. Ottawa: Minister of Supply and Services Canada, 1980.

American-Arab Anti-Discrimination Committee. *ADC Resources*. Washington, D.C.: Anti-Discrimination Committee, 1984.

American Council for Judaism. *Christian Opinion on Jewish Nationalism and a Jewish State*. Philadelphia: American Council for Judaism, 1944a.

————. *Zionism and Judaism*. Philadelphia: American Council for Judaism, 1944b.

————. *The Anglo-American Committee of Inquiry*. New York: American Council for Judaism, 1946.

American Jewish Committee. *Ethnic Lobbying: An American Tradition*. New York: American Jewish Committee, Institute of Human Relations, 1976.

————. *The Arab Boycott and American Law: A Brief Guide for Companies Active in the Middle East*. New York: American Jewish Committee, 1979.

————. *Decades of Decisions: A Brief History of the American Jewish Committee*. New York: American Jewish Committee, Institute of Human Relations, 1983.

American Jewish Congress. *American Law vs. the Arab Boycott: A Memorandum to the President of the United States*. New York: American Jewish Congress, 1975.

Arnold, Abraham J. *Jewish Life in Canada*. Edmonton: Hurtig Publishers, 1976.

Bailey, Harry A., Jr., and Katz, Ellis, eds. *Ethnic Group Politics*. Columbus, Ohio: Charles E. Merrill Publishing, 1969.

Bauer, Raymond A.; de Sola Pool, Ithiel; and Dexter, Lewis Anthony. *American Business and Public Policy: The Politics of Foreign Trade*. New York: Atherton Press, 1964.

Bavly, Dan, and Salpeter, Eliahu. *Fire in Beirut: Israel's War in Lebanon with the PLO*. New York: Stein and Day, 1984.

Benesh, John. "Canadian Images of the Middle East: Conflict and Implication for Canada's Middle East Foreign Policy to 1977." Master's thesis, School of International Affairs, Carleton University, Ottawa, 1979.

Bentley, Arthur F. *The Process of Government*. Bloomington, Ind.: Principia Press, 1908.

Bercuson, David J. *Canada and the Birth of Israel*. Toronto: University of Toronto Press, 1985.

Berger, Elmer. *Why I Am a Non-Zionist*. Flint, Mich.: Myron Winegarden, 1942.

———. *A Partisan History of Judaism*. New York: Devin-Adair Company, 1945.

———. *The Jewish Dilemma*. New York: Devin-Adair Company, 1951.

———. *Judaism or Jewish Nationalism? The Alternatives to Zionism*. New York: Bookman Associates, 1957.

———. *Memoirs of an Anti-Zionist Jew*. Beirut: Institute for Palestine Studies, n.d.

Berlin, William S. *On the Edge of Politics: The Roots of Jewish Political Thought in America*. Westport, Conn.: Greenwood Press, 1978.

Bessin, Shira Herzog, and Kaufman, David, eds. *Canada-Israel Friendship: The First Thirty Years*. Toronto: Canada-Israel Committee, 1979.

Bessin, Shira Herzog, and Willmot, Robert. *Issues and Answers: A Handbook for Community Advocacy*. Toronto: Canada-Israel Committee, 1984.

Blitzer, Wolf L. *Between Washington and Jerusalem: A Reporter's Notebook*. New York: Oxford University Press, 1985.

Bookbinder, Hyman, and Abourezk, James A. (moderated by David Shipler). *Through Different Eyes: Two Leading Americans, A Jew and an Arab, Debate U.S. Policy in the Middle East*. Bethesda, Md.: Adler and Adler, 1987.

Brecher, Michael. *Decisions in Crisis: Israel, 1967 and 1973*. Berkeley and Los Angeles: University of California Press, 1980.

Brewer, Thomas L. *American Foreign Policy*. Englewood Cliffs, N.J.: Prentice-Hall, 1980.

Brookings Institution. *Toward Peace in the Middle East: Report of a Study Group*. Washington, D.C.: Brookings Institution, 1975.

Brzezinski, Zbigniew. *Power and Principle: Memoirs of the National Security Adviser, 1977–1981*. New York: Farrar, Strauss, Giroux, 1983.

Canada-Israel Committee. *The Arab Boycott: Implications for Canada*. Montreal: Canada-Israel Committee, 1976a.

———. *Canadian Foreign Policy in the Middle East*. Ottawa: Canada-Israel Committee, 1976b.

———. *Middle East Agenda and Government Policy*. Ottawa: Canada-Israel Committee, 1977.

———. *Briefing Book: "Celebrating Forty Years of Canada-Israel Friendship."* Ottawa: Canada-Israel Committee, 1988a.

———. *On Violence in the Territories and the Pursuit of Regional Peace*. Toronto: Canada-Israel Committee, 1988b.

————. *The Canadian Government and Effective Community Action*. Toronto: Canada-Israel Committee, 1988c.

————. "Jerusalem: An Historic and Legal Review." Toronto: Canada-Israel Committee. Mimeo. N.d.

Canada-Palestine Committee. *The PLO and the Toronto Crime Conference*. Ottawa: Canada-Palestine Committee, 1975.

Carter, Jimmy. *Keeping Faith: Memoirs of a President*. New York: Bantam Books, 1982.

Chafets, Ze'ev. *Double Vision: How the Press Distorts America's Views of the Middle East*. New York: Morrow and Company, 1985.

Chill, Dan S. *The Arab Boycott of Israel: Economic Aggression*. New York: Praeger Publishers, 1976.

Clement, Wallace. *The Canadian Corporate Elite: An Analysis of Economic Power*. Toronto: McClelland and Stewart, 1975.

Cohen, Bernard C. *The Press and Foreign Policy*. Princeton, N.J.: Princeton University Press, 1963.

Cohen, Naomi W. *Not Free to Dissent: The American Jewish Committee, 1906–1966*. Philadelphia: Jewish Publication Society of America, 1972.

————. *American Jews and the Zionist Idea*. New York: Ktav Publishing House, 1975.

Cotler, Irwin. *Report of the Commission of Economic Coercion and Discrimination*. Montreal: 1974b.

Dahl, Robert A. *Congress and Foreign Policy*. New York: Harcourt, Brace and Co., 1950.

————. *A Preface to Democratic Theory*. Chicago: University of Chicago Press, 1956.

————. *Who Governs? Democracy and Power in an American City*. New Haven, Conn.: Yale University Press, 1961.

————. *Pluralist Democracy in the United States*. Chicago: Rand McNally and Company, 1967.

————. *Democracy in the United States: Promise and Performance*. 3d ed. Chicago: Rand McNally and Company, 1976.

————. *Dilemmas of Pluralist Democracy: Autonomy vs. Control*. New Haven, Conn.: Yale University Press, 1982.

Daly, John Charles, ed. *What Should Be the Role of Ethnic Groups in U.S. Foreign Policy?* Washington, D.C.: American Enterprise Institute for Public Policy Research, 1980.

Davidowicz, L., and Goldstein, L. *Politics in a Pluralist Democracy*. New York: American Jewish Committee, Institute of Human Relations, 1963.

Davis, Moshe, ed. *The Yom Kippur War: Israel and the Jewish People*. New York: Arno Press; Jerusalem: Institute of Contemporary Jewry, 1974.

Dayan, Moshe. *Story of My Life: An Autobiography*. New York: Warner Books, 1976.

————. *Breakthrough: A Personal Account of the Egypt-Israel Negotiations*. New York: Alfred A. Knopf, 1981.

Dewitt, David B., and Kirton, John J. *Canada As a Principal Power: A Study in Foreign Policy and International Relations*. Toronto: John Wiley and Sons Canada, 1983a.

Drinan, Robert F. *Honor the Promise: America's Commitment to Israel*. Garden City, N.Y.: Doubleday and Company, 1977.

Eayrs, James. *Canada in World Affairs: October 1955 to June 1957*. Toronto: Oxford University Press, 1959.

————. *The Art of the Possible: Government and Foreign Policy in Canada*. Toronto: University of Toronto Press, 1961.

Eckstein, Harry. *Pressure Group Politics: The Case of the British Medical Association*. London: George Allen and Unwin, 1960.

Ehrmann, Henry W., ed. *Interest Groups on Four Continents*. Pittsburgh: University of Pittsburgh Press, 1958.

Elazar, Daniel J. *Decision-Making in the American Jewish Community*. Philadelphia: Jewish Community Studies Group, 1972.

————. *Community and Polity: The Organizational Dynamics of American Jewry*. Philadelphia: The Jewish Publication Society of America, 1980.

Elliott, Jean Leonard, ed. *Immigrant Groups: Minority Canadians*, vol. 2. Scarborough, Ont.: Prentice-Hall of Canada, 1971.

Emerson, Steven J. *The American House of Saud: The Secret Petrodollar Connection*. New York: Watts, 1985.

Feuerwerger, Marvin C. *Congress and Israel: Foreign Aid Decision-Making in the House of Representatives, 1969–1976*. Westport, Conn.: Greenwood Press, 1979.

Findley, Paul. *They Dare to Speak Out: People and Institutions Confront Israel's Lobby*. Westport, Conn.: Lawrence Hill and Company, 1985.

Ford, Gerald R. *A Time to Heal: The Autobiography of Gerald R. Ford*. New York: Harper and Row, 1979.

Forrest, A. C. *The Unholy Land*. Toronto: McClelland and Stewart, 1971.

Fuchs, Lawrence. *The Political Behavior of American Jews*. Glencoe, Ill.: Free Press, 1956.

————, ed. *American Ethnic Politics*. New York: Free Press, 1968.

Garson, G. David. *Group Theories of Politics*. Sage Library of Social Research, vol. 61, Beverly Hills, Calif.: 1978.

Geltman, Max. *The Confrontation: Black Power, Anti-Semitism, and the Myth of Integration*. Englewood Cliffs, N.J.: Prentice-Hall, 1970.

Gephart, Jerry C., and Siegel, Michael. "A Study in Persuasion: The Arab and Israeli Propaganda Campaigns in America." Ph.D. diss., University of Utah, 1973.

Gerson, Louis L. *The Hyphenate in Recent American Politics and Diplomacy*. Lawrence, Kans.: University of Kansas Press, 1964.

Ghareeb, Edward. *Split Vision: Arab Portrayal in the U.S. Media*. Washington, D.C.: Institute of Middle Eastern and North American Affairs, 1977.

Gilboa, Eytan. *American Public Opinion toward Israel and the Arab-Israeli Conflict*. Lexington, Mass.: Lexington Books, 1987.

Glazer, Nathan, and Moynihan, Daniel Patrick. *Beyond the Melting Pot: The Negroes, Puerto Ricans, Jews, Italians, and Irish of New York City*. 2d ed. Cambridge, Mass.: MIT Press, 1970.

Glazer, Nathan, and Young, Ken, eds. *Ethnic Pluralism and Public Policy: Achieving Equality in the United States and Britain*. Toronto: Lexington Books/D.C. Heath and Company, 1983.

Glock, Charles, and Stark, Rodney. *Christian Beliefs and Anti-Semitism*. New York: Harper and Row, 1966.

Golan, Matti. *The Secret Conversations of Henry Kissinger: Step-by-Step Diplomacy in the Middle East*. New York: Quadrangle/The New York Times Book Company, 1976.

Goldin, Milton, *Why They Give*. New York: Macmillan, 1976.

Gottesman, Eli, ed. *Canadian Jewish Reference Book*. Ottawa: Supply and Services Canada, 1964.

Green, Stephen. *Taking Sides: America's Secret Relations with a Militant Israel*. New York: Macmillan, 1984.

Grose, Peter. *Israel in the Mind of America*. New York: Alfred A. Knopf, 1983.

Haig, Alexander M. *Caveat: Realism, Reagan and Foreign Policy*. New York: Macmillan, 1984.

Halperin, Samuel. *The Political World of American Zionism*. Detroit: Wayne State University Press, 1961.

Halpern, Ben. *The Idea of the Jewish State*. Cambridge, Mass.: Harvard University Press, 1961.

———. *Jews and Blacks: The Classic American Minorities*. New York: Herder and Herder, 1971.

Louis Harris and Associates. *A Survey of the Attitudes of Americans Toward the Arab-Israel Conflict and Toward Jews in the United States*. 1974.

Hart, Arthur Daniel, ed. *The Jewish in Canada*. Toronto: Jewish Publications, 1926.

Hershberg, Marshall Amnon. "Ethnic Interest Groups and Foreign Policy: A Case Study of the Activities of the Organized Jewish Community in Regard to the 1968 Decision to Sell Phantom Jets to Israel." Ph.D. diss., University of Pittsburgh, 1983.

Hertzberg, Arthur, ed. *The Zionist Idea*. New York: Atheneum, 1979.

Howe, Russell, and Trott, Sarah. *The Power Peddlers*. New York: Doubleday, 1977.

Huff, Earl Dean. "Zionist Influences Upon U.S. Foreign Policy: A Study of American Policy toward the Middle East from the Time of the Struggle for Israel to the Sinai Conflict." Ph.D. diss., University of Idaho, 1971.

Humphreys, David. *Joe Clark: A Portrait*. Ottawa: Deneau and Greenberg, 1978.

Hurewitz, J. C., ed. *Oil, the Arab-Israel Dispute, and the Industrial World: Horizons of Crisis*. Boulder, Colo.: Westview Press, 1976.

Isaac, Real Jean. *Breira: Counsel for Judaism*. New York: Americans for a Safe Israel, 1977.

Isaacs, Stephen D. *Jews and American Politics*. Garden City, N.Y.: Doubleday and Company, 1974.

Ismael, Tareq, ed. *Canadian Arab Politics: Policy and Perspective*. Ottawa: Jerusalem International Publishing House, 1984.

———, ed. *Canada and the Arab World*. Edmonton: University of Alberta Press, 1986.

Kalb, Marvin, and Kalb, Bernard. *Kissinger*. Boston: Little, Brown and Co., 1974.

Kallen, Evelyn. *Spanning the Generations: A Study in Jewish Identity*. Toronto: Longmans Canada, 1977.

Karetzky, Stephen, and Goldman, Peter E. *The Media's War against Israel*. New York: Steimatzky/Shapolsky, 1986.

Kay, Zachariah. *Canada and Palestine: The Politics of Non-Commitment*. Jerusalem: Israel Universities Press, 1978.

Kegley, Charles W., Jr., and Wittkopf, Eugene R. *American Foreign Policy: Patterns and Process*. New York: St. Martin's Press, 1979.

———, eds. *The Domestic Sources of American Foreign Policy: Insights and Evidence*. New York: St. Martin's Press, 1988.

Kenen, I. L. *Israel's Defense Line: Her Friends and Foes in Washington*. Buffalo, N.Y.: Prometheus Books, 1981.

Kissinger, Henry A. *Years of Upheaval*. Boston: Little, Brown and Co., 1982.

Krasner, Stephen D. *Defending the National Interest: Raw Materials Investments and U.S. Foreign Policy*. Princeton, N.J.: Princeton University Press, 1978.

Liebman, Arthur. *Jews and the Left*. New York: John Wiley and Sons, 1979.

Liebman, Charles S. *The Ambivalent American Jew: Politics, Religion and Family in American Jewish Life*. Philadelphia: Jewish Publication Society of America, 1973.

Lilienthal, Alfred M. *What Price Israel?* Chicago: Henry Regnery, 1953.

————. *There Goes the Middle East*. New York: Devin-Adair Company, 1957.

————. *The Other Side of the Coin: An American Perspective on the Arab-Israeli Conflict*. New York: Devin-Adair Company, 1965.

————. *The Zionist Connection: What Price Peace?* New York: Dodd, Mead and Company, 1978.

Lindblom, Charles E. *The Intelligence of Democracy*. New York: Free Press, 1965.

Lowi, Theodore J. *The End of Liberalism: The Second Republic of the United States*, 2d ed. New York: Norton, 1979.

Lyon, Peyton V., and Ismael, Tareq, eds. *Canada and the Third World*. Toronto: Macmillan of Canada, 1976.

Lyon, Peyton V.; Ismael, Tareq; and Tomlin, Brian. *Canada as an International Actor*. Toronto: Macmillan of Canada, 1979.

Martire, Gregory, and Clark, Ruth. *Anti-Semitism in the United States: A Study of Prejudice in the 1980s*. New York: Praeger Publishers, 1982.

Massoud, Muhammad Said. *I Fought As I Believed: An Arab Canadian Speaks Out on the Arab-Israel Conflict*. Montreal: Canadian Arab Federation, 1976.

Matthews, Robert, and Pratt, Cranford, eds. *Church and State: The Christian Churches and Canadian Foreign Policy*. Toronto: Canadian Institute for International Affairs, 1983.

Mehdi, Beverlee Thomas, ed. *The Arabs in America, 1492–1979*. Dobbs Ferry, N.Y.: Oceana Publications, 1978.

Milbrath, Lester W. *The Washington Lobbyists*. Chicago: Rand McNally and Company, 1963.

————. *Political Participation*. Chicago: Rand McNally and Company, 1965.

Moore, John Norton, ed. *The Arab-Israeli Conflict: Readings*. Princeton, N.J.: Princeton University Press, 1979.

Munton, Don, ed. *Groups and Governments in Canadian Foreign Policy. Proceedings of a Conference, Ottawa, June 9–11, 1982*. Toronto: Canadian Institute of International Affairs, 1985.

Nelson, W. H., and Prittie, Thomas. *The Economic War against the Jews*. New York: Random House, 1977.

Neusner, Jacob, *Israel in America: A Too-Comfortable Exile?* Boston: Beacon Press, 1985.

Nordlinger, Eric A. *On the Autonomy of the Democratic State*. Cambridge, Mass.: Harvard University Press, 1981.

Nossal, Kim Richard. *The Politics of Canadian Foreign Policy*. 2d ed. Scarborough, Ont.: Prentice-Hall of Canada, 1989.

O'Brien, Lee. *American Jewish Organizations and Israel*. Washington, D.C.: Institute for Palestine Studies, 1986.

Ogene, F. Chidogie. *Interest Groups and the Shaping of Foreign Policy*. New York: St. Martin's Press, 1983.

Orfalea, Gregory. *Before the Flames: A Quest for the History of Arab Americans.* Austin: University of Texas Press, 1988.

Paris, Erna. *Jews: An Account of Their Experience in Canada.* Toronto: Macmillan of Canada, 1980.

Plaut, W. Gunther. *Unfinished Business: An Autobiography.* Toronto: Lester and Orpen Dennys, 1981b.

Pollock, David. *The Politics of Pressure: American Arms and Israel Policy since the Six Day War.* Westport, Conn.: Greenwood Press, 1982.

Porter, Jack Nusan, ed. *The Sociology of American Jews: A Critical Anthology.* Washington, D.C.: University Press of America, 1978.

Porter, John. *Vertical Mosaic.* Toronto: University of Toronto Press, 1965.

Presthus, Robert. *Elite Accommodation in Canadian Politics.* Toronto: Macmillan of Canada, 1973.

————. *Elites in the Policy Process.* London: Cambridge University Press, 1974a.

————. *Cross-National Perspectives: United States and Canada.* Leiden, The Netherlands: E. J. Brill, 1977.

Pross, A. Paul, ed. *Pressure Group Behaviour in Canadian Politics.* Toronto: McGraw-Hill Ryerson, 1975.

Quandt, William B. *Decade of Decisions. American Policy toward the Arab-Israeli Conflict, 1967–1976.* Berkeley, Calif.: University of California Press, 1977.

————. *Saudi Arabia in the 1980s: Foreign Policy, Security and Oil.* Washington, D.C.: Brookings Institution, 1981.

Rabin, Yitzhak. *The Rabin Memoirs.* London: Weidenfeld and Nicolson, 1979.

Rabinovich, Itamar. *The War for Lebanon, 1970–1983.* Ithaca, N.Y.: Cornell University Press, 1984.

Raphael, Marc Lee, ed. *Understanding American Jewish Philanthropy.* New York: Ktav Publishing House, 1979.

Reich, Bernard. *Quest for Peace: United States-Israel Relations and the Arab-Israel Conflict.* New Brunswick, N.J.: Transaction Books, 1977.

————. *Israel: Land of Tradition and Conflict.* Boulder, Colo.: Westview Press, 1985.

Riddell-Dixon, Elizabeth, ed. *The Domestic Mosaic: Domestic Groups and Canadian Foreign Policy.* Toronto: Canadian Institute of International Affairs, 1985.

Rosenau, James N. *Public Opinion and Foreign Policy.* New York: Random House, 1961.

————. *Domestic Sources of Foreign Policy.* New York: Free Press, 1967.

Rosenberg, Stuart E. *The Jewish Community in Canada: A History.* 2 vols. Toronto: McClelland and Stewart, 1970–71.

Sachar, Howard M. *A History of Israel from the rise of Zionism to Our Times.* New York: Alfred A. Knopf, 1976.

————. *A History of Israel. Vol. 2, From the Aftermath of the Yom Kippur War.* New York: Oxford University Press, 1987.

Sack, B. G. *History of the Jews in Canada.* Translated by Ralph Novek. Montreal: Harvest House, 1965.

Safran, Nadav. *From War to War: The Arab-Israeli Confrontation, 1948–1967.* Indianapolis, Ind.: Pegasus, Bobbs-Merrill, 1969.

————. *Israel: The Embattled Ally.* Cambridge, Mass.: Belknap Press of Harvard University Press, 1981.

Said, Abdul Aziz, ed. *Ethnicity and U.S. Foreign Policy*. rev. ed. New York: Praeger Publishers, 1981.

Said, Edward. *The Question of Palestine*. New York: Vintage, 1980.

Sampson, Anthony. *The Seven Sisters: The Great Oil Companies and the World They Made*. New York: Viking, 1977.

Savage, Ralph Lee. "Israeli and American Jewish Attitudes in 1971 on the Future of Israel's Conquered Territories." Ph.D. diss., University of Southern Mississippi, 1973.

Schattschneider, Elmer Eric. *Politics, Pressure, and the Tariff*. Englewood Cliffs, N.J.: Prentice-Hall, 1937.

Schiff, Ze'ev, and Ya'ari, Ehud. *Israel's Lebanon War*. Translated by Ina Friedman. New York: Simon and Schuster, 1984.

Schneider, William. *Anti-Semitism and Israel: A Report on American Public Opinion*. Washington, D.C.: American Jewish Committee, 1978.

Selznick, Gertrude, and Steinberg, Stephen. *The Tenacity of Prejudice: Anti-Semitism in Contemporary America*. New York: Harper and Row, 1969.

Sherbiny, Naiem A., and Tessler, Mark A., eds. *Arab Oil: Impact on the Arab Countries and Global Implications*. New York: Praeger Publishers, 1976.

Siegel, Arthur. *Politics and the Media in Canada*. Toronto: McGraw-Hill Ryerson, 1983.

Simpson, Jeffrey. *Discipline of Power: The Conservative Interlude and the Liberal Restoration*. Toronto: Personal Library, 1980.

Slater, Robert. *Rabin of Israel: A Biography*. London: Robson Books, 1977.

Slonim, Reuben. *Family Quarrel*. Toronto: McGraw-Hill Ryerson, 1976.

Spanier, John, and Nogee, Joseph, eds. *Congress, the Presidency and American Foreign Policy*. New York: Pergamon Press, 1981.

Spiegel, Steven L. *The Other Arab-Israeli Conflict: Making America's Middle East Policy, from Truman to Reagan*. Chicago: University of Chicago Press, 1985.

Stanfield, Robert L. *Final Report of the Special Representative of the Government of Canada Respecting the Middle East and North Africa*. Ottawa: Government of Canada, 1980.

Stanislawski, Howard J. *The Arab Boycott: Policies and Perspectives*. Montreal: Canada-Israel Committee, 1977.

————. "Elites, Domestic Interest Groups, and International Interests in the Canadian Foreign Policy Decision-making Process: The Arab Economic Boycott of Canadians and Canadian Companies Doing Business with Israel." Ph.D. diss., Brandeis University, 1981b.

Stein, Janice Gross, and Dewitt, David B., eds. *The Middle East at the Crossroads: Regional Forces and External Powers*. Oakville, Ontario: Mosaic Press, 1983.

Stember, Charles Herbert, ed. *Jews in the Mind of America*. New York: Basic Books, 1966.

Stern, Paula. Water's Edge: Domestic Politics and the Making of American Foreign Policy. Westport, Conn.: Greenwood Press, 1979.

Takach, George Steven. "Clark and the Jerusalem Embassy Affair: Initiation and Constraint in Canadian Foreign Policy." Master's thesis, School of International Affairs, Carleton University, Ottawa, 1980.

Tapper, Lawrence F. *A Guide to Sources for the Study of Canadian Jewry*. Ottawa: Department of Supply and Services, 1978.

Taras, David. "Canada and the Arab-Israeli Conflict: A Study of the Yom Kippur War and the Domestic Political Environment.'' Ph.D. Diss., University of Toronto, 1983.

Taras, David, and Goldberg, David H., eds. *The Domestic Battleground: Canada and the Arab-Israeli Conflict*. Montreal: McGill-Queen's University Press, 1989.

Teslik, Kennan Lee. *Congress, the Executive Branch, and Special Interests: The American Response to the Arab Boycott of Israel*. Westport, Conn.: Greenwood Press, 1982.

Thompson, Fred, and Stanbury, W. T. *The Political Economy of Interest Groups in the Legislative Process in Canada*. Occasional Paper no. 9. Montreal: Institute for Research on Public Policy, 1979.

Thordarson, Bruce. *Trudeau and Foreign Policy: A Study in Decision-Making*. Toronto: Oxford University Press, 1972.

Tivnan, Edward. *The Lobby: Jewish Political Power and American Foreign Policy*. New York: Simon and Schuster, 1987.

Trice, Robert Holmes. ''Domestic Political Interests and American Policy in the Middle East: Pro-Israel, Pro-Arab, and Corporate Non-Governmental Actors and the Making of American Foreign Policy, 1966–1971.'' Ph.D. diss., University of Wisconsin, Madison, 1974.

———. *Interest Groups and the Foreign Policy Process: U.S. Policy in the Middle East*. Berkeley, Calif.: Sage Publications, 1976b.

Truman, David. *The Governmental Process: Political Interests and Public Opinion*. New York: Alfred A. Knopf, 1951.

Tsukashima, Ronald T. *The Social and Psychological Correlations of Black Anti-Semitism*. San Francisco: R. and E. Research Associates, 1978.

Tucker, Michael. *Canadian Foreign Policy: Contemporary Issues and Themes*. Toronto: McGraw-Hill Ryerson, 1980.

Urofsky, Melvin I. *American Zionism from Herzl to the Holocaust*. Garden City, N.Y.: Anchor Press/Doubleday and Company, 1975.

———. *We Are One! American Jewry and Israel*. Garden City, N.Y.: Anchor Press/ Doubleday and Company, 1978.

Vance, Cyrus. *Hard Choices: Critical Years in America's Foreign Policy*. New York: Simon and Schuster, 1983.

Waller, Harold M. *The Canadian Jewish Community: A National Perspective*. Philadelphia: Center for Jewish Community Studies, Temple University, 1977.

Watanabe, Paul Y. *Ethnic Groups, Congress, and American Foreign Policy: The Politics of the Turkish Arms Embargo*. Westport, Conn.: Greenwood Press, 1984.

Waugh, Earle H.; Abu-Laban, Baha; and Qureski, Regula B., eds. *The Muslim Community in North America*. Edmonton: University of Alberta Press, 1984.

Waxman, Chaim I. *America's Jews in Transition*. Philadelphia: Temple University Press, 1983.

Weinfeld, Morton; Shaffir, William; and Cotler, Irwin, eds. *The Canadian Jewish Mosaic*. Toronto: John Wiley and Sons Canada, 1981.

Weizman, Ezer. *The Battle for Peace*. New York: Bantam Books, 1981.

Weizmann, Chaim. *Trial and Error: The Autobiography of Chaim Weizmann, the First President of Israel*. New York: Harper and Brothers, 1949.

Windmueller, Steven Fred. ''American Jewish Interest Groups: Their Role in Shaping United States Foreign Policy in the Middle East. A Study of Two Time Periods.'' Ph.D. diss., University of Pennsylvania, 1973.

Yankelovich, Skelly, and White. *Anti-Semitism in the United States*. American Jewish Committee, 1981.

ARTICLES

Abella, Irving. "Innocent Abroad: The Strange Case of Ambassador Theodore Arcand." *Middle East Focus* 5, no. 3 (September 1982): 3–4.

———. "Why It's Not All Israel's Fault." *Toronto Star*, January 17, 1988a, A15.

———. "Family Ties." *Saturday Night*, June 1988b, 15–16.

———. "Canada and the Arab-Israeli Conflict." In *The Domestic Battleground*, edited by David Taras and David H. Goldberg, 227–48. Montreal: McGill-Queen's University Press, 1989.

Abu-Laban, Baha. "Arab-Canadians and the Arab-Israeli Conflict." *Arab Studies Quarterly* 10 (Winter 1988): 104–126.

Abu Rudeneh, Odeh. "The Jewish Factor in U.S. Politics." *Journal of Palestine Studies* 10, no. 4 (Summer 1972): 92–107.

Adams, Michael, and Dasko, Donna. "Poll on Israel Finds Polity Unpopular." *Globe and Mail*, March 30, 1988, A1.

Adelman, Howard. "Clark and the Canadian Embassy in Israel." *Middle East Focus* 2 (March 1980): 6–18.

Ages, Arnold. "Antisemitism: The Uneasy Calm." In *The Canadian Jewish Mosaic*, edited by Morton Weinfeld, William Shaffir and Irwin Cotler, 383–95. Toronto: John Wiley and Sons Canada, 1981.

Aikenhead, Sherrie, "A Community's Torment." *MacLeans*, April 4, 1988, 13–14.

"American Jews and Blacks Developing Joint Programs." *Canadian Jewish News*, September 5, 1985, 23.

"American Jews and Israel: A Symposium." *Commentary* 85, no. 2 (February 1988): 21–75.

"The Arab Lobby: David in a David and Goliath Role." *New York Times*, October 28, 1983, A10.

Arnold, Abraham J. "The Mystique of Western Jewry." In *The Canadian Jewish Mosaic*, edited by Morton Weinfeld, William Shaffir, and Irwin Cotler, 259–72. Toronto: John Wiley and Sons, 1981.

Averick, Sara M. *U.S. Policy toward Jerusalem, the Capital of Israel*. AIPAC Papers on U.S.-Israel Relations, 6. Washington, D.C.: AIPAC, 1984.

Ball, George W. "How To Save Israel In Spite of Herself." *Foreign Affairs* 55, no. 3 (April 1977): 453–71.

———. "The Coming Crisis in Israeli-American Relations." *Foreign Affairs* 58, no. 2 (Winter 1979/1980): 231–56.

Barberis, Mary. "The Arab-Israeli Battle on Capital Hill." *Virginia Quarterly Review* 52 (Spring 1976): 205–23.

Bard, Mitchell. "The Influence of Ethnic Interest Groups on American Middle East Policy." In *The Domestic Sources of American Foreign Policy: Insights and Evidence*, edited by Charles W. Kegley, Jr. and Eugene R. Wittkopf, 57–69. New York: St. Martin's Press, 1988.

Barrett, Laurence I. "The Diaspora's Discontent: U.S. Jews Are Leaning on Shamir to Bend His Rigid Policies." *Time*, April 3, 1989, 18–19.

Belkaoui, Janice Monti. "Images of Arabs and Israelis in the Prestige Press, 1966–1974." *Journalism Quarterly* 55 (Winter 1978): 732–38.

Bercuson, David J. "Canada and Jerusalem: An Historical Overview." *Middle East Focus* 4, no. 3 (September 1981): 7–10.

———. "Serving the National Interest: Canada's Palestine Policy, 1940–1949." *Middle East Focus* 6, no. 5 (January 1984): 12–16, 26–27.

———. "The Zionist Lobby and Canada's Palestine Policy, 1941–1948." In *The Domestic Battleground*, edited by David Taras and David H. Goldberg, 17–36. Montreal: McGill-Queen's University Press, 1989.

———. "Canada's Middle East Policy in Historical Perspective." *Middle East Focus*, special issue (forthcoming).

Berman, Julius. "American Jewry's Consensus on Israel." *Forward*, July 16, 1984, 17.

Bick, Myer. "The Yom Kippur War . . . CIC Activities." *Canadian Zionist*, November/December 1973.

Biggart, Nicole Woolsey. "Management Style as Strategic Interaction: Case of Governor Ronald Reagan." *Journal of Applied Behavioural Science* 17, no. 3 (1981): 291–307.

Blair, Peggy. *A U.S.-Israel Free Trade Area: How Both Sides Gain.* AIPAC Papers on U.S.-Israel Relations, 9. Washington, D.C.: AIPAC, 1984.

Blitzer, Wolf. "The AIPAC Formula." *Moment Magazine* 6, no. 10 (November 1981a): 22–28.

———. "No Ill Feeling About AWACS Officials Reassure American Jews." *Canadian Jewish News*, November 19, 1981b, 7.

———. "Report from Washington—II: Measuring Clout." *Present Tense* 10, no. 3 (Spring 1983): 17–19.

"B'nai B'rith Praises Reagan's Plan for Settling Palestinian Problem." *New York Times*, September 9, 1982, A1.

Booth, John Nicholls. "How Zionists Manipulate Your News." *United Church Observer*, March 1972, 7.

Canada. Department of External Affairs. *Statements*, October 16, 1973.

———. *Statements*, June 23, 1979.

———. *Statements*, 88/18, March 10, 1988.

Canada. House of Commons. *Debate*, May 8, 1975.

———. *Debate*, October 29, 1979.

———. *Debate*, January 19, 1988.

Canada. Standing Senate Committee on Foreign Affairs. *Report on Canada's Relations with the Countries of the Middle East and North America*, June 1985.

Canada-Israel Committee. "The CBC and the Middle East: A Commentary." Submission to the Canadian Radio-Television and Telecommunications Commission Hearings on the CBC's French and English Radio and Television Network license renewal application, April 1978.

———. *Excerpts from the Canada-Israel Committee Policy Statement.* Ottawa: CIC, June 1982.

"Canada's Mid-East Policy: A Heated Summer." *Canadian Middle-East Digest* 6, no. 6 (September-October 1982): 1–3.

Carus, W. Seth. *Israel and the U.S. Navy.* AIPAC Papers on U.S.-Israel Relations, 4. Washington, D.C.: AIPAC, 1983.

————. *U.S. Procurement of Israeli Defense Goods and Services.* AIPAC Papers on U.S.-Israel Relations, 8. Washington, D.C.: AIPAC, 1984.

Clarke, Patricia, and Courtenay, Carla. "Has g-d A Lobby in Ottawa?" *United Church Observer*, February 15, 1967, 26–28.

Clarke, S. D. "Canada and the American Value System." In *The Canadian Political Process: A Reader.* Rev. ed., edited by Richard Schultz, Orest Khrulak, and Sydney I. Pobihushchy, 61–68. Toronto: Holt, Rinehart and Winston, 1973.

Cleveland, Harlan. "The Domestication of International Affairs and Vice Versa." *Annals of the American Academy of Political and Social Science* 442 (1979): 125–37.

Cohn, Werner. "English and French Canadian Opinion on Jews and Israel: Some Poll Data." *Canadian Ethnic Studies* 11, no. 2 (1979): 31–48.

Cotler, Irwin. "Canada: Overview." In *The Yom Kippur War: Israel and the Jewish People*, edited by Moshe Davis, 101–6. New York: Arno Press; Jerusalem: Institute of Contemporary Jewry, 1974a.

Cotler, Irwin, and Wisse, Ruth. "Quebec Jews: Caught in the Middle." *Commentary* 64 (September 1977): 55–59.

Cox, David. "Leadership Change and Innovation in Canadian Foreign Policy: The 1979 Progressive Conservative Government." *International Journal* 37, no. 4 (Autumn 1982): 555–83.

Davidowicz, Lucy. "A Century of Jewish History, 1881–1981: The View from America." In *American Jewish Year Book, 1982*, 3–98. Philadelphia: Jewish Publication Society of America, 1983.

Davis, Eric L. "Legislative Liaison in the Carter Administration." *Political Science Quarterly* 94, no. 2 (Summer 1979): 187–301.

Dewitt, David B. "Intifada, Canadian Foreign Policy Adjustments, and the Position of the Canadian Jewish Community." 57th General Assembly, Council of Jewish Federations, New Orleans, November 18, 1988 (author's copy).

Dewitt, David B., and Kirton, John J. "Canadian Foreign Policy towards the Middle East, 1947–1980: International, Domestic and Governmental Determinants." Paper presented at the Canadian-Arab Relations Conference, University of Calgary, Calgary, Alberta, June 22–25, 1981.

————. "Media and Canadian Foreign Policy Towards the Middle East: Lebanon 1982." Paper presented at the Conference on Media and Foreign Policy, University of Windsor, October 27–29, 1983b.

————. "Canada and Mideast Realities." *International Perspectives* (January/February 1984): 19–21.

————. "Foreign Policy Making towards the Middle East: Parliament, the Media and the 1982 Lebanon War." In *The Domestic Battleground*, edited by David Taras and David H. Goldberg, 167–85. Montreal: McGill-Queen's University Press, 1989.

Dine, Thomas A. "The U.S. in the Middle East: A Forceful or Fearful Foreign Policy?" Paper presented at the AIPAC 22d Annual Policy Conference, Washington, D.C., May 1981a.

————. "A Call to Political Action." Paper presented at the National Association of Jewish Legislators Meetings, State Senate Chamber, State Capitol, Atlanta, Georgia, July 1981b.

————. "The United States in the Middle East: Problems and Prospects." Paper presented at the AIPAC Georgia Workshop on Politics, Atlanta, Georgia, February 1983a.

———. "U.S.-Israel Relations: Stopping the Deterioration." Paper presented at the AIPAC Georgia Workshop on Politics, Atlanta, Georgia, February 1983b.

———. "The Way Jews Are Seen from the White House." Paper presented at the Westchester Reform Temple, Scarsdale, New York, March 1983c.

———. "Reconstructing the Relationship." Paper presented at the AIPAC Alabama Workshop on Politics, Birmingham, Alabama, May 1983d.

———. "Citizen Action and American Foreign Policy." Paper presented at the AIPAC Annual Policy Conference, Washington, D.C., June 1983e.

———. "Syria's War Against Lebanon: America's Response." Paper presented at the Israel Bonds Dinner, Corpus Christi, Texas, September 1983f.

———. "Political Action: Our Common Agenda." Paper presented at the AIPAC-NAACP Conference, Washington, D.C., November 1983g.

———. "A Muscular Minority." Paper presented at the Main Line Reform Temple, Philadelphia, Pennsylvania, December 1983h.

———. "The Errors of Arabism." Paper presented at the AIPAC Metropolitan Committee, New York City, April 1984a.

———. "Hope and Foreboding: The Future of the U.S.-Israel Relationship." Paper presented at the AIPAC Policy Conference, Washington, D.C., April 1984b.

Eayrs, James. "Canadian Policy and Opinion during the Suez Crisis." *International Journal* 12, no. 2 (Spring 1957): 97–108.

Eckstein, Harry. "Case Studies and Theory in Political Science." In *Handbook of Political Science: Strategies of Inquiry*. Vol. 7, edited by Fred. I. Greenstein and Nelson W. Polsby, 79–137. Reading, Mass.: Addison-Wesley, 1975.

Ehrmann, Henry W. "Interest Groups." In *International Encyclopedia of the Social Sciences*. Vol. 7, edited by David L. Sills, 486–92. New York: Macmillan/Free Press, 1968.

Eldersveld, Samuel J. "American Interest Groups: A Survey of Research and Some Implications for Theory and Method." In *Interest Groups on Four Continents*, edited by Henry W. Ehrmann, 173–96. Pittsburgh: University of Pittsburgh Press, 1958.

Emerson, Steven J. "The American House of Saud: I—The Petro-dollar Connection." *New Republic* 186, no. 7 (February 17, 1982a): 18–25.

———. "The American House of Saud: II—The Aramco Connection." *New Republic* 186, no. 20 (May 19, 1982b): 11–16.

———. "The American House of Saud: III—Dutton of Arabia." *New Republic* 186, no. 24 (June 16, 1982c): 18–23.

Erskine, Hazel. "The Polls: Western Partisanship in the Middle East." *Public Opinion Quarterly* 33 (Winter 1968–1969): 627–40.

Farrell, William E. "The Arab Lobby: 'David in a David-Goliath Role.' " *New York Times*, October 28, 1983, A10.

Fein, Leonard. "A New Zionism." *Moment* 14, no. 3 (April 1989): 48–53.

Ferman, David. "CLC Paper Criticizes Israel." *Canadian Jewish News*, May 19, 1988, 12.

Fialka, John J. "Jewish Groups Increase Campaign Donations, Target Them Precisely." *Wall Street Journal*, August 3, 1983, 1, 12.

Fisher, Allen M. "Realignment of the Jewish Vote?" *Political Science Quarterly* 94, no. 1 (Spring 1979a): 97–116.

————. "Where is the New Jewish Conservatism?" *Society* 16, no. 4 (May-June 1979b): 5, 15–18.

Friedman, Murray. "A New Direction for American Jews." *Commentary* 72, no. 6 (December 1981): 37–44.

————. "AWACS and the Jewish Community." *Commentary* 73, no. 4 (April 1982): 29–33.

Fuchs, Lawrence H. "Minority Groups and Foreign Policy." *Political Science Quarterly* 74 (1959): 161–75.

————. "Ethnicity and Foreign Policy." Paper presented at the Third Annual University of Wisconsin Conference on Ethnicity and Public Policy, Green Bay, Wisconsin, 1982.

Gailey, Phil. "Pro-Israel Lobby's Low-Key Power." *New York Times*, March 24, 1984, A8.

Garnham, David. "The Oil Crisis and U.S. Attitudes toward Israel." In *Arab Oil: Impact on the Arab Countries and Global Implications*, edited by Naiem A. Sherbiny and Mark A. Tessler, 295–304. New York: Praeger Publishers, 1976.

————. "Factors Influencing Congressional Support for Israel during the 93rd Congress." *Jerusalem Journal of International Relations* 2 (Spring 1977): 23–45.

Garson, G. David. "On the Origins of Interest Group Theory." *American Political Science Review* 68 (December 1974): 1505–19.

George, Alexander L. "Case Studies and Theory Development: The Method of Structured, Focussed Comparison." In *Diplomacy: New Approaches in History, Theory and Policy*, edited by Paul Gordon Lauren, 43–68. New York: Free Press, 1979.

Gershman, Carl. "The Andrew Young Affair." *Commentary* 68, no. 5 (November 1979): 25–33.

Gerson, Louis L. "The Influence of Hyphenated Americans on U.S. Diplomacy." In *Ethnicity and U.S. Foreign Policy*. Rev. ed., edited by Abdul Aziz Said, 19–31. New York: Praeger Publishers, 1981.

Gilboa, Eytan. "Israel's Image in American Public Opinion." *Middle East Review* 21, no. 3 (Spring 1989): 25–37.

Glick, Stephen P. *Israeli Medical Support for the U.S. Armed Forces*. AIPAC Papers on U.S.-Israel Relations, 5. Washington, D.C.: AIPAC, 1983.

Goldberg, David H. "Interest Groups and Foreign Policy Making: Canada and Palestine, 1946–1948." *Journal of the Canadian Jewish Historical Society* 6–7 (Spring 1982): 26–37.

————. "Keeping Score: From the Yom Kippur War to the Palestinian Uprising." In *The Domestic Battleground*, edited by David Taras and David H. Goldberg, 102–24. Montreal: McGill-Queen's University Press, 1989.

Goldberg, David H., and Taras, David. "Collision Course: Clark, Canadian Jews and the Palestinian Uprising." In *The Domestic Battleground*, edited by David Taras and David H. Goldberg, 207–26. Montreal: McGill-Queen's University Press, 1989.

Goott, Amy Kaufman, and Rosen, Steven J. *The Campaign to Discredit Israel*. 1st ed., AIPAC Papers on U.S.-Israel Relations, 3. Washington, D.C.: AIPAC, 1983.

Gwertzman, Bernard. "Leading Pro-Israeli Lobbyist Sees 'A Lot of Value' in Reagan's Plan." *New York Times*, September 7, 1982, A1.

Halperin, Mark. "American Jews and Israel: Seizing a New Opportunity." *New York Times Magazine*, November 7, 1982, 34–37, 84–86, 96–97, 100.

Hayes, David. "Toronto Jews, Israel and the Media: An Agonizing Debate Investigated."
    Toronto Life, August 1988, 31–35, 56, 60, 62.
Hayes, Saul. "Some Differences between Canadian and U.S. Jewry." *Viewpoints* 10
    (March 1966): 3–10.
———. "Canada: Overview." In *The Yom Kippur War: Israel and the Jewish People*,
    edited by Moshe Davis, 101–6. New York: Arno Press; Jerusalem: Institute of
    Contemporary Jewry, 1974.
———. "Are Jews of Quebec an Endangered Species?" *Journal of the Jewish Historical
    Society of Canada* 1, no. 1 (April 1977): 24–34.
———. "Canadian Politics and the Jewish Community." *Viewpoints* 10 (Fall 1979):
    17–22.
Hershman, Robert, and Griggs, Henry, Jr. "American Television News and the Middle
    East." *Middle East Journal* 35, no. 4 (Autumn 1981): 481–91.
Hertzberg, Arthur. "Israel and American Jewry." *Commentary* 44, no. 2 (August 1967):
    69–73.
Hillmer, Anne Trowell. " 'Here I am in the Middle': Lester Pearson and the Origins of
    Canada's Diplomatic Involvement in the Middle East." In *The Domestic Battle-
    ground*, edited by David Taras and David H. Goldberg, 125–43. Montreal: McGill-
    Queen's University Press, 1989.
Himmelfarb, Milton. "The Jewish Vote (Again)." *Commentary* 55, no. 6 (June 1973):
    81–85.
Horowitz, Irving Louis. "Ethnic Politics and U.S. Foreign Policy." In *Ethnicity and
    U.S. Foreign Policy.* 2d ed., edited by Abdul Aziz Said, 217–40. New York:
    Praeger Publishers, 1981.
Howe, Irving. "American Jews and Israel." *Tikkun*, May/June 1989, 71–74.
Ibrahim, Saad. "American Domestic Factors and the October War." *Journal of Palestine
    Studies* 4, no. 1 (Autumn 1974): 55–81.
Indyk, Martin; Kupchan, Charles; and Rosen, Steven J. *Israel and the U.S. Air Force.*
    AIPAC Papers on U.S.-Israel Relations, 2. Washington, D.C.: AIPAC, 1983.
Isaac, Real Jean. "Liberal Protestants Versus Israel." *Midstream*, October 1981, 6–9.
Ismael, Tareq Y. "Canada and the Middle East." *Behind the Headlines* 32, no. 5
    (December 1973).
Iyengar, Shanto, and Suleiman, Michael. "Trends in Public Support for Egypt and Israel
    1956–1978." *American Politics Quarterly* 8 (January 1980): 36–60.
"Jewish Group Protests Israeli Invasion." *Montreal Gazette*, July 10, 1982, A3.
"Jews Discuss Common Ground with Leaders of United Church." *Montreal Gazette*,
    August 13, 1982, A3.
Kay, Zachariah. "The Canadian Press and Palestine: A Survey, 1939–1948." *Interna-
    tional Journal* 18, no. 3 (Summer 1962–1963): 361–73.
Keenleyside, T. A.; Soderlund, W. C.; and Burton, B. E. "A Tilt to Indifference: The
    Press and Canadian Foreign Policy in the Middle East (Autumn 1982)" *Middle
    East Focus* 8, no. 2 (July 1985): 6–14.
"Keeping a Watchful Eye on Parliament Hill, Where Canada's Middle East Policy is
    Determined, Is the Major Job of The Canada-Israel Committee." *Canadian Zi-
    onist*, September 1983.
Kegley, Charles W., Jr., and Wittkopf, Eugene R. "The Reagan Administration's World-
    view." *Orbis* 26 (Spring 1982): 223–44.

————. "Beyond Consensus: The Domestic Context of American Foreign Policy." *International Journal* 38, no. 1 (Winter 1982–1983): 77–106.

Kessler, Jonathan, and Schwaber, Jeff. *The AIPAC College Guide: Exposing the Anti-Israel Campaign on Campus.* AIPAC Papers on U.S.-Israel Relations, 7. Washington, D.C.: AIPAC, 1984.

Kirton, John J. "Foreign Policy Decision-Making in the Trudeau Government: Promise and Performance." *International Journal* 33, no. 2 (Spring 1978): 287–311.

Kirton, John J., and Dimock, Blair. "Domestic Access to Government in the Canadian Foreign Policy Process, 1968–1982." *International Journal* 39, no. 1 (Winter 1983–1984): 68–98.

Kirton, John J.; Barei, Jack; and Smokum, Eli. "A Continuing Concern: Canadian Television News Coverage of the Middle East in the Winter of 1982–83." *Middle East Focus* 8, no. 2 (July 1985): 15–20.

Kirton, John J., and Lyon, Peyton. "Perceptions of the Middle East in the Department of External Affairs and Mulroney's Policy, 1984–1988." In *The Domestic Battleground*, edited by David Taras and David H. Goldberg, 186–206. Montreal: McGill-Queen's University Press, 1989.

Kittle, Robert. "For Pro-Israel Lobby, the Stiffest Test Yet." *U.S. News and World Report*, September 14, 1981, 36.

Kuniholm, Bruce R. "Carrots or Sticks? The Question of United States Influence over Israel." *International Journal* 38, no. 4 (Autumn 1983): 700–12.

Lanouette, William J. "The Many Faces of the Jewish Lobby in America." *National Journal*, May 13, 1978a, 748–56.

————. "Representing the Arab Point of View." *National Journal*, May 13, 1978b, 745.

Latham, Earl. "The Group Basis of Politics: Notes for a Theory." *American Political Science Review* 66 (June 1952): 376–97.

Lipset, Seymour Martin. "Revolution and Counterrevolution: The United States and Canada." In *The Revolutionary Theme in Contemporary America*, edited by Thomas Ford, 21–64. Lexington, Ky.: University Press of Kentucky, 1965.

————. "The 'Jewish Lobby' and the National Interest." *New Leader*, November 16, 1981, 8–10.

Lowi, Theodore J. "Making Democracy Safe for the World: National Politics and Foreign Policy." In *Domestic Sources of Foreign Policy*, edited by James N. Rosenau, 295–331. New York: Free Press, 1967.

Lyon, Peyton V. "Israeli Invasion." *Globe and Mail*, June 22, 1982a, 6.

————. "Canada's Middle East Tilt." *International Perspectives* (September-October 1982b): 3–5.

————. "Canada's Middle East Tilt." In *Canadian Arab Politics: Policy and Perspective*, edited by Tareq Ismael, 37–44. Ottawa: Jerusalem International Publishing House, 1984.

————. "Canada and Palestinian Self-Determination." *International Perspectives* 17, no. 2 (March/April 1988): 17–18.

Manning, Bayless. "The Congress, the Executive and Intermestic Affairs: Three Proposals." *Foreign Affairs* 55 (January 1977): 306–24.

Mathias, Charles McC., Jr. "Ethnic Groups and Foreign Policy." *Foreign Affairs* 59, no. 5 (Summer 1981): 975–98.

McNaught, Kenneth. "Who Controls Foreign Policy? American and Canadian Contrasts." *Behind the Headlines* 9, no. 3 (September 1954).

Medjuck, Sheva, and Lazar, Morty M. "Existence on the Fringe: The Jews of Atlantic Canada." In *The Canadian Jewish Mosaic*, edited by Morton Weinfeld, William Shaffir and Irwin Cotler, 241–58. Toronto: John Wiley and Sons Canada, 1981.

Milbrath, Lester W., "Interest Groups and Foreign Policy." In *Domestic Sources of Foreign Policy*, edited by James N. Rosenau, 231–51. New York: Free Press, 1967.

Mintz, Alan. "The People's Choice: A Demurral on Breira." *Response* 32 (Winter 1976–1977): 5–10.

Morris, Roger. "Beirut—and the Press—Under Siege." *Columbia Journalism Review* (November-December 1982): 23–33.

Muravchik, Joshua. "Misrepresenting Lebanon." *Policy Review* (Winter 1983): 11–66.

Naff, Alixa. "Arabs in America: A Historical Overview." In *Arabs in the New World: Studies in American Arab Communities*, edited by Sameer Y. Abraham and Nabeel Abraham, 9–29. Detroit: Wayne State University, 1983.

Naidu, A. G. "Jewish Factor in U.S. Foreign Policy." *Foreign Affairs Reports—The Indian Council of World Affairs* 39, no. 1 (January 1980): 1–28.

Needelman, Marvin. "The Arab Boycott: Principles vs. Petrodollars." *Viewpoints* 9, no. 2 (1975): 4–11.

Noble, Paul C. "Where Angels Fear to Tread: Canada and the Status of the Palestinians, 1967–1980." Paper presented at the Canadian-Arab Relations Conference, University of Calgary, Calgary, Alberta, June 24, 1981.

———. "Canada and the Palestinian Question." *International Perspectives* (September-October 1983): 3–7.

Nossal, Kim Richard. "Analyzing the Domestic Sources of Canadian Foreign Policy." *International Journal* 39, no. 1 (Winter 1983–1984): 1–22.

"An Open Letter to the Canadian People." *Vancouver Sun*, October 13, 1973, 7.

Penn, M. J., and Schoen, D. E. "American Attitudes toward the Middle East." *Public Opinion* 11 (May-June 1988): 45–48.

Percy, Charles H. "The Partisan Gap." *Foreign Policy*, no. 45 (Winter 1981–1982): 3–15.

Peretz, Martin. "Lebanon Eyewitness." *New Republic* 187, no. 5 (August 2, 1982): 15–23.

Perlmutter, Amos. "Begin's Rhetoric and Sharon's Tactics." *Foreign Affairs* 61, no. 1 (Fall 1982): 67–83.

Plaut, W. Gunther. "Battles for Jerusalem—Canadian Style: How Clark's Promise Almost Split Community." *Canadian Jewish News*, September 24, 1981a, 1.

Power, Paul F. "Ethnic Groups and the 'National Interest.' " Prepared for delivery at the 1984 annual meeting of the American Political Science Association, Washington, D.C., August-September 1984.

"The Presidency: How Reagan Decides." *Time*, December 13, 1982, 10–17.

Presthus, Robert. "Interest Groups and the Canadian Parliament: Activity, Interest, Legitimacy, and Influence." *Canadian Journal of Political Science* 4 (December 1971): 444–60.

———. "Interest Group Lobbying: Canada and the United States." *Annals of the American Academy of Political and Social Science* 413 (1974b): 44–57.

"Pro-Israel Lobby's Low-Key Power." *New York Times*, March 24, 1984, A8.

"Prominent American Jews Support Israel but Some Condemn Its Leaders." *New York Times*, September 22, 1982, A16.

"A Promise Delayed." *Canadian Jewish News*, June 28, 1979, 2.

Raab, Earl S. "Is the Jewish Community Split?" *Commentary* 74, no. 5 (November 1982): 21–25.

Roberts, Steven V. "Arab Lobby's Specialty: Soft Sell, Tough Message." *New York Times*, April 30, 1978. 4.

Rose, Alan. "Addressing the Federal Governance." *Viewpoints* 11, no. 4 (Spring 1980): 8–12.

Rosen, Steven J. *The Strategic Value of Israel*. AIPAC Papers on U.S.-Israel Relations, 1. Washington, D.C.: AIPAC, 1982.

Rosen, Steven J., and Abramowitz, Yosef I. *How Americans Feel about Israel*. AIPAC Papers on U.S.-Israel Relations, 10. Washington, D.C.: AIPAC, 1984.

Rosenbaum, Aaron David. "The AWACS Aftermath: No Victory—But Not Quite a Defeat." *Moment Magazine* 7, no. 1 (December 1981): 13–22, 57–58.

Rosenfeld, Stephen S. "Dateline Washington: Anti-Semitism and U.S. Foreign Policy." *Foreign Policy* no. 47 (Summer 1982): 172–183.

———. "Report from Washington—I: AIPAC." *Present Tense* 10, no. 3 (Spring 1983): 15–16.

Rosenfield, Geraldine. "The Polls: Attitude toward American Jews." *Public Opinion Quarterly* 46, no. 3 (Fall 1982): 431–43.

Rucker, Patricia. "Jewish Senators Abstain from Foreign Affairs Vote." *Canadian Jewish News*, June 13, 1985, 1, 13.

Sajoo, Amyn B. "Much Ado about Tilting: Canada and the Palestinians." *International Perspectives* 17, no. 5 (September/October 1988): 9–11.

Salisbury, Robert H. "Interest Groups." In *Handbook of Political Science*, edited by Fred I. Greenstein and Nelson W. Polsby, 2:171–228. Reading, Mass.: Addison-Wesley Publishing Company, 1975.

Sander, Gordon. "(Petro)Dollars for Scholars." *Moment Magazine* 3, no. 9 (September 1978a): 15–19.

———. "The Buying of America: A Tale of Three Cities." *Moment Magazine* 3, no. 10 (October 1978b): 27–32.

———. "The Arab Lobby Comes of Age." *Moment Magazine* 3, no. 11 (November 1978c): 15–18.

Schiff, Ze'ev. "Lebanon: The Green Light." *Foreign Policy* no. 50 (Spring 1983): 73–85.

Shanks, Hershel. "Leonard Fein's New Zionism: An Inspiring Vision or a Flawed Argument." *Moment Magazine* 14, no. 3 (April 1989): 4–6.

Sheheen, Jack G. "The Influence of the Arab Stereotype on American Children." In *The Arab World and Arab Americans*, edited by Sameer Y. Abraham and Nabeel Abraham, 53–56. Detroit: Wayne State University, 1981.

———. *ABSCAM: Arabiamenia in America*. Anti-Discrimination Committee Publication, no. 1. Washington, D.C.: ADC, n.d.

Sigler, John. "The Palestinian Uprising." *International Perspectives* 17, no. 4 (July/August 1988): 15–17.

———. "Canada and the Arab-Israeli Conflict." In *The Domestic Battleground*, edited by David Taras and David H. Goldberg, 227–48. Montreal: McGill-Queen's University Press, 1989.

Simon, Rita J. "The Print Media's Coverage of War in Lebanon." *Middle East Review* 16, no. 1 (Fall 1983): 5–6.

Slade, Shelley. "The Image of the Arab in America: Analysis of a Poll on American Attitudes." *Middle East Journal* 35, no. 2 (Spring 1981): 143–62.

Spiegel, Fredelle Z. "The Arab Lobby." *American Professors for Peace in the Middle East: Background Paper*, November 1981.

Spiegel, Steven L. "Carter and Israel." *Commentary* (July 1977): 35–40.

———. "The Carter Approach to the Arab-Israeli Dispute." In *The Middle East and the U.S.: Perceptions and Policies*, edited by Haim Shaked and Itamar Rabinovich, 93–117. New Brunswick, N.J.: Transaction Books, 1980.

———. "The Middle East: A Consensus of Error." *Commentary* 73, no. 3 (March 1982): 15–24.

———. "Religious Components of U.S. Middle East Policy." *Journal of International Affairs* 36 (Fall-Winter 1982–1983): 235–246.

———. "Ethnic Politics and the Formulation of U.S. Policy toward the Arab-Israel Dispute." Prepared for delivery at the annual meeting of the American Political Science Association, Washington, D.C., September 1984.

Stairs, Denis. "The Foreign Policy of Canada." In *World Politics*, edited by James N. Rosenau, Kenneth Thompson, and Robert Boyd, 178–98 New York: Free Press, 1976.

———. "The Press and Foreign Policy in Canada." *International Journal* 31, no. 2 (Spring 1976): 223–43.

———. "Public Opinion and External Affairs: Reflections on the Domestication of Canadian Foreign Policy." *International Journal* 31, no. 2 (1977–1978).

———. "The Nature and Role of Interest Groups and Domestic Policies in the Canadian Foreign Policy Process." Notes for presentation to CPSA-CIIA Panel on "Interest Groups and Public Policies, Domestic and Foreign," University of Ottawa, June 1982a.

———. "The Political Culture of Canadian Foreign Policy." *Canadian Journal of Political Science* 15, no. 4 (December 1982b): 667–90.

Stanbury, William T. "Lobbying and Interest Group Representation in the Legislative Process." In *The Legislative Process in Canada: The Need for Reform*, edited by William Neilson and James C. Macpherson, 167–207. Montreal: Institute for Research on Public Policy, 1978.

Stanislawski, Howard J. "Habitat proved to be 'diplomatic disaster.' " *Canadian Jewish News*, July 2, 1976, 5.

———. "Canadian Jewry and Foreign Policy in the Middle East." In *Canadian Jewish Mosaic*, edited by Morton Weinfeld, William Shaffir, and Irwin Cotler, 397–413. Toronto: John Wiley and Sons Canada, 1981a.

———. "Ethnic Interest Group Activity in the Canadian Foreign Policy Making Process: A Case Study of the Arab Boycott." In *The Middle East at the Crossroads: Regional Forces and External Powers*, edited by Janice Gross Stein and David B. Dewitt, 200–220. Oakville, Ontario: Mosaic Press, 1983.

———. "Domestic Interest Groups and Canadian and American Policy: The Case of the Arab Boycott." In *International Conflict and Conflict Management*, edited by Robert Matthews, Arthur Rubinoff, and Janice Stein, 137–47. Scarborough, Ontario: Prentice-Hall of Canada, 1984.

———. "Canadian Corporations and Their Middle East Interests." In *The Domestic*

Battleground, edited by David Taras and David H. Goldberg, 63–85. Montreal: McGill-Queen's University Press, 1989.

Stein, Janice Gross. "Canada: Evenhanded Ambiguity." In *Oil, the Arab-Israel Dispute, and the Industrial World: Horizons of Crisis*, edited by J. C. Hurewitz, 96–109. Boulder, Colo.: Westview Press, 1976.

———. "Canadian Foreign Policy in the Middle East after the October War." *Social Praxis* 4, no. 3/4 (1976–1977): 271–97.

Steinberg, Blema S. "American Foreign Policy in the Middle East 1948–1982: The Relationship between Interests and Behaviour." Paper presented at the Annual Conference of the International Studies Association, Mexico City, Mexico, April 1983a.

———. "American Foreign Policy in the Middle East: A Study in Changing Priorities." In *The Middle East at the Crossroads*, edited by Janice Gross Stein and David B. Dewitt, 111–44. Oakville, Ontario: Mosaic Press, 1983b.

Steiner, Henry J. "Pressures and Principles—The Politics of the Anti-Boycott Legislation." *Georgia Journal of International and Comparative Law* 8, no. 3 (1978).

"Study Finds Pro-Israel PAC's Active in '84 Races." *New York Times*, August 16, 1984, B10.

Suleiman, Michael W. "National Stereotypes as Weapons in the Arab-Israeli Conflict." *Journal of Palestine Studies* 3, no. 3 (Spring 1974): 109–21.

Syrkin, Marie. "How Israel Affects American Jews." *Midstream* 19, no. 5 (May 1973): 26–31.

Takach, George Steven. "Clark and the Jerusalem Embassy Affair: Initiative and Constraint in Canadian Foreign Policy." In *The Domestic Battleground*, edited by David Taras and David H. Goldberg, 144–66. Montreal: McGill-Queen's University Press, 1989.

Taras, David. "Parliament and Middle East Interest Groups: The Politics of Canadian and American Diplomacy during the October 1973 War." *Middle East Focus* 6, no. 5 (January 1984): 17–24.

———. "A Church Divided: A. C. Forrest and the United Church's Middle East Policy." In *The Domestic Battleground*, edited by David Taras and David H. Goldberg, 86–101. Montreal: McGill-Queen's University Press, 1989.

Taras, David, and Gottlieb Taras, Daphne. "The Canadian Media, Domestic Interest Groups, and Middle East Reporting: The Effects of Structural Bias." *International Journal* 42 (1986–1987): 536–58.

Terry, Janice, and Mendenhall, Gordon. "1973 U.S. Press Coverage on the Middle East." *Journal of Palestine Studies* 4, no. 1 (August 1984): 120–33.

Thorburn, H. G. "Pressure Groups in Canadian Politics." *Canadian Journal of Economics and Political Studies* 30 (1965): 157–74.

Tischler, Fred. "Canada, the Middle East, and the Arab Israeli Conflict." *Journal of the Canadian Jewish Historical Society*, 6–7, (1982–1983): 1–25.

Trice, Robert H. "American Interest Groups after October 1973." In *Oil, the Arab-Israeli Dispute, and the Industrial World: Horizons of Crisis*, edited by J. C. Hurewitz, 79–95. Boulder, Colo.: Westview Press, 1976a.

———. "Congress and the Arab-Israeli Conflict: Support for Israel in the U.S. Senate, 1970–1973." *Political Science Quarterly*, vol. 92, no. 3 (Fall 1977a): 443–63.

———. "Domestic Interest Groups and the Arab-Israeli Conflict: A Behavioral Analysis." In *Ethnicity and U.S. Foreign Policy.* 1st ed., 117–38. Edited by Abdul Aziz Said. New York: Praeger Publishers, 1977b.

Troper, Harold. "Canadian Jews and the 'Dual Loyalty' Canard." *Comment* (April 1988): 1–3.

Tucker, Robert W. "The Middle East: "Carterism without Carter?" *Commentary* 72, no. 3 (September 1981a): 27–30.

———. "Appeasement and the AWACS." *Commentary* 72, no. 6 (December 1981b): 25–30.

Turck, Nancy. "The Arab Boycott of Israel." *Foreign Affairs* 55, no. 3 (April 1977): 472–93.

Umar, Yusuf, and Brynen, Rex. "The Revolution called *intifada.*" *International Perspectives* 17, no. 5 (September/October 1988): 6–8.

Urofsky, Melvin I. "The Lobbying Life." *Midstream* 28, no. 7 (August-September 1982): 63–64.

"U.S. Jews and Israel: The Basic Consensus." *New York Times*, September 28, 1982, A22.

"U.S. Jews Debate Ties with Israel." *New York Times*, September 10, 1982, A10.

Utting, Gerald. "Lobbyists: Who Speaks on the Mideast?" *Toronto Sunday Star*, July 18, 1982, F4.

Von Riekhoff, Harald. "The Impact of Prime Minister Trudeau on Foreign Policy." *International Journal* 33, no. 2 (Spring 1978): 267–86.

Waller, Harold M. "The Governance of the Jewish Community in Montreal," *Canadian Jewish Community Reports*, no. 5. Philadelphia: Center for Jewish Community Studies, Temple University, 1974.

———. "Power in the Jewish Community." In *Canadian Jewish Mosaic*, edited by Morton Weinfeld, William Shaffir and Irwin Cotler, 151–70. Toronto: John Wiley and Sons Canada, 1981a.

———. "A Re-Examination of Zionism in Canada." In *Canadian Jewish Mosaic*, edited by Morton Weinfeld, William Shaffir and Irwin Cotler, 343–58. Toronto: John Wiley and Sons Canada, 1981b.

———. "The Montebello Mystery." *Jerusalem Letter/Viewpoints*. Jerusalem Center for Public Affairs. August 1, 1988.

Waller, Harold M., and Weinfeld, Morton. "The Jews of Quebec and 'Le Fait Francais.' " In *Canadian Jewish Mosaic*, edited by Morton Weinfeld, William Shaffir and Irwin Cotler, 415–40. Toronto: John Wiley and Sons Canada, 1981.

Waxman, Chaim I. "The Fourth Generation Grows Up: The Contemporary American Jewish Community." *Annals of the American Academy of Political and Social Science* 454 (March 1981): 70–85.

Weinfeld, Morton. "The Jews of Quebec: Perceived Anti-Semitism, Segregation, and Emigration." *The Jewish Journal of Sociology* 22 (June 1980): 5–20.

———. "My Lai and Shatilla." *Middle East Focus* 5, no. 6 (March 1983): 8–11.

"What Jewish Community Feels on Lebanon." *Toronto Star*, September 24, 1982, A21.

Zerker, Sally F. "Silliness No Answer to Mid-East Tensions," *Toronto Star*, May 26, 1988, A18.

Zogby, James. *The Other Anti-Semitism: The Arabs as Scapegoats.* Anti-Discrimination Committee Publication, no. 3. Washington, D.C.: ADC, n.d.

INTERVIEWS

Abdallah, A. Director, Palestine Information Office. Ottawa. May 1984.

Abugov, Dr. Bert. Secretariat, National Budgeting Conference (Council of Jewish Federations). Toronto. January 1989.

Amitay, Morris. Former Executive Director, American Israel Public Affairs Committee (AIPAC). Washington, D.C. May-June 1984.

Bessin, Shira Herzog. Former National Executive Director, Canada-Israel Committee (CIC). Toronto. March 1989.

Bick, Myer. Former National Executive Director, CIC. Montreal. March 1984.

Bookbinder, Hyman. Former Washington Representative, American Jewish Committee. Washington, D.C. May-June 1984.

Dimant, Frank. Executive Vice-President, B'nai B'rith Canada. Toronto. June 1986.

Dine, Thomas. Executive Director, AIPAC. Washington, D.C. May-June 1984.

*Former Assistant to the Secretary of State of External Affairs. Ottawa. April 1984.

Gray, Herb. Member of Parliament. Ottawa. April 1984.

Kenen, I. L. Former Executive Director, AIPAC. Washington, D.C. May-June 1984.

May, Norman. Former National Chairman, CIC. Toronto. March 1984.

*Official of the Middle East Division, Department of External Affairs. Ottawa. February 1984.

Plaut, Rabbi W. Gunther. Former President, Canadian Jewish Congress (CJC), and Former National Chairman, CIC. Toronto. February 1984.

Resnick, Mark. Former National Executive Director, CIC. Ottawa. February 1984.

Rose, Alan. Executive Vice-President, CJC. Montreal. March 1984.

Rosenbaum, Aaron David. Former Research Director, AIPAC. Washington, D.C. May-June 1984.

Sharp, Mitchell. Former Secretary of State for External Affairs. Ottawa. March 1984.

Stanfield, Robert L. Former Leader of the Progressive Conservative Party of Canada. Ottawa. May 1984.

Willmot, Robert. Former National Executive Director, Canada Israel-Committee. Toronto. March 1989.

*Anonymity requested.

Index

About the Author

DAVID HOWARD GOLDBERG is National Executive Director, Canadian Professors for Peace in the Middle East. He coedited and contributed several chapters to *The Domestic Battleground: Canada and the Arab-Israeli Conflict* and he is the publisher of *Middle East Focus*.